Face to Face with Levinas

Edited by Richard A. Cohen

State University of New York Press

Published by
State University of New York Press, Albany

Printed in the United States of America

For information, address State University of New York Press,
State University Plaza, Albany, N.Y. 12246

Library of Congress Cataloging in Publication Data

Main entry under title:

Face to face with Levinas.

   (SUNY series in philosophy)

   1. Levinas, Emmanuel—Addresses, essays, lectures.
2. Philosophy—Addresses, essays, lectures. I. Cohen,
Richard A., 1950-   II. Series.
B2430.L484F33 1986   194   85-17361
ISBN 0-88706-258-X
ISBN 0-88706-259-8 (pbk.)

10 9 8 7 6 5 4 3 2 1

Contents

Preface

Levinas has written his own brief intellectual bibliography, "Signature."[1] His biography, complete up to 1981, can be found in *Emmanuel Levinas* by Roger Burggraeve.[2]

The present collection, however, does not require any previous knowledge of Levinas. Indeed, the interview with Levinas included in it, conducted by Richard Kearney, is an excellent summary review of his philosophy. The authors who have contributed to this collection know Levinas' work thoroughly: their articles come from many years' meditation upon it.

Much is at stake in such meditations and in their fruits. Taking up philosophy's central tradition, Levinas raises anew the question of the limits and nature of knowledge, the question of the status of thought itself. What is unique about Levinas' answer is that it binds thought not in the name of the *true*, but in the name of the *good*. Levinas does not demand that thought be more rigorous or more in tune with being, but that it be more thoughtful; heedful of the social, and therefore moral, conditions that govern it. Levinas demands that thought be humble.

Levinas' response to the end of metaphysics is not Nietzsche's "pandemonium of free spirits," but a call to maturation. Reasonableness requires greater responsibilities than were dreamed of by *ratio*. Levinas insists on these greater responsibilities, within and beyond reason. The articles in this collection are challenged by this profound insistence, seduced by its force, yet not ready to succumb without protest. In this intellectual hesitation, they articulate a critical confrontation. Bound yet free, they are deep responses.

Putting this collection together has required much generosity from many people. I am especially grateful to all the contributors who have so generously given of their thought, and also to the translators who have contributed their time and effort to a trying task. I would like to thank Carol Bresnock and Diane Brunamonti of Penn State at Scranton for typing many parts of the manuscript. I would like to thank Alphonso Lingis and Edith Wyschogrod, who from the start — and all along — have encouraged me to do this project. The entire collection is a gift of gratitude for Levinas' work, which inspires it throughout.

Richard A. Cohen
Owings Mills, MD

Notes

1. Levinas, "Signature," ed. and annotated by Adriaan Peperzak, trans. M.E. Petrisko, *Research in Phenomenology* VIII, 1978, 175–189.

2. Roger Burggraeve, *Emmanuel Levinas*, The Center for Metaphysics and Philosophy of God, Institute of Philosophy, Kardinaal Mercierplein 2, 3000, Louvain, Bergium, 1982.

Acknowledgments

"Dialogue with Emmanuel Levinas" is the result of a series of interviews conducted, edited, and translated by Richard Kearney and reviewed by Levinas. It appeared in Richard Kearney, *Dialogues with Contemporary Continental Thinkers* (Manchester: Manchester University Press, 1984), 49–69.

"Bad Conscience and the Inexorable," by Emmanuel Levinas, translated by Richard A. Cohen, first appeared under the title "La mauvaise conscience et l'inexorable" in *Exercises de la patience,* no. 2 (Winter 1981): 109–113, in an issue devoted to Maurice Blanchot. It is reprinted with some changes in *De Dieu qui vient à l'idée* by Levinas (Paris: Vrin, 1982) 258–265.

"Our Clandestine Companion," by Maurice Blanchot, translated by David B. Allison, appeared under the title "Notre compagne clandestine" in *Textes pour Emmanuel Levinas,* ed. F. Laruelle (Paris: Jean-Michel Place, 1980), 79–87.

"Reason as One for Another: Moral and Theoretical Argument," by Steven G. Smith, appeared in the *Journal of the British Society for Phenomenology,* no. 3 (October 1981): 231–244.

"Levinas' Question," by Charles William Reed, was written for this collection.

"Levinas' Logic," by Jean-François Lyotard, translated by Ian McLeod, was published in abbreviated form under the title "Logique de Levinas" in *Textes pour Emmanuel Levinas,* 127–150. It will eventually be included in a larger work by Lyotard.

"An Ethical Transcendental Philosophy," by Theodore de Boer, translated by Alvin Plantinga, is a revised version of a chapter from de Boer's *Tussen filosofie en profetie* (Baarn: Ambo, 1976).

"Skepticism and Reason," by Jan de Greef, translated by Dick White, was written for this collection. Under the title "Scepticism et raison" it appeared in the *Revue Philosophique de Louvain*, 3 (1984).

"Some Remarks on Hegel, Kant, and Levinas," by Adriaan Peperzak, was first read at a colloquium on Levinas held at the State University of New York at Stony Brook, April 2, 1982.

"Levinas and Derrida: The Question of the Closure of Metaphysics," by Robert Bernasconi, is a revised version of a paper read at the Stony Brook Levinas colloquium of April 2, 1982.

"The Sensuality and the Sensitivity," by Alphonso Lingis, has been written for this collection.

"The Fecundity of the Caress," by Luce Iriguray, translated by Carolyn Burke, a fragment of which appeared in *Land* 2 (February 1982), first appeared in *Exercises de la patience*, 5 (Spring 1983): 119–137, in an issue devoted to "Le sujet exposé." It also appeared as the final chapter of Irigaray's *Ethique de la différence sexuelle* (Paris: Minuit, 1984), 173–199.

All articles used by permission of the authors.

Key to Abbreviations of Levinas' Texts

DEE/EE — *De l'existent à l'existence* (Paris: Fontaine, 1947)/ *Existence and Existents*, trans. by A. Lingis (The Hague: Nijhoff, 1978).

DEHH — *En découvrant l'existence avec Husserl et Heidegger*, 2d ed. (Paris: Vrin, 1967).

TeI/TI — *Totalité et Infini* (The Hague: Nijhoff, 1961)/ *Totality and Infinity* trans. by A. Lingis (The Hague: Nijhoff, 1969; Pittsburgh: Duquesne, 1969).

DL
DL (2d) — *Difficile Liberté* (Paris: Albin Michel, 1963; 2d enlarged and revised ed. 1976).

QLT — *Quatre lectures talmudiques* (Paris: Minuit, 1968).

HAH — *Humanisme de l'autre homme* (Montpellier: Fata Morgana, 1972).

AEAE/OBBE — *Autrement qu' être ou au-delà de l'essence* (The Hague: Nijhoff, 1974)/*Otherwise than Being or Beyond Essence*, trans. by A. Lingis (The Hague: Nijhoff, 1981).

Additional abbreviations are indicated as used in separate articles.

RICHARD A. COHEN

Introduction

Is an ethical philosophy primarily philosophical, a true discourse that happens to be about moral phenomena? Or is such a philosophy primarily ethical, an edifying discourse designed to stimulate good behavior, an exhortation, instruction or prescription rather than an explanation, description or denotation? Knowing that the drowning child must be saved, even when coupled with knowing how to save the child, is not the same as saving the child, unless knowing and doing are synonymous, which in our world they are not. For Levinas goodness comes first. His philosophy aims to pronounce this goodness, to articulate and emphasize it, and thus to realign its relation to the true. His thought is not simply an articulation, but a peculiar ethical exacerbation of language which bends the true to the good.

The issue between the true and the good is one of priority. Each claims absolute priority. If truth is primary then the criteria of epistemology, of cognition and knowledge, take precedence over moral standards. Knowledge interests dominate. Truth absorbs and transforms goodness to its own purposes, in more or less subtle ways, even when it claims not to. Aristotle and Hegel discover that the highest good ultimately surpasses the responsibilities and duties of citizenship, friendship and love. For these thinkers what is most needful is for thought to think itself. Such thought, however (and typically), *includes* citizenship, love, and the other *less exalted* human activities and relations, which are oriented toward and by

1

knowledge. Today, to take another example, one often hears scientists lay claim to a "value-free" language, that is to say, to a language beholden only to itself, to its own criteria. The deconstruction inaugurated by Derrida, too — so apparently at odds with science as with all naivite — is only a more recent instance in a long tradition of the self-absorption of knowledge.

But if the good were somehow primary in philosophy and life, and the standards of ethics took precedence over those of epistemology, then knowledge, for its part, would apparently be legitimately outraged. Is one not justified in fearing that the quest for truth would be hampered by moral scruples? Would it not be shackled by the nonfreedom of moral obedience? In the final account knowledge cannot distinguish moral scruple from tyranny or from cowardice; it has yet to learn one true morality, yet to see its proofs. In place of universal truth, or the quest for universal truth, one would have instead the contending particularities and vagaries of history: class truths, female truths, Islamic truths, and so on, each claiming moral superiority in a war of all against all.

Epistemology and ethics only seem able to distort one another unrecognizably.

But is the opposition of ethics and epistemology an opposition of two systems on the same plane? Truth is not the other of ethics in the same sense that goodness is the other of epistemology. The false is the other of the true; evil is the other of good. How are true, false, good, and evil related? Nietzsche proposes that ethics and epistemology have converged in the goodness that the latter finds in truth and not in falsity. Nietzsche will challenge this epistemological preference for the goodness of truth. Heidegger sets out to show that ethics and epistemology converge in "onto-theo-logy," in the eminence given to one being over all other beings. He rejects the very form of this superiority. Levinas proposes that ethics and epistemology converge in a moral righteousness that is not the rightness of the true but that makes truth possible. For knowledge such a condition is an *exteriority*, but for ethics it is *better* than knowledge. Ethics would not be a legitimate or illegitimate epistemological power or weakness, in the Nietzschean or Heideggerian sense, but the responsibility of the knower prior to, and the condition of, knowing.

Knowing cannot know such a condition. Socrates requires that we pause to know what right and wrong are before we act — but can this pause ever end? Cain asks if he is his brother's keeper and is thus *already* condemned. Knowledge, even when about morality, is insufficient, inadequate, inappropriate — and inasmuch as these terms of "criticism" are themselves products of knowledge, they too are insufficient. This does not, however, imply that ethics is an ignorance, a stupidity, for ignorance is but the other side of knowledge. Rather, for Levinas "it is time the abusive confusion of foolishness with morality were denounced."[1] Knowledge must once again be reexamined.

For knowledge to be knowledge it must turn upon itself, retrieve its project, deliberate, probe, and prove. In such a quest Socrates' dictum — know thyself — is unnecessary: all knowledge is self-knowledge. Self-knowledge is the telos, the auto-nomy at the origin of knowing. Whether it takes the empirical or the transcendental turn, knowledge must reject any authority as external and alien if that authority cannot pass through its evidence-checkpoint. *Evidence*, as Husserl understood, is the "principle of principles," the legitimizing instance of knowledge. Knowing must always decide *beforehand* what will count as knowledge. Hence knowledge and method are inseparable. Even when an entire paradigm of knowledge shifts, however unpredictable the shift may be it always makes sense retrospectively. Knowledge cannot be taken by surprise. Thus it is not the specific evidential standard upheld at any particular time that makes knowledge insufficient from the ethical standpoint, but its usurpation of priority itself. Its "beforehand" *already* excludes the import of ethics and thus, also, undermines knowing's claim to wholeness.

But in its own way such a failing is not altogether unknown by knowledge. Knowledge has never, even to its own satisfaction, reasoned out its origins, or reasoned itself out of its origins. Since its inception in ancient Greece this failure has trapped it between the cold logic of Parmenides and the fiery madness of Heraclitus. That is to say, on the one hand, knowledge can claim to contain its own origin, to be one and whole, but only at cost of sacrificing the way to becoming knowledgeable, the path from finitude to perfection, from the world of change, appearance, multiplicity to the perfect unity of the one. Here being and thinking are one: eternal, unchanging, indivisible. From the formulations of Parmenides, to Pythagoras, to Spinoza, knowledge remains eternally only itself, pure, divine — the rest is illusion, indeed, the illusion of illusion, for

illusion has no being. But when, on the other hand, knowledge
attempts to look outside of itself for its origin it falls into an abyss
of infinite regress, of a flux verging on chaos and held from chaos
for no good reason. From the formulations of Heraclitus to Hume
to Nietzsche, this tendency of thought contains itself only with an
evanescent hollow laughter, fading into the appearance of appearance of appearance of . . . naught. Thus knowledge, by its own
lights, is torn between being and nothingness, positivity and negativ-
ity, a too perfect purity and a too imperfect impurity. Like an oyster,
the irritation of knowledge over its fundamental incompleteness
secretes a pearl: *myth*. From the formulations of Plato to those of
Hegel philosophy attempts an impossible synthesis by means of more
or less disguised myths of beginning and end. But myth only succeeds in appropriating and distorting the genuine import of knowing's lack of origin — for "in truth" here knowledge encounters the
ethical situation upon which it uncomfortably rests. Knowledge,
however, is so far willing to deny its own essential frustration, so far
willing to defend its freedom and autonomy, that it wills the "make
believe," wills the false for the sake of the true.

But this desperate addiction to *mythos* should teach the *logos*
something about its limits, about the meaning of the disruption it
finds so intolerable yet so inevitable. Ethics does not satisfy
knowledge, it is not a myth, it is precisely what disrupts knowledge
and myth. The ineradicable ethical movement beyond knowledge is
not a movement on the plane of knowledge, reason, themes or
representation. Nor is it a movement of creative imagination, *poesis*,
or displacement. Ethics, for Levinas, is not a movement toward the
light or away from the light. Rather it is a trembling movement, that
cannot be measured, toward the height and destitution of the other
person.

Ethical necessity escapes knowledge not because it occurs in a
different territory, another world, but because it is exerted *through* but
not contained *in* themes. Its force is not that of the sufficiency of
reasons. Nor is its force that of a myth or ideology that props up
knowledge in its weak moments. The assertion that "A logically or
politically implies B" can be shown to arise out of shared presuppositions. Through such assertions knowers join together in the
relevance of transpersonal truths, truths true for you as well as for
me. But there is a prior question about these transpersonal truths.

This prior question concerns the epistemological criteria but cannot, without circularity, be settled by them.

For Levinas the lack of epistemological regulation here caught sight of is a positive event. Moral force cannot be reduced to cognitive cogency, to *acts* of consciousness or will. One *can* always refuse its claim; that is, once can be evil — and the capacity to rationalize such refusal is certainly without limit. Ethical necessity lies in a different sort of refusal, a refusal of concepts. It lies in prethematic demands that are necessarily lost in the elaboration of themes. Ethical necessity lies in social obligation prior to thematic thought, in a disturbance suffered by thematizing thought. "The conceptualization of this last refusal of conceptualization is not contemporaneous with this refusal; it transcends this conceptualization."[2] Ethics occurs as an unsettling of being and essence, as the "otherwise than being or beyond essence," whose *otherwise* and *beyond* cannot be thematized because goodness is better than the true and the false. This is not because ethics makes some truths better and others worse, but because it disrupts the entire project of knowing with a higher call, a more severe "condition": responsibility.

What is prior to the apriori conditions for cognition is neither the thematizing project itself, the ever escaping set of all sets, nor an antecedent attunement to being. It is the relationship with the alterity of the other person in an obligation to respond to that other, a responsibility to and for the other person that comes from him but is mine. The unassumable other of discourse — a discourse that can be true or false, beautiful or ugly, spoken or written — is the other person. This other is the ethical other, irreducible to what is known and outside the dominion of autonomy and freedom. The other, without "doing" anything, obligates the self prior to *what* the other says. It is this obligation, this responsibility to respond to the other that is, paradoxically, the unspoken first word prior to the first word spoken.

Thought retains a positive though residual awareness of this obligation. Though its telos is self-knowledge it does not think of itself or by itself. Its words are not merely its own formulations of itself in a vocal material. Nor is thought the auto-nomous movement of a system of signs. One says something *to* someone. The dative is an essential, irreducible aspect of all meaningful discourse, even if it escapes the most scrutinizing thematization, indeed, precisely inasmuch as it escapes all thematization. To acknowledge it one must go beyond what one can grasp in themes. Movement toward the other must not be confused, then, with the epistemological search for a moment of immediacy, an irrefragable origin, a pure given. Such immediacy has been shown to be contradictory time and again (by Adorno, by Sellars, by Derrida, et al.). Knowledge will not be humbled by an immediacy it knows — rightfully — to be mediated. But knowledge of itself knows of no sufficient reason to set its sufficient reasons in motion. Rather, it only knows sufficient reasons — it *knows* nothing more compelling than reason. Knowledge wants only more knowledge, wider and more firmly established knowledge. Yet its freedom is always in search of more freedom, more autonomy. It moves, but its movement is always homecoming, even in its difficulties and uncompleted programs, across however vast a territory of accomplishments and tasks, no matter how many researchers share in its adventure. Its transcendence is always reducible to that of intentionality, never going beyond the confines of noeses and noemas. What is lacking to reason is its very *raison d'être*, its why. The movement that sustains knowledge while remaining outside of knowledge is that of the ethical situation.

The ethical situation is excessive. The originality of Levinas' ethical philosophy lies in the very exorbitance of its claim. Precisely the excess of the ethical claim is what both contests knowledge and, as a nonepistemic contestation, makes for the seriousness of the ethical situation itself. The ethical situation is a unique relation, a relation without distance or union: the *proximity* of the one for the other, the *face to face*. Each of its four components is excessive, both its "terms": (1) the alterity of the other person and (2) the passivity of the self, and their "relations": (3) the other's command and (4) my responsibility to respond. All four of these inseparable yet distinguishable elements are exorbitant, excessive, yet irreducible to knowledge and freedom. They are *infinite* in the sense Descartes gives to this term in his third Meditation when he writes that "in some way I have in me the notion of the infinite earlier than the finite" and that "the strength of my mind . . . is in some measure dazzled by the sight." Levinas borrows the word "infinite" from Descartes to characterize the alterity of the other, my own passivity, the other's command, and my responsibility. Let us look at these four components of the ethical situation in turn.

1. Ethics exceeds knowledge by beginning in what lacks an origin, a radical exteriority: the absolute alterity of the other person.

For Levinas what makes the other person other is not a unique attribute or a unique combination of attributes but the "quality" of alterity itself. The other is other because his alterity is absolute, indeterminate and indeterminable. Of course, the other is always a specific other, a fellow citizen, a widow, an orphan, a magistrate, but the other is never only that, never only a phenomenon. The utter nakedness of the other's face pierces all significations, historical or otherwise, that attempt to mask or comprehend it.

2. Ethics exceeds knowledge in its "terminus," an "agency" without its own origin, a radical passivity: the inalienable responsibility to respond to the other person. The radical alterity of the other person contacts the subject beneath and prior to its powers and abilities, including its acts of consciousness. Prior to the reciprocal relations that may voluntarily or traditionally bind one to another, prior to the reasons the subject may propose in response to the other, prior to the respect one may have for the other, and prior to the sensuous receptivity that may welcome the other, the self is *subjected* to the excessive alterity of the other. In relation to the other the self is reconditioned, desubstantialized, put into question. Put into relation to what it cannot integrate, the self is made to be itself "despite itself." Hence one is "in some sense," as Descartes says, — a sense indeterminable by knowing — for the other before being for oneself. Hence one is radically passive in a superlative passivity equal only to the superlative alterity of the other person.

3. The ethical relation holds together what knowing can not hold together: the absolute alterity of the other person and the absolute passivity of the self despite-itself. The other's alterity is experienced as a command, an order which as it orders ordains the self into its inalienable selfhood. It is the other who "awakens" the subject from the abilities which make the life of the ego continuous and ultimately complacent, a homecoming. The other disturbs, pierces, ruptures, disrupts the immanence into which the subject falls when free of unassimilable alterity. The other, then, contacts the self from a height and a destitution: from the height of alterity itself and from the destitution to which the frailty and ultimately the mortality of the human condition make the other destined. The unspoken message which appears in the face of the other is: do not kill me; or, since the message has no ontological force, but is the very force of morality: you *ought* not kill me; or, since the alterity of the other's face is alterity itself: thou shalt not kill.

4. Subjected to subjectivity by the excessive alterity of the other
and the demand this places on me, the I becomes responsible:
responsible to and for the other. Here again, responsibility is not an
attribute of the self, but the self itself, the self-despite-itself is responsible to and for the other. In the face of the other, and only in the
face of the other, the self becomes noninterchangeable, non-
substitutable, which is to say, it becomes inalienably itself, "in the
first person," responsible. To be oneself is to be for the other. Further,
the responsibility to respond to the other is an infinite responsibility,
one which increases the more it is fulfilled, for the other is not an
end that can be satisfied. The self is responsible for all the frailty of
the other, the other's hungers, wounds, desires; and for the very
responsibility of the other — I am my brother's keeper; as well as for
the very death of the other, so that the other may not die alone,
forsaken.

Excessive alterity, excessive passivity, excessive demand, excessive responsibility — these are the components of the ethical situation that Levinas draws to the attention of philosophy. The relevance
of such a situation cannot be that of a "new" theme or a potential
theme. Rather, ethics is the essentially nonencompassable context,
the nonplace, the u-topia, within which knowing "takes place." The
identities, themes, reflections and reasons of knowledge occur within
the exorbitant context of the nonidentifiable, nonrepresentable, nonthematizable, nonreflective, unjustified proximity of one face to
another. Cutting knowledge (with a wound) diagonally, as it were,
ethics is that absolute from out of which emerges the relative exteriority and interiority of knowledge — evidence and intentionality —
without being on the same plane as itself, thus without submitting
to the constraints of epistemology.

Knowledge is not thereby degraded. Indeed it is an important
product of the ethical situation itself and has tremendous ethical
significance beyond its natural tendency to cover up its beginnings.
Knowledge emerges from the ethical situation owing to exigencies
within that situation itself. The excess of the ethical relation needs
limitations "to breathe," one might say, but in truth it needs limitations because the world contains more than two people. We do not
live in the garden of Eden. More than ethics is required in order to
be good, *justice* is also required. The subject realizes that the absolute
other is also other relative to others, and that its own inalienable,
infinite responsibility for the other is also a responsibility to others

and a responsibility like others'. In this way the value of justice, of *equality*, emerges from the originary unequalled and *unequal* ethical relation. The demands of justice arise from out of the ethical situation and at the same time pose a danger for that situation. The danger of justice, *injustice*, is the forgetting of the human face. The human face "regulates," is the goodness of justice itself. "The fact that the other, my neighbor, is also a third party with respect to another, who is also a neighbor, is the birth of thought, consciousness, justice and philosophy. The unlimited initial responsibility, which justifies this concern for justice, for oneself, and for philosophy can be forgotten. In this forgetting consciousness is a pure egoism. But egoism is neither first nor last."[3]

Levinas' writings, then, are paradoxical. As philosophy they must justify themselves, but their justification lies beyond the text, not in a reference, a signified, but in what is essentially elusive: goodness, sincerity. Knowledge must be of the true. It cannot be "corrected" by knowing the good for the good is good insofar as it is *outside* knowledge. This is precisely the trouble with knowledge, in a double sense: by essence it cannot know the good, but it is disturbed by the good, by the ethical plenitude that encompasses and escapes it. Hence Levinas' writings are condemned to incessantly speak *about* the good, about the "*to* the other" of ethical discourse. His writings are signs of lost traces. Levinas admits this paradox: signs of non-signs, sense of nonsense, justification of the unjustifiable. Yet it is by raising this paradox, by invoking its nonmeasurable movement, that his writings make sense in transgressing sense. The absence of the ethical subject is the ethical subject-matter whose escape is the "evidence" that animates Levinas' writings. Can this tenuous exercise bring seriousness to knowledge? Can knowledge, on the other hand, take it seriously?

It is the impropriety of Levinas' ethical claims that draws together the articles selected for this collection: they are caught with their guard down, struck by the anteriority of the ethical claim, challenged by it into thought, *wondering* which comes first, the thought or the challenge, the statement or its moral force, questioning anew what it means to come first, what it means to "do" philosophy.

Part II of this collection, "From Ethics to Philosophy," then is both its center and heart. Here lies the issue: the question of the relation of ethics to thought, the problem of a thought which must somehow think the unthinkable, the paradoxical language of the good in philosophy. Steven G. Smith, Charles William Reed, Theodore de Boer and Jan de Greef, examine Levinas from within, as it were, in an attempt to precisely pinpoint those crucial moments when what cannot be said is said, and to articulate the nonepistemic conditions that make them possible. Jean-Francois Lyotard and Robert Bernasconi are no less interested in these moments, but illuminate them in relation to Kant's notion of respect and the elusiveness of Derridaian semiology respectively.

Part I, "Proximity," and Part III, "Contexts," "contain" the uneasy paradoxes of the center. Richard Kearney's interview provides a concise overview of the wide range of Levinas' thought. "Bad Conscience and the Inexorable," by Levinas, affords a glimpse of his thought at work. Blanchot's brief remarks offer a sensitive appreciation by one of France's leading literary critics and a life long personal friend of Levinas. Adriaan Peperzak and Alphonso Lingis draw us outside the central debate to explore other lines opened up by Levinas' thought, in its relation to Hegel, Kant and Heidegger, Luce Irigaray, too, explores alternative lines, taking ethical alterity to the alterity of the erotic encounter.

Collections such as this gather around original thought, not merely to be warmed by its radiance, but to radiate, to light various ways, and to indicate distances traversed and distances yet to be traveled. Levinas challenges thought to rethink its proper righteousness, to grapple with the forever unstable unity of being and the better than being.

Notes

1. AEAE 162/OBBE 126.

2. AEAE 163/OBBE 127.

3. AEAE 165/OBBE 128.

Part I

Proximity

EMMANUEL LEVINAS AND RICHARD KEARNEY

1. Dialogue with Emmanuel Levinas

Richard Kearney: Perhaps you could retrace your philosophical itinerary by identifying some of the major influences on your thought?

Emmanuel Levinas: Apart from the great masters of the history of philosophy — in particular Plato, Descartes, and Kant — the first contemporary influence on my own thinking was Bergson. In 1925, in Strasbourg University, Bergson was being hailed as France's leading thinker. For example, Blondel, one of his Strasbourg disciples, developed a specifically Bergsonian psychology quite hostile to Freud — a hostility that made a deep and lasting impression on me. Moreover, Bergson's theory of time as concrete duration (*la durée concrète*) is, I believe, one of the most significant, if largely ignored, contributions to contemporary philosophy. Indeed, it was this Bergsonian emphasis on temporality that prepared the soil for the subsequent implantation of Heideggerian phenomenology into France. It is all the more ironic, therefore, that in *Being and Time* Heidegger unjustly accuses Bergson of reducing time to space. What is more, in Bergson's *Creative Evolution*, one finds the whole notion of technology as the destiny of the Western philosophy of reason. Bergson was the first to contrast technology, as a logical and necessary expression of scientific rationality, with an alternative form of human expression that he called creative intuition or impulse — the *élan vital*. All of Heidegger's celebrated analyses of our technological era as the logical culmination of Western metaphysics and its forgetfulness of being came after Bergson's reflections on the subject. Bergson's importance to contemporary Continental thought has been somewhat obfuscated; he has been suspended in a sort of limbo; but I believe it is only a temporary suspension.

> Could you describe how, after Bergson, you came under the influence of the German phenomenologists, Husserl and Heidegger?

It was in 1927 that I first became interested in Husserl's phenomenology, which was still unknown in France at that time. I traveled to the University of Freiburg for two semesters in 1928–29 and studied phenomenology with Husserl and also, of course, with Heidegger, who was then the leading light in German philosophy after the publication of *Being and Time* in 1927. Phenomenology represented the second, but undoubtedly most important, philosophical influence on my thinking. Indeed, from the point of view of philosophical method and discipline, I remain to this day a phenomenologist.

> How would you characterize the particular contribution of phenomenology to modern philosophy?

The most fundamental contribution of Husserl's phenomenology is its methodical disclosure of how meaning comes to be, how it emerges in our consciousness of the world, or more precisely, in our becoming conscious of our intentional rapport (*visée*) with the world. The phenomenological method enables us to discover meaning within our lived experience; it reveals consciousness to be an intentionality always in *contact* with objects outside of itself, other than itself. Human experience is not some self-transparent substance or pure *cogito*; it is always intending or tending towards something in the world that preoccupies it. The phenomenological method permits consciousness to understand its own preoccupations, to reflect upon itself and thus discover all the hidden or neglected horizons of its intentionality. In other words, by returning to the implicit horizons of consciousness, phenomenology enables us to explicate or unfold the full intentional meaning of an object, which would otherwise be presented as an abstract and isolated entity cut off from its intentional horizons. Phenomenology thus teaches us that consciousness is at once tied to the object of its experience and yet free to detach itself from this object in order to return upon itself, focusing on those *visées* of intentionality in which the object emerges as *meaningful*, as part of our lived experience. One might say that phenomenology is a way of becoming aware of where we are in the world, a *sich besinnen* that consists of a recovery of the origin of meaning in our life world, or *Lebenswelt*.

> Your second major work was entitled *En découvrant l'existence avec Husserl et Heidegger*. If Husserl introduced you to the phenomenological method, how would you assess your debt to Heidegger?

Heidegger's philosophy was a shock for me, and for most of my contemporaries in the late twenties and thirties. It completely altered the course and character of European philosophy. I think that one cannot seriously philosophize today without traversing the Heideggerian path in some form or other. *Being and Time*, which is much more significant and profound than any of Heidegger's later works, represents the fruition and flowering of Husserlian phenomenology. The most far-reaching potentialities of the phenomenological method were exploited by Heidegger in this early work, particularly in his phenomenological analysis of 'anguish' as the fundamental mood of our existence. Heidegger brilliantly described how this existential mood, or *Stimmung*, revealed the way in which we are attuned to being. Human moods, such as guilt, fear, anxiety, joy, or dread, are no longer considered as mere physiological sensations or psychological emotions, but are now recognized as the ontological ways in which we feel and find our being-in-the-world, our being-there, as *Befindlichkeit*.

> This phenomenological analysis of our existential moods was, of course, something that you yourself used to original effect in your descriptions of such human dispositions as need, desire, effort, laziness, and insomnia in *Existence and Existents*. But to return to Husserl and Heidegger, how would you define the main difference of *style* in their employment of phenomenology?

Husserl's approach was always more abstract and ponderous — one really had to have one's ears cocked if one wished to understand his lectures! Husserl was primarily concerned with establishing and perfecting phenomenology as a method, that is, as an epistemological method of describing how our logical concepts and categories emerge and assume an essential meaning. What is the relation between our logical judgments and our perceptual experience? This was Husserl's question — and phenomenology was his method of responding by means of rigorous and exact descriptions of our intentional modes of consciousness. Phenomenology was thus a way of suspending our preconceptions and prejudices in order to disclose how essential truth and meaning are generated; it was a methodical return to the beginnings, to the origins, of knowledge. On the other hand, Heidegger, the young disciple, brought the phenomenological method to life and gave it a contemporary style and relevance. Heidegger's existential analyses possessed a poetic quality and force that enchanted and astonished the mind, while preserving all the while the rigorous contours of the master's method. So that I would say, by way of summary, that if it was Husserl who opened up for me the radical possibilities of a phenomenological analysis of knowledge, it was Heidegger who first gave these possibilities a positive and concrete grounding in our everyday existence; Heidegger showed that the phenomenological search for eternal truths and essences ultimately originates in *time*, in our temporal and historical existence.

> Your first study of phenomenology, *The Theory of Intuition in Husserl's Phenomenology*, published in 1930, was the first complete work on Husserl in French. Your seminal study of Heidegger in *La Revue philosophique* in 1932 was another milestone in contemporary French philosophy. Sartre and Merleau-Ponty were soon to follow suit, exploring further possibilities of the phenomenological method known today as French existentialism. As the discreet inaugurator of the French interest in phenomenology, what exactly was your relationship with Sartre and Merleau-Ponty?

I have always admired the powerful originality of Merleau-Ponty's work, however different from my own in many respects, and had frequent contact with him at Jean Wahl's philosophical meetings in the *Collége de Philosophie* in the thirties and forties, and also whenever I contributed to *Les Temps Modernes* while he was still coeditor with Sartre. But it was Sartre who guaranteed my place in eternity by stating in his famous obituary essay on Merleau-Ponty that he, Sartre, "was introduced to phenomenology by Levinas." Simone de Beauvoir tells how it happened, in one of her autobiographical works. One day in the early thirties, Sartre chanced upon a copy of my book on Husserl in the Picard bookshop just opposite the Sorbonne. He picked it up, read it, and declared to de Beauvoir, "This is the philosophy I wanted to write!" Afterwards he reassured himself that my analysis was far too didactic and that he could do better himself! And so he applied himself to a sustained study of Husserl and Heidegger. The result was a host of enterprising phenomenological analyses, ranging from *Imagination* (1936) to *Being and Nothingness* (1943). I was extremely interested in Sartre's phenomenological analysis of the 'other', though I always regretted that he interpreted it as a threat and a degradation, an interpretation that also found expression in his fear of the God question. In fact, Sartre's rejection of theism was so unequivocal that his final statements, in the *Nouvel Observateur* interviews just before his death, about the legitimacy of Jewish history as a belief in the existence of God seemed incredible to those who knew him or had studied him. In Sartre the phenomenon of the other was still considered, as in all Western ontology, to be a modality of unity and fusion, that is, a reduction of the other to the categories of the same. This is described by Sartre as a teleological project to unite and totalize the for-itself and the in-itself, the self and the other-than-self. It is here that my fundamental philosophical disagreement with Sartre lay. At a personal level, I always liked Sartre. I first met him in Gabriel Marcel's house just before the war and had further dealings with him after the war on the controversial question of Israel's existence. Sartre had refused the Nobel Prize for Literature, and I felt that someone who had the courage to reject such a prize for ethical reasons had certainly conserved the right to intervene and to try to persuade Nasser, the Egyptian leader at the time, to forego his threats to Israel and embark upon dialogue. What I also admired in Sartre was that his philosophy was not confined to purely conceptual issues but was open to the possibility of ethical and political commitment.

What are the origins of the religious dimensions in your own thinking?

I was born in Lithuania, a country where Jewish culture was intellectually prized and fostered and where the interpretation and exegesis of biblical texts was cultivated to a high degree. It was here that I first learned to read the Bible in Hebrew. It was at a much later date, however, that I became actively interested in Jewish thought. After the Second World War, I encountered a remarkable master of Tal-

mudic interpretation here in Paris, a man of exceptional mental
agility, who taught me how to read the Rabbinic texts. He taught me
for four years, from 1947 to 1951, and what I myself have written in
my *Talmudic Lectures* has been written in the shadow of his shadow.
It was this postwar encounter that reactivated my latent — I might
even say dormant — interest in the Judaic tradition. But when I
acknowledge this Judaic influence, I do not wish to talk in terms of
belief or nonbelief. *Believe* is not a verb to be employed in the first
person singular. Nobody can really say *I believe* — or *I do not believe*
for that matter — that God exists. The existence of God is not a
question of an individual soul's uttering logical syllogisms. It cannot
be proved. The existence of God, the *Sein Gottes*, is sacred history
itself, the sacredness of man's relation to man through which God
may pass. God's existence is the story of his revelation in biblical
history.

> How do you reconcile the phenomenological and religious dimen-
> sions of your thinking?

I always make a clear distinction, in what I write, between philosophical and confessional texts. I do not deny that they may ultimately have a common source of inspiration. I simply state that it
is necessary to draw a line of demarcation between them as distinct methods of exegesis, as separate languages. I would never, for
example, introduce a Talmudic or biblical verse into one of my
philosophical texts, to try to prove or justify a phenomenological
argument.

> Would you go so far as to endorse Heidegger's argument that gen-
> uine philosophical questioning requires one to suspend or bracket
> one's religious faith? I am thinking in particular of Heidegger's
> statement in his *Introduction to Metaphysics* that a religious thinker
> cannot ask the philosophical question, "Why is there something
> rather than nothing?" — since he already possesses the answer:
> "Because God created the world." Hence Heidegger's conclusion
> that a religious (in the sense of Christian or Jewish) philosophy is
> a square circle, a contradiction in terms.

For me the essential characteristic of philosophy is a certain, specifically Greek, way of thinking and speaking. Philosophy is primarily
a question of language; and it is by identifying the subtextual lan-

guage of particular discourses that we can decide whether they are philosophical or not. Philosophy employs a series of terms and concepts — such as *morphe* (form), *ousia* (substance), *nous* (reason), *logos* (thought) or *telos* (goal), etc. — that constitute a specifically Greek lexicon of intelligibility. French and German, and indeed all of Western philosophy, is entirely shot through with this specific language; it is a token of the genius of Greece to have been able to deposit its language thus in the basket of Europe. But although philosophy is essentially Greek, it is not exclusively so. It also has sources and roots that are non-Greek. What we term the Judeo-Christian tradition, for example, proposed an alternative approach to meaning and truth. The difficulty is, of course, to *speak* of this alternative tradition, given the essentially Greek nature of philosophical language. And this difficulty is compounded by the fact that Judeo-Christian culture has, historically, been incorporated into Greek philosophy. It is virtually impossible for philosophers today to have recourse to an unalloyed religious language. All one can say is that the Septuagint is not yet complete, that the translation of biblical wisdom into the Greek language remains unfinished. The best one can do by way of identifying the fundamental difference between the Greek and biblical approaches to truth is to try to define the distinctive quality of Greek philosophy before the historical incursion of Jewish and Christian cultures. Perhaps the most essential distinguishing feature of the language of Greek philosophy was its equation of truth with an *intelligiblity of presence*. By this I mean an intelligiblity that considers truth to be that which is present or copresent, that which can be gathered or synchronized into a totality that we would call the world or *cosmos*. According to the Greek model, intelligibility is what can be rendered present, what can be represented in some eternal here and now, exposed and disclosed in pure light. To equate truth thus with presence is to presume that however different the two terms of a relation might appear (e.g., the Divine and the human) or however separated over time (e.g., into past and future), they can ultimately be rendered commensurate and simultaneous, the same, contained in a history that totalizes time into a beginning or an end, or both, which is presence. The Greek notion of being is essentially this presence.

Would you agree, then, with Heidegger's critique of Western metaphysics as a philosophy of presence?

I don't think Heidegger is entirely consistent on this point. For me, Heidegger never really escaped from the Greek language of intelligibility and presence. Even though he spent much of his philosophical career struggling against certain metaphysical notions of presence — in particular the objectifying notion of presence as *Vorhandenheit*, which expresses itself in our scientific and technological categorization of the world — he ultimately seems to espouse another, more subtle and complex, notion of presence as *Anwesen*, that is, the coming-into-presence of being. Thus, while Heidegger heralds the end of the metaphysics of presence, he continues to think of being as a coming-into-presence; he seems unable to break away from the hegemony of presence that he denounces. This ambiguity also comes to the surface when Heidegger interprets our being-in-the-world as history. The ultimate and most authentic mission of existence or *Dasein* is to recollect (*wiederholen*) and totalize its temporal dispersal into past, present, and future. *Dasein* is its history to the extent that it can interpret and narrate its existence as a finite and contemporaneous story (*histoire*), a totalizing copresence of past, present, and future.

> How does the ethical relation to the other, so central a theme in your philosophy, serve to subvert the ontology of presence in its Greek and Heideggerian forms?

The interhuman relationship emerges with our history, with our being-in-the-world, as intelligibility and presence. The interhuman realm can thus be construed as a part of the disclosure of the world as presence. But it can also be considered from another perspective — the ethical or biblical perspective that transcends the Greek language of intelligibility — as a theme of justice and concern for the other as other, as a theme of love and desire, which carries us beyond the infinite being of the world as presence. The interhuman is thus an interface: a double axis where what is 'of the world' qua *phenomenological intelligibility* is juxtaposed with what is 'not of the world' qua *ethical responsibility*. It is in this ethical perspective that God must be thought, and not in the ontological perspective of our being-there or of some supreme being and creator correlative to the world, as traditional metaphysics often held. God, as the God of alterity and transcendence, can only be understood in terms of that interhuman dimension which, to be sure, emerges in the phenomenological-ontological perspective of the intelligible world, but which cuts through and perforates the totality of presence and points towards the absolutely other. In this sense one could say that biblical thought has, to some extent, influenced my ethical reading of the inter-human, whereas Greek thought has largely determined its philo-sophical expression in language. So that I would maintain, against Heidegger, that philosophy can be ethical as well as ontological, can be at once Greek and non-Greek in its inspiration. These two sources of inspiration coexist as two different tendencies in modern philosophy, and it is my own personal task to try to identify this dual origin of meaning — *der Ursprung der Sinnhaften* — in the interhuman relationship.

> One of the most complex, and indeed central, themes in your philosophy is the rapport between the interhuman and time. Could you elucidate this rapport by situating it in terms of the ethics/ontology distinction?

I am trying to show that man's ethical relation to the other is ultimately prior to his ontological relation to himself (egology) or to the totality of things that we call the world (cosmology). The rela-tionship with the other is *time*: it is an untotalizable diachrony in which one moment pursues another without ever being able to retrieve it, to catch up with, or coincide with it. The non-simultaneous and nonpresent are my primary rapport with the other in time. Time means that the other is forever beyond me, irreducible to the synchrony of the same. The temporality of the interhuman opens up the meaning of otherness and the otherness of meaning. But because there are more than two people in the world, we invari-ably pass from the ethical perspective of alterity to the ontological perspective of totality. There are always at least three persons. This means that we are obliged to ask who the other is, to try to objec-tively define the undefinable, to compare the incomparable, in an effort to juridically hold different positions together. So that the first type of simultaneity is the simultaneity of equality, the attempt to reconcile and balance the conflicting claims of each person. If there were only two people in the world, there would be no need for law courts because I would always be responsible for and before, the other. As soon as there are three, the ethical relationship with the other becomes political and enters into the totalizing discourse of ontology. We can never completely escape from the language of ontology and politics. Even when we deconstruct ontology we are obliged to use its language. Derrida's work of deconstruction, for example, possesses the speculative and methodological rigor of the philosophy that he is seeking to deconstruct. It's like the argument of the skeptics: how can we know that we can't know anything? The greatest virtue of philosophy is that it can put itself in question, try to deconstruct what it has constructed, and unsay what it has said. Science, on the contrary, does not try to unsay itself, does not interrogate or challenge its own concepts, terms, or foundations; it forges ahead, progresses. In this respect, science attempts to ignore language by constructing its own abstract nonlanguage of calculable symbols and formulae. But science is merely a secondary bracketing of philosophical language, from which it is ultimately derived; it can never have the last word. Heidegger summed this up admirably when he declared that science *calculates* but does not *think*. Now what I am interested in is precisely this ability of philosophy to think, to question itself, and ultimately to unsay itself. And I wonder if this capacity for interrogation and for unsaying (*dédire*) is not itself derived from the preontological interhuman relationship with the other. The fact that philosophy cannot fully totalize the alterity of meaning in some final presence or simultaneity is not for me a deficiency or fault. Or to put it another way, the best thing about philosophy is that it fails. It is better that philosophy fail to totalize meaning — even though, as ontology, it has attempted just this — for it thereby remains open to the irreducible otherness of transcendence. Greek ontology, to be sure, expressed the strong sentiment that the last word is unity, the many becoming one, the truth as synthesis. Hence Plato defined love — *eros* — as only *half*-divine, insofar as it lacks the full coincidence or unification of differences that he defined as divinity. The whole romantic tradition in European poetry tends to conform to this platonic ontology by inferring that love is perfect when two people become *one*. I am trying to work against this identification of the divine with unification or totality. Man's relationship with the other is *better* as difference than as unity: sociality is better than fusion. The very value of love is the impossibility of reducing the other to myself, of coinciding into sameness. From an ethical perspective, two have a better time than one (*on s'amuse mieux à deux*)!

Is it possible to conceive of an eschatology of noncoincidence wherein man and God could coexist eternally without fusing into oneness?

But why eschatology? Why should we wish to reduce time to eternity? Time is the most profound relationship that man can have with God, precisely as a going towards God. There is an excellence in time that would be lost in eternity. To desire eternity is to desire to perpetuate oneself, to go on living as oneself, to *be* always. Can one conceive of an eternal life that would not suspend time or reduce it to a contemporaneous presence? To accept time is to accept death as the impossibility of presence. To be in eternity is to be *one*, to be *oneself* eternally. To be in time is to be for God (*être à Dieu*), a perpetual leave taking (*adieu*).

But how can one be for God or go towards God as the absolutely other? Is it by going towards the human other?

Yes, and it is essential to point out that the relation implied in the preposition *towards* (*à*) is ultimately a relation derived from time. Time fashions man's relation to the other, and to the absolutely other or God, as a diachronic relation irreducible to correlation. 'Going towards God' is not to be understood here in the classical ontological sense of a return to, or reunification with, God as the beginning or end of temporal existence. 'Going towards God' is meaningless unless seen in terms of my primary going towards the other person. I can only go towards God by being ethically concerned by and for the other person. I am not saying that ethics predisposes belief. On the contrary, belief presupposes ethics as the disruption of our being-in-the-world that opens us to the other. The ethical exigency to be responsible for the other undermines the ontological primacy of the meaning of being; it unsettles the natural and political positions we have taken up in the world and predisposes us to a meaning that is other than being, that is otherwise than being (*autrement qu'être*).

What role does your analysis of the 'face' (*visage*) of the other play in this disruption of ontology?

The approach to the face is the most basic mode of responsibility. As such, the face of the other is verticality and uprightness; it spells a relation of rectitude. The face is not in front of me (*en face de moi*) but above me; it is the other before death, looking through and exposing death. Secondly, the face is the other who asks me not to let him die alone, as if to do so were to become an accomplice in his death. Thus the face says to me: you shall not kill. In the relation to the face I am exposed as a usurper of the place of the other. The celebrated 'right to existence' that Spinoza called the *conatus essendi* and defined as the basic principle of all intelligibility is challenged by the relation to the face. Accordingly, my duty to respond to the other suspends my natural right to self-survival, *le droit vitale*. My ethical relation of love for the other stems from the fact that the self cannot survive by itself alone, cannot find meaning within its own being-in-the-world, within the ontology of sameness. That is why I prefaced *Otherwise than Being or Beyond Essence* with Pascal's phrase, " 'That is my place in the sun.' That is how the usurpation of the whole world began." Pascal makes the same point when he declares that "the self is hateful." Pascal's ethical sentiments here go against the ontological privileging of 'the right to exist'. To expose myself to the vulnerability of the face is to put my ontological right to existence into question. In ethics, the other's right to exist has primacy over my own, a primacy epitomized in the ethical edict: you shall not kill, you shall not jeopardize the life of the other. The ethical rapport with the face is asymmetrical in that it subordinates my existence to the other. This principle recurs in Darwinian biology as the "survival of the fittest" and in psychoanalysis as the natural instinct of the 'id' for gratification, possession, and power — the *libido dominandi*.

So I owe more to the other than to myself . . .

Absolutely, and this ethical exigency undermines the Hellenic endorsement, still prevalent today, of the *conatus essendi*. There is a Jewish proverb which says that "the other's material needs are my spiritual needs"; it is this disproportion, or assymmetry, that characterizes the ethical refusal of the first truth of ontology — the struggle to *be*. Ethics is, therefore, *against nature* because it forbids the murderousness of my natural will to put my own existence first.

Does going towards God always require that we go against nature?

God cannot appear as the cause or creator of nature. The word of God speaks through the glory of the face and calls for an ethical conversion, or reversal, of our nature. What we call lay morality, that is, humanistic concern for our fellow human beings, already speaks the voice of God. But the moral priority of the other over myself could not come to be if it were not motivated by something beyond nature. The ethical situation is a human situation, beyond human nature, in which the idea of God comes to mind (*Gott fällt mir ein*). In this respect, we could say that God is the other who turns our nature inside out, who calls our ontological will-to-be into question. This ethical call of conscience occurs, no doubt, in other religious systems besides the Judeo-Christian, but it remains an essentially religious vocation. God does indeed go against nature, for He is not of this world. God is other than being.

> How does one distill the ethico-religious meaning of existence from its natural or ontological sedimentation?

But your question already assumes that ethics is derived from ontology. I believe, on the contrary, that the ethical relationship with the other is just as primary and original (*ursprünglich*) as ontology — if not more so. Ethics is not derived from an ontology of nature; it is its opposite, a meonotology, which affirms a meaning beyond being, a primary mode of non-being (*me-on*).

> And yet you claim that the ethical and the ontological coexist as two inspirations without Western philosophy?

In Greek philosophy one can already discern traces of the ethical breaking through the ontological, for example in Plato's idea of the 'good existing beyond being' (*agathon epekeina tes ousias*). (Heidegger, of course, contests this ethical reading of the good in Plato, maintaining that it is merely one among other descriptions of being itself.) One can also cite in this connection Descartes' discovery of the 'idea of the infinite,' which surpasses the finite limits of human nature and the human mind. And similarly, supra-ontological notions are to be found in the Pseudo-Dionysian doctrine of the *via eminentiae*, with its surplus of the divine over being, or in the Augustinian distinction in the *Confessions* between the truth that challenges (*veritas redarguens*) and the ontological truth that shines (*veritas lucens*), and so on.

> Do you think that Husserl's theory of temporality points to an otherness beyond being?

However radically Husserl's theory of time may gesture in this direction, particularly in *The Phenomenology of Internal Time Consciousness*, it
remains overall a *cosmological* notion of time; temporality continues
to be thought of in terms of the present, in terms of an ontology of
presence. The present (*Gegenwart*) remains for Husserl the central-
izing dimension of time, the past and the future being defined in
terms of intentional representations (*Vergegenwärtigen*). To be more
precise, the past, Husserl claims, is retained by the present, and the
future is precontained in, or protended by, the present. Time past
and time future are merely modifications of the present; and this
double extension of the present into the past (retention) and the
future (protension) reinforces the ontology of presence as a seizure
and appropriation of what is other or transcendent. Heidegger, who
actually edited Husserl's lectures on time, introduced an element of
alterity into his own phenomenological description of time in *Being
and Time*, when he analyzed time in terms of our anguish before
death. Temporality is now disclosed as an ecstatic being-towards-
death, which releases us from the present into an ulimate horizon of
possibles, rather than as a holding or seizing or retaining of the
present.

> But is not Heidegger's analysis of temporality as a being-towards-
> death still a subtle form of extending what is *mine*, of reducing the
> world to *my* ownmost (*eigenst*) authentic (*eigentlich*) existence? Death
> is for Heidegger always *my* death. *Dasein* is always the being that
> is *mine*.

This is the fundamental difference between my ethical analysis of
death and Heidegger's ontological analysis. Whereas for Heidegger
death is *my* death, for me it is the *other's* death. In *The Letter on
Humanism*, Heidegger defines *Dasein* in almost Darwinian fashion as
"a being that is concerned for its own being." In paragraph nine of
Being and Time, he defines the main characteristic of *Dasein* as that
of *mineness* (*Jemeinigkeit*) — the way in which being becomes mine, imposes or imprints itself on me. *Jemeinigkeit*, as the possession of my
being as *mine*, precedes the articulation of the *I*. *Dasein* is only 'I' (*Ich*)
because it is already *Jemeinigkeit*. I become I only because I possess
my own being as primary. For ethical thought, on the contrary, *the
self*, as this primacy of what is mine, is *hateful*. Ethics is not, for this
reason, a depersonalizing exigency. I am defined as a subjectivity, as

a singular person, as an 'I', precisely because I am exposed to the other. It is my inescapable and incontrovertible answerability to the other that makes me an individual 'I'. So that I become a responsible or ethical 'I' to the extent that I agree to depose or dethrone myself — to abdicate my position of centrality — in favor of the vulnerable other. As the Bible says: "He who loses his soul gains it." The ethical I is a being who asks if he has a right to be! — who excuses himself to the other for his own existence.

> In the structuralist and poststructuralist debates that have tended to dominate Continental philosophy in recent years, there has been much talk of the disappearance, or the demise, of the subject. Is your ethical thought an attempt to preserve subjectivity in some form?

My thinking on this matter goes in the opposite direction from structuralism. It is not that I wish to preserve, over and against the structuralist critique, the idea of a subject who would be a substantial or mastering center of meaning, an idealist, self-sufficient *cogito*. These traditional ontological versions of subjectivity have nothing to do with the meontological version of subjectivity that I put forward in *Otherwise than Being*. Ethical subjectivity dispenses with the idealizing subjectivity of ontology, which reduces everything to itself. The ethical 'I' is subjectivity precisely insofar as it kneels before the other, sacrificing its own liberty to the more primordial call of the other. For me, the freedom of the subject is not the highest or primary value. The heteronomy of our response to the human other, or to God as the absolutely other, precedes the autonomy of our subjective freedom. As soon as I acknowledge that it is 'I' who am responsible, I accept that my freedom is anteceded by an obligation to the other. Ethics redefines subjectivity as this heteronomous responsibility, in contrast to autonomous freedom. Even if I deny my primordial responsibility to the other by affirming my own freedom as primary, I can never escape the fact that the other has demanded a response from me *before* I affirm my freedom not to respond to his demand. Ethical freedom is *une difficile liberté*, a heteronomous freedom obliged to the other. Consequently, the other is the richest and the poorest of beings: the richest, at an ethical level, in that it always comes before me, its right-to-be preceding mine; the poorest, at an onto-logical or political level, in that without me it can do nothing — it is utterly vulnerable and exposed. The other haunts our ontological existence and keeps the psyche awake, in a state of vigilant insomnia. Even though we are ontologically free to refuse the other, we remain forever accused, with a bad conscience.

> Is not the ethical obligation to the other a purely negative ideal, impossible to realize in our everyday being-in-the-world? After all, we live in a concrete historical world governed by ontological drives and practices, be they political and institutional totalities or technological systems of mastery, organization, and control. Is ethics practicable in human society as we know it? Or is it merely an invitation to apolitical acquiescence?

This is a fundamental point. Of course we inhabit an ontological world of technological mastery and political self-preservation. Indeed, without these political and technological structures of organization we would not be able to feed mankind. This is the great paradox of human existence: we must use the ontological *for the sake of the other*; to ensure the survival of the other we must resort to the technico-political systems of means and ends. This same paradox is also present in our use of language, to return to an earlier point. We have no option but to employ the language and concepts of Greek philosophy, even in our attempts to go beyond them. We cannot obviate the language of metaphysics, and yet we cannot, ethically speaking, be satisfied with it: it is necessary but not enough. I disagree, however, with Derrida's interpretation of this paradox. Whereas he tends to see the deconstruction of the Western metaphysics of presence as an irredeemable crisis, I see it as a golden opportunity for Western philosophy to open itself to the dimension of otherness and transcendence beyond being.

> Is there any sense in which language can be ethical?

In *Otherwise than Being* I pose this question when I ask: "What is saying without a said?" Saying is ethical sincerity insofar as it is exposition. As such, this *saying* is irreducible to the ontological definability of the *said*. Saying is what makes the self-exposure of sincerity possible; it is a way of giving everything, of not keeping anything for oneself. Insofar as ontology equates truth with the intelligibility of total presence, it reduces the pure exposure of saying to the totalizing closure of the said. The child is a pure exposure of expression insofar as it is pure vulnerability; it has not yet learned to dissemble, to deceive, to be insincere. What distinguishes human language from animal or child expression, for example, is that the human speaker can remain silent, can refuse to be exposed in sincerity. The human being is characterized as human not only because he is a being who can speak but also because he is a being who can lie, who can live in the duplicity of language as the dual possibility of exposure and deception. The animal is incapable of this duplicity; the dog, for instance, cannot suppress its bark, the bird its song. But man can repress his saying, and this ability to keep silent, to withhold oneself, is the ability to be political. Man can give himself in saying to the point of poetry — or he can withdraw into the nonsaying of lies. Language as *saying* is an ethical openness to the other; as that which is *said* — reduced to a fixed identity or synchronized presence — it is an ontological closure to the other.

> But is there not some sort of 'morality' of the *said* that might reflect the ethics of *saying* in our everyday transactions in society? In other words, if politics cannot be ethical insofar as it is an expression of our ontological nature, can it at least be 'moral' (in your sense of that term)?

This distinction between the ethical and the moral is very important here. By morality I mean a series of rules relating to social behavior and civic duty. But while morality thus operates in the socio-political order of organizing and improving our human survival, it is ultimately founded on an ethical responsibility towards the other. As *prima philosophia*, ethics cannot itself legislate for society or produce rules of conduct whereby society might be revolutionized or transformed. It does not operate at the level of the manifesto or *call to order*; it is not a *savior vivre*. When I talk of ethics as a 'dis-interestedness', I do not mean that it is indifference; I simply mean that it is a form of vigilant passivity to the call of the other, which precedes our interest in being, our *inter-est*, as a being-in-the-world attached to property and appropriating what is other than itself to itself. Morality is what governs the world of political 'inter-estedness', the social interchanges between citizens in a society. Ethics, as the extreme exposure and sensitivity of one subjectivity to another, becomes morality and hardens its skin as soon as we move into the political world of the impersonal 'third' — the world of government, institutions, tribunals, prisons, schools, committees, and so on. But the norm that must continue to inspire and direct the moral order is the ethical norm of the interhuman. If the moral-political order totally relinquishes its ethical foundation, it must accept all forms of society, including the facist or totalitarian, for it can no longer evaluate or discriminate between them. The state is usually better than anarchy — but not always. In some instances, — fascism or totalitarianism, for example — the political order of the state may have to be challenged in the name of our ethical responsibility to the other. This is why ethical philosophy must remain the first philosophy.

> Is not the ethical criterion of the interhuman employed by you as a sort of messianic eschatology, wherein the ontological structures of possession and totality would be transcended towards a face-to-face relation of pure exposure to the absolutely other?

Here again I must express my reservations about the term eschatology. The term *eschaton* implies that there might exist a finality, an end (*fin*) to the historical relation of difference between man and the absolutely other, a reduction of the gap that safeguards the alterity of the transcendent, to a totality of sameness. To realize the *eschaton* would therefore mean that we could seize or appropriate God as a *telos* and degrade the infinite relation with the other to a finite fusion. This is what Hegelian dialectics amounts to, a radical denial of the rupture between the ontological and the ethical. The danger of eschatology is the temptation to consider the man–God relation as a state, as a fixed and permanent state of affairs. I have described ethical responsibility as *insomnia* or *wakefulness* precisely because it is a perpetual duty of vigilance and effort that can never slumber. Ontology as a state of affairs can afford sleep. But love cannot sleep, can never be peaceful or permanent. Love is the incessant watching over of the other; it can never be satisfied or contented with the bourgeois ideal of love as domestic comfort or as the mutual possession of two people living out an *egoisme-á-deux*.

> If you reject the term "eschatology", would you accept the term "messianic" to describe this ethical relation with the other?

Only if one understands messianic here according to the Talmudic maxim that "the doctors of the law will never have peace, neither in this world nor in the next; they go from meeting to meeting, discussing always — for there is always more to be discussed." I could not accept a form of messianism that would terminate the need for discussion, that would end our watchfulness.

> But are we not ethically obliged to struggle for a perfect world of peace?

Yes, but I seek this peace not for *me* but for the other. By contrast, if I say that "virtue is its own reward," I can only say so *for myself*; as soon as I make this a standard for the other I exploit him, for what I am then saying is: be virtuous towards me — work for me, love me, serve me, and so on — but don't expect anything from me in return. That would be rather like the story of the Czar's mother who goes to the hospital and says to the dying soldier: "You must be very happy to die for your country." I must always demand more of myself than of the other; and this is why I disagree with Buber's description of the I-Thou ethical relation as a symmetrical copresence. As Alyosha Karamazov says in *The Brothers Karamazov* by Dostoyevsky, "We are all responsible for everyone else — but I am more responsible than all the others." And he does not mean that every 'I' is more responsible than all the others, for that would be to generalize the law for everyone else — to demand as much from the other as I do from myself. This essential asymmetry is the very basis of ethics: not only am I more responsible than the other but I am even responsible for everyone else's responsibility!

> How does the God of ethics differ from the 'God of the philosophers', that is, the God of traditional ontology?

For ethics, it is only in the infinite relation with the other that God passes (*se passe*), that traces of God are to be found. God thus reveals himself as a trace, not as an ontological presence — such as Aristotle defined as a self-thinking-thought and scholastic metaphysics defined as an *Ipsum Esse Subsistens* or *Ens Causa Sui*. The God of the Bible cannot be defined or proved by means of logical predictions and attributions. Even the superlatives of wisdom, power, and causality advanced by medieval ontology are inadequate to the abso-

lute otherness of God. It is not by superlatives that we can think of
God, but by trying to identify the particular interhuman events that
open towards transcendence and reveal the traces where God has
passed. The God of ethical philosophy is not God the almighty
being of creation, but the persecuted God of the prophets who is
always in relation with man and whose difference from man is never
indifference. This is why I have tried to think of God in terms of
desire, a desire that cannot be fulfilled or satisfied — in the
etymological sense of *satis*, measure. I can never have enough in my
relation to God, for he always exceeds my measure, remains forever
incommensurate with my desire. In this sense, our desire for God is
without end or term: it is interminable and infinite because God
reveals himself as absence rather than presence. Love is the society
of God and man, but man is happier, for he has God as company
whereas God has man! Furthermore, when we say that God cannot
satisfy man's desire, we must add that the nonsatisfaction is itself
sublime! What is a defect in the finite order becomes an excellence
in the infinite order. In the infinite order, the absence of God is better than his presence, and the anguish of man's concern and searching for God is better than consummation or comfort. As
Kierkegaard put it, "The need for God is a sublime happiness."

> Your analysis of God as an impossibility of being or being-present
> would seem to suggest that the ethical relation is entirely utopian
> and unrealistic.

This is the great objection to my thought. "Where did you ever see
the ethical relation practiced?" people say to me. I reply that its being
utopian does not prevent it from investing our everyday actions of
generosity or goodwill towards the other: even the smallest and most
commonplace gestures, such as saying "after you" as we sit at the din-
ner table or walk through a door, bear witness to the ethical. This
concern for the other remains utopian in the sense that it is always
'out of place' (*u-topos*) in this world, always other than the 'ways of the
world'; but there are many examples of it in the world. I remember
meeting once with a group of Latin American students, well versed
in the terminology of Marxist liberation and terribly concerned by
the suffering and unhappiness of their people in Argentina. They
asked me rather impatiently if I had ever actually witnessed the uto-

pian rapport with the other that my ethical philosophy speaks of. I replied, "Yes, indeed — here in this room."

> So you would maintain that Marxism bears witness to a utopian inspiration?

When I spoke of the overcoming of Western ontology as an "ethical and prophetic cry" in *"God and Philosophy,"* I was in fact thinking of Marx's critique of Western idealism as a project to understand the world rather than to transform it. In Marx's critique we find an ethical conscience cutting through the ontological identification of truth with an ideal intelligibility and demanding that theory be converted into a concrete praxis of concern for the other. It is this revelatory and prophetic cry that explains the extraordinary attraction that the Marxist utopia exerted over numerous generations. Marxism was, of course, utterly compromised by Stalinism. The 1968 Revolt in Paris was a revolt of sadness, because it came after the Khruschev Report and the exposure of the corruption of the Communist Church. The year 1968 epitomized the joy of despair, a last grasping at human justice, happiness, and perfection — after the truth had dawned that the communist ideal had degenerated into totalitarian bureaucracy. By 1968 only dispersed groups and rebellious pockets of individuals remained to seek their surrealist forms of salvation, no longer confident of a collective movement of humanity, no longer assured that Marxism could survive the Stalinist catastrophe as the prophetic messenger of history.

> What role can philosophy serve today? Has it in fact reached that end, spoken of by so many contemporary continental philosophers?

It is true that philosophy, in its traditional forms of ontotheology and logocentrism — to use Heidegger's and Derrida's terms — has come to an end. But it is not true of philosophy in the other sense of critical speculation and interrogation. The speculative practice of philosophy is by no means near its end. Indeed, the whole contemporary discourse of overcoming and deconstructing metaphysics is far more speculative in many respects than is metaphysics itself. Reason is never so versatile as when it puts itself in question. In the contemporary end of philosophy, philosophy has found a new lease on life.

EMMANUEL LEVINAS

2. *Bad Conscience and the Inexorable*

> *The ego responsible for the Other, ego without ego, is fragility itself, to the point of being put into question through and through as I, without identity, responsible for the one to whom he cannot give a response, respondent who is not a question, question which relates to the Other without any longer waiting for a response from him. The other does not respond.*
>
> Maurice Blanchot
> The Writing of Disaster

1. Starting with *intentionality*, consciousness is understood as a modality of the voluntary. The word *intention* suggests this, and thus the label *acts* conferred on the unities of intentional consciousness is justified. On the other hand, the intentional structure of consciousness is characterized by representation. Representation would be at the basis of all consciousness, whether theoretical or nontheoretical. Brentano's thesis remains true for Husserl, despite all the exactitude he brought to it and the care with which he surrounded it with the notion of objectivizing acts. Consciousness implies presence, position-before-itself, that is, mundaneness, the fact of being-given, and exposure to the grasp, hold, comprehension, appropriation. Is not intentional consciousness, then, the detour through which perseverance-in-being is concretely exercised, the active appropriation on the scene where the being of beings unfolds, is reassembled, and is manifested? Consciousness would be the very scenario of the incessant effort of *esse* with a view to this *esse* itself, a quasi-tautological exercise of the *conatus*, to which the formal signification of that privileged verb one names, without due consideration, "auxiliary," is reduced.

But a consciousness *directed* onto the world and its objects, structured as intentionality, is also in addition *indirectly* consciousness of itself: consciousness of the active-ego that represents the world and objects, as well as consciousness of its very acts of representation, consciousness of mental activity. However indirect, this consciousness is immediate but without intentional aim, an implicit and pure accompaniment. It is nonintentional, to be distinguished from the interior perception to which it is apt to be converted. The latter reflective consciousness *takes for objects* the ego, its states, and mental acts. This is a reflective consciousness, where consciousness directed onto the world seeks help against the inevitable naiveté of its intentional rectitude, which is forgetful of the indirectly lived and the nonintentional and its horizons, forgetful of what accompanies it.

In philosophy one is then borne — perhaps too quickly — to consider this lived element as a still nonexplicit knowledge or a still confused representation that reflection will bring to full light. It would be the obscure context of the thematized world that reflection, intentional consciousness, will convert into clear and distinct data, like those presenting the perceived world itself.

Nevertheless, it is not forbidden to wonder if, under the gaze of reflective consciousness taken for self-consciousness, the nonintentional, lived in counterpoint to the intentional, conserves and delivers its veritable meaning. The critique traditionally applied to introspection has always suspected a modification that the consciousness called "spontaneous" would undergo under the scrutinizing, thematizing, objectivizing, and indiscreet eye of reflection, as a violation and misappreciation of some secret. This critique is always refuted, but it is always reborn.

What happens, then, in this nonreflective consciousness that one takes solely as prereflective and that, implicit, accompanies intentional consciousness, aiming intentionally in reflection at the selfsame, as if the thinking ego appeared in the world and belonged there? What can this alleged confusion, this implication, in any manner positively signify? Are there not grounds to distinguish between the *envelopment* of the particular within a concept, the *implied* of the presupposed in a notion, the *potentiality* of the possible in a horizon on the one side, and the *intimacy* of the nonintentional in prereflective consciousness?

2. Is the "knowledge" of the prereflective self-consciousness, properly speaking, *knowing*? The confused and implicit consciousness preceding every intention — or returning from every intention — is not an act, but pure passivity. It is not only pure passivity

because of its being-without-having-chosen-to-be or because of its fall into an entanglement of possibles already realized before any assumption, as in Heideggerian *Geworfenheit*. It is a "consciousness" that rather than signifying a knowledge of self, is an effacement, or discretion, of presence. It is bad conscience: without intentions, without aims, without the protective mask of the character beholding himself in the mirror of the world, reassured and posing. Without name, without situation, without titles. Presence that dreads presence, denuded of all attributes. Nudity that is not that of the unveiling or the uncovering of truth. In its nonintentionality, on this side of all willing, before all fault, in its nonintentional identification, identity recedes before its affirmation, before what the identification's return to self can admit of insistence. Bad conscience or timidity: accused without guilt, responsible for its very presence. Reserve of the noninvested, the nonjustified, the "stranger on the earth," according to the expression of the Psalmist, without country or abode, who does not dare to enter. The interiority of the mental is perhaps originally this. Not in the world but in question. By reference to and in "memory" of what the ego, which is already posited and affirmed, or made firm, in the world and in being, remains ambiguous enough, or enigmatic enough, to acknowledge itself as "hateful," to use Pascal's term, in the very manifestation of its emphatic identity of ipseity, in language, in the saying-I. The superb priority of the A *is* A — principle of intelligibility and meaningfulness — that sovereignty, that freedom in the human ego, is also, if one can say, the advent of humility. Putting into question the affirmation and firming up of being, which is found right up to the famous and facilely rhetorical quest for the "meaning of life," as if the ego in-the-world, which has already taken meaning from the vital psychic and social finalities, were getting back to its bad conscience.

Nonintentional prereflective consciousness could not be described as taking cognizance of this passivity, as though one could already distinguish in it a subject's reflection, positing itself as an "indeclinable nominative," assured of its legitimacy of being, and "dominating" the timidity of the nonintentional as some childishness of the spirit to be overcome, or as an attack of weakness occurring to an impassible psychism, The nonintentional is straightaway passivity; in some way the accusative is its first "case." To speak truly, this passivity, which is not the correlate of any action, describes less the "bad conscience" of the nonintentional than it lets itself be described by it. Bad conscience is not the finitude of existing signified in anguish. My death, which is always premature, puts the being that as being perseveres in being into check, but this scandal does not rattle the good conscience of being, nor the morality founded on the inalienable right of the *conatus*. In the passivity of the nonintentional, in the very mode of its spontaneity, before any formulation of "metaphysical" ideas on this subject, the very justice of the position in being that is affirmed by intentional thought, knowledge, and appropriation of the now (*main-tenant*) is put into question: being as bad conscience; being in question, but also having to respond to the question — the birth of language; to have to speak, to have to say "I," to be in the first person, to be precisely me; but, then, in the affirmation of the ego's being, to have to respond to its right to be.

3. To have to respond to its right to be — not by reference to the abstraction of some anonymous law, some juridicial entity, but in fear for the Other (*Autrui*). My "in the world," my "place in the sun," my at homeness, have they not been the usurpation of the places belonging to the other man already oppressed and starved by me? Fear of all that my existing, despite its intentional and conscious innocence, can accomplish of violence and murder. Fear that rises up behind my "self-consciousness" and whatever, towards good conscience, are the qualms of pure perseverance in being. Fear that comes to me from the face of the Other. Extreme uprightness of the face of the neighbor, rending the plastic forms of the phenomenon. Uprightness of an exposure unto death, without defense; and, before all language and mimicry, a demand to me addressed from the bottom of an absolute solitude; demand addressed or order signified, a putting into question of my presence and my responsibility.

Fear and responsibility for the other man's death, even if the ultimate meaning of this responsibility for the Other's death were a responsibility before the inexorable and, in the last extremity, the obligation not to let the other man face death alone. Even if, facing death, where the very uprightness of the face that calls me finally fully reveals both its exposure without defense and its very facing itself, even if, in the last extremity, the not-letting-the-other-man-alone consists, in this confrontation and impotent meeting, only of responding "Here I am" (*me voici*) to the demand that summons me. This is, without doubt, the secret of sociality and, in its ultimate gratuity and vanity, love for the neighbor, love without concupiscence.

Fear for the Other, for the neighbor's death, is my fear, but there is nothing in it of fear *for* myself. It thus contrasts strongly with the admirable phenomenological analysis that *Being and Time* proposes on affectivity: a reflective structure where emotion is always *about* something moving, but also *for* itself, where emotion consists in being moved — in being frightened, being glad, being sad, and so on. It is a double "intentionality" of the *about* and the *for*, which participate in the emotion par excellence: anxiety, being-towards-death, where finite being is moved *about* its finitude *for* this very finitude. Fear for the other man does not come back to anxiety for *my* death. It overflows the ontology of Heideggerian *Dasein*. The ethical trouble of being — beyond its good conscience of being "with a view to that very being" whose end and scandal are marked by being-towards-death, but where it does not awaken scruples.

Within the "naturalness" of "being-with-a-view-to-that-very-being," in relation to which all things, as *Zuhandenes* (readiness to hand), and even the other man, seem to take on meaning, essential nature is put into question. It is a reversal starting from the face of the Other, where at the very heart of the phenomenon in its light there is signified a *surplus* of meaningfulness that one could designate as glory. Does not what is called the "word of God" come to me in the demand that summons me and appeals to me and, before any invitation to dialogue, that rends apart the form under which the individual, who resembles me, appears to me and alone is shown in order to become the face of the other man? In relation to all the affectivity of being-in-the-world, there is the novelty of a nonindifference for me of the absolutely different, other, nonrepresentable, nongraspable, that is, the Infinite that assigns me, rending apart the representation under which beings of the human genus manifest themselves in order to designate me, in the face of the Other, without possible escape, as the unique and the elect. Call of God, it does not set up a *relation* between me and Him who has spoken to me; it does not set up what, under whatever title, would be a conjunction, a coexistence, a synchrony, however ideal, between terms. The Infinite could not bear meaning for a thought that goes to a term, and the "God bless" (*à-Dieu*)[1] is not a finality. Perhaps beyond being, the word *glory* signifies this irreducibility of the "God bless" or the fear of God to the eschatological which for humans interrupts the consciousness that was going to being in its ontological perseverance, or to the death it takes for the ultimate thought. The alternative of being and nothingness is not ultimate. The "God bless" is not a process of being; in the call I am sent back to the other man through whom this call signifies, to the neighbor for whom I have to fear.

Behind the affirmation of being's persisting analytically, or animally, in its being — where the ideal vigor of the identity that is identified, affirmed, and firmed up in the lives of individual human beings and in their struggle for existence, is vital, conscious, and rational — the wonder of the ego claimed by God in the face of the neighbor, the wonder of the I relieved of its self and fearing God, is thus like the suspension of the eternal and irreversible return, both of the identical to itself and of the intangibility of its logical and ontological privilege. Suspension of its ideal priority, negator of all alterity, excluding the third person. Suspension of war and politics, which pass themselves off as the relation of the same to the other. In the deposition by the ego of its ego's sovereignty, in its modality of hateful ego, the ethical has meaning, but so, too, it is likely, does the very spirituality of the soul. The human, or human interiority, is the return to the interiority of nonintentional consciousness, to bad conscience, to its possibility of dreading injustice more than death, of preferring injustice sustained to injustice committed, and to what justifies being to what secures it. To be or not to be — this is probably not the question par excellence.

"Everything is in the hands of God, except the fear of God," says Reb Hanina, quoted on an ancient page of the Talmud (Tractate *Berakhot* 33B). The fear of God would be man's business. The fear that, in its omnipotence, the omnipotent God of theology cannot not inspire in the creature is thus not the fear of God that, according to the words of Reb Hanina, is "the unique treasure of the treasury of Heaven."

Note

1. The term *à-Dieu*, which could be literally translated as "to-God," is also a hyphenated and accented version of the common French word *adieu*, used at partings to mean "good-bye," "farewell," or "God bless." Only the latter, *God bless*, retains the reference to the divine that is at the etymological root of *adieu* and that is the emphatic point of Levinas' special construction. In spoken French *à-Dieu* and *adieu* would be indistinguishable. — Trans.

3. Our Clandestine Companion

Twenty years ago Levinas wrote, "For everyone, this century will have witnessed the end of philosophy" — yet, by ending this very same phrase with an exclamation point, he modified and possibly reversed its sense. This punctual addition was particularly welcome since, having been destined to bring philosophy back down to earth, our epoch will perhaps be remembered as one of the richest in philosophers (if the word *rich* still passes as pertinent), marked throughout by philosophical investigation and by an unparalleled rivalry among the sciences, literature, and philosophy, all of which necessarily gives philosophy the last word — and averts its demise.

All, Shamefully, Gloriously

Whether shamefully, gloriously, mistakenly, or by default, we are all philosophers; especially when we submit whatever seems philosophical (a term chosen to avoid emphasizing "philosophy" as such) to a questioning so radical that the entire tradition would have to be called forth in its support. But I would add (while repeating the warning of Bacon and Kant: *de nobis ipsis silemus*[1]) that, as soon as I encountered — a happy encounter, in the strongest sense — Emmanuel Levinas, more than fifty years ago, it was with a sort of testimony that I persuaded myself that philosophy was life itself, youth itself, in its unbridled — yet nonetheless reasonable — passion, renewing itself continually and suddenly by an explosion of new and enigmatic thoughts or by still unknown names, who would later shine forth as prodigious figures.

Philosophy would henceforth be our companion day and night, even by losing its name, by becoming literature, scholarship, the lack thereof, or by standing aside. It would be the clandestine friend we always respected, loved, which meant we were not bound by it — all the while giving us to believe that there was nothing awakened in us, vigilant unto sleep, not due to our difficult friendship. Philosophy or love. But philosophy is precisely not an allegory.

An Invincible Skepticism

Levinas wrote (and some of these quotes are from memory) that skepticism was invincible. While easily refuted, the refutation leaves skepticism intact. Is it really contradicted when it openly uses reasons that it destroys? Contradiction is also the essence of skepticism: just as it combats every dogmatism openly, by exposing its unsatisfactory or onerous presuppositions (origin, truth, value, authenticity, the exemplary or proper, etc.), so does it do so in an implicit way, referring itself back to a 'dogmatism' so absolute that every assertion is threatened (this is already to be observed in the ancient skeptics and in Sextus Empiricus.) This doesn't mean that one should take pleasure in that maniacal and pathetic sort of nihilism Lyotard rightly denounces and for which, once and for all, nothing is of *value*. Once again, this would be a kind of rest or security. What is at fault with nihilism — a term without vigor or rigor — is not knowing its own weaknesses and always stopping prematurely. The invincible skepticism that Levinas admits shows that his own philosophy, his metaphysics (these names so easily disparaged), affirms nothing that is not overseen by an indefatigable adversary, one to whom he does not concede but who obliges him to go further, not beyond reason into the facility of the irrational or towards a mystical effusion, but rather towards another reason, towards the other as reason or demand. All this appears in each of his books. Doubtless, he follows the same path; but in each case, the unexpected emerges to render the path so new or so ancient that, following it along, we are struck as by a blow to the heart — the heart of a reason — that makes us say within ourselves, "But I've also thought that; I *must* think it."

Valéry: "The Other Man, a Fundamental Concept"

Some thinkers are perhaps more naive than others: Descartes more naive than Leibniz; Plato more naive than Plato. Heidegger, this thinker of our own time, is so bereft of naiveté that he has to have disciples to put it into perspective, disciples, moreover, who can't be called upon to excuse him from what happened in 1933 (but this last point is so serious that one cannot be content with an episodic allusion: Nazism and Heidegger, this is a wound in thought itself, and each of us is profoundly wounded — it will not be dealt with by preterition). Philosophical naiveté is perhaps inseparable from philosophical evidence, since the latter brings forth the most recent (what is newest in the oldest) and because what it says or *advances* there necessarily lends itself to critique: what is advanced is vulnerable, yet nonetheless it is the most important. When Levinas asked if ontology were fundamental (excluding other issues here, and for other reasons, which precede those of Heidegger — who also came to object to these two terms, in the same way that he puts the word *being* under erasure), in a certain way he posed a naive question, one that was unexpected and unheard of, because it broke with what seemed to have renewed philosophy and also because he was the first to have contributed to understanding and transmitting this thought. Raising the question, then, Levinas broke with himself. By this move, when Levinas pronounced the word *other* and the relation of the I to the Other as exorbitant, as an infinite or transcendent relation, one that could not be grasped by a reflection on being and beings, given that the whole of Western philosophy had been traditionally oriented by the privilege accorded to the Same, to the Self-Same, or more abruptly, to identity, it became obvious that subsequent criticism would judge his affirmation naive and would accumulate objections to refute it (as is said of K. in *The Castle*: he always refuted everything). All the same, it is the critique that was naive — not to understand what was decisive or difficult in this exigency, an exigency that made reason (even practical reason) ill at ease, without repudiating it in the meantime, however.

I recall the following from Valéry's *Notebooks* (Valéry, this hardly naive writer, who nevertheless is, sometimes happily, sometimes unhappily, especially when he sets out to malign philosphy, which he doesn't know very well anyway): "The systems of the philosophers,

which I hardly know, seem generally trifling.", which is clearly a presentiment of the Other's importance, even if he expresses it somewhat inadequately: "Other, a similar other, or perhaps a double of
myself [but, precisely, the other cannot be an alter ego], this is the
most mesmerizing abyss, the most recurrent question, the most cun-
ning obstacle . . . . Thus," Valéry remarkably adds, "the other
man . . . remains a fundamental conception."

Questioning Language

I am sure that Levinas does not mind philosophizing in ways
that might seem somewhat unfashionable. Philosophy is, if anything,
untimely, and to characterize his work as novel is what would least
agree with him. Nonetheless, while restoring metaphysics and ethics
to an eminence they formerly, if not unwittingly, enjoyed, Levinas
anticipates, or follows out in his own way, the preoccupations that are
preeminently (or, unfortunately) those of our time. For example, he
never fails to question the domain of language in a crucial, astute
way, one that has for so long been neglected by the philosophical
tradition. Valéry, for example, thought he could put philosophy in a
difficult situation by claiming that "philosophy and all the rest is only
a peculiar use of words" and that "every metaphysics results from a
poor use of words." The remark gets clarified when he explains his
own conception of language, what might be called an existential
view, namely, that what counts is that the "lived [réelle], internal
experience" conceals a conceptually ordered system, a system of
notations and conventions that goes far beyond "the quite particular
and personal phenomenon." Beyond the singular phenomenon itself,
then, such a view conveys the general value of truth or law. In other
words, Valéry reproaches philosophy for being what he will demand
that literature and poetry be: the possibility of language, the invention of a second-degree language ("to think in a form that one would
have invented"), without the "foolish and indomitable pretension" of
making it seem one could get out of the situation by having this
language pass for thought. It is true that Valéry will add (a warning
that still holds for the best linguists when they concern themselves
with poetics) that "every investigation about Art and Poetry tends to
make necessary what is essentially arbitrary." Thus, he points out the
temptations or "mimological perversions" that arise when necessity is

equated with the appearance, or the effect, of necessity — a somewhat enigmatic attempt of discursive mutation, all the same.

Irreducible Diachrony

What matters to Levinas is something else, and it is only involved indirectly — happily, should I say? — in linguistic research. If there is an extreme dissymmetry between "me and the Other" (expressed in his impressive remark that "the Other is always closer to God than I," who preserves His power, whatever is understood by the unnameable name of God), if the infinite relation between me and other might nonetheless be a relation of language, if it is allowed me, I who am scarcely myself, to have a relation with the extreme other — the closest and farthest — through speech, then there could not fail to result certain exigencies that might reverse or overturn speech itself, even if this were only the following: the Other or other can not be thematized. All of which is to say, I will not speak of the other or about the other, but I will speak — if I speak — *to* the Other (i.e., to the stranger, the poor, him who has no speech, even the master, bereft of mastery), not to inform him or to transmit knowledge to him — a task for ordinary language — but rather to invoke him (this other so other that his mode of address is not "you" but "he"), to render him witness by a manner of speaking that doesn't efface the infinite distance, but is speech by this distance, a speech born of the infinite.

In each of his books Levinas continually refines, by an ever more rigorous reflection, what was said on this subject in his *Totality and Infinity*: what, properly, had been *said*, that is, thematized, and thus was always already said, instead of remaining to be said. From this one of the persistent and insoluble problems of philosophy derives: how can philosophy be talked about, opened up, and presented, without, by that very token, using a particular language, contradicting itself, mortgaging its own possibility? Must not the philosopher be a writer, and thus forego philosophy, even while pointing out the philosophy implicit in writing? Or, just as well, to pretend to teach it, to master it — that is, this venture of a non-mastered, oral speech, all the while demeaning himself from time to time by *writing* books? How can one maintain the dissymmetry, the intersubjectively qualified (and wrongly so) curvature of space, the

infinity of a speech born of the infinite? Levinas will go furthest, in
the text entitled "The Saying and the Said," a text that speaks to us,
just as if the extraordinary itself spoke to us, about something I have
no intention or ability to take up or sum up. One simply has to read
it, and meditate upon it. Indeed, I can somewhat evasively recall that
if the said is always already said, then the Saying is never only to be
said, something that does not privilege the future (the future present
of the future), nor is it even — at least, this is how I interpret it —
a prescription as edict. Rather, it is what no ego can take upon itself
and safeguard in its keep: it can only be done by giving it up. Saying
is giving, loss (yes, loss), but, and I might add, loss within the impossibility of loss pure and simple. By the said, we belong to order, to
the world (the cosmos), and we are present to the other with whom
we deal as equals. We are contemporaries.

Somewhere in Saying, however, we are uprooted from that
order, without which order itself might serenely disappear into
disorder. Such is the noncoincidence with the Other: the impossibility of being together in a simple simultaneity, the necessity (the
obligation) of assuming a time not of the present, what Levinas will
term the "*irreducible diachrony*," which is not a lived temporality, but
rather is marked as a lapse (or absence) of time. This is what Saying
entails in our responsibility towards the other, a responsibility so
beyond measure that we are given over to it passively, at the limit of
all patience — rather than being capable of responding to it autono-
mously, out of our pretension to be subjects. On the contrary, we are
subjected, we are exposed (an exposure that is not of presence or of
unconcealment) and revealed as *ourselves* at risk, thoroughly obsessed
or besieged to the point of "substitution" — the one who practically
doesn't exist existing only for the other — in the "*one for the other*" relation. Such a relation mustn't be thought of as an identification, since
it doesn't occur by way of being; nor is this relation simply one of
nonbeing, for it nonetheless gauges the incommensurable. The relation is one of positive impropriety, of strangeness and interruption;
and yet, it is a *substitution* of one for the other, a difference as
nonindifference.

Indiscretion Towards the Unsayable

I recall several of Levinas' phrases, the resonance of which is
that of philosophy itself — an appeal of reason for the awakening of

another reason, the recollection of speaking within the said — this ancillary language that nonetheless claims not to subdue the *exception*: "Indiscretion towards the unsayable. Maybe this will be the task of philosophy." Or again, "Perhaps philosophy is only the exaltation of language, within which words (subsequently) condition the very stability of religion, science, and, technology." From this point we can foresee the requirements raised for language, namely, to enunciate the Saying. But this is an activity only in appearance if it prolongs (in a nonself-possessing hold) the uttermost passivity. The enigma of a Saying is like that of a God speaking within man — within this man who counts on no God, for whom there is no home, who is exiled from all worlds, who has no hidden world, and who in the end doesn't even have language as an abode (at least to any greater extent than by having it merely to speak in the affirmative or negative). This is why Levinas — getting back to the thought of an invincible skepticism — will also say (if I'm not mistaken) that "language is already skepticism." And here the accent should perhaps be placed on the *already*, not only because language would be inadequate or essentially negative, or even because it would surpass the limits of thought, but also, and perhaps just as well, precisely because of this relation with the ex-cessive, insofar as this relation bears the trace of what has happened in a nonpresence, a trace that has left no traces of what is always already effaced, but bearing it, nonetheless, beyond being. Thus, language itself would be skepticism; thought of in this sense, indeed, it would not allow satisfaction with absolute knowledge or allow transparent communication. Because of this, it would be a language to overtax the whole of language, precisely by not exceeding it: it would be the language of the epoché, or, according to Jean-Luc Nancy, it would be one of lapse or syncopation. To a certain extent then (and how much is unclear), the skepticism of language undermines every guarantee, by reason of which it does not enclose us in what it would pretend ought to be the case, namely, a sure set of conditions.

The Divine Comedy

I hardly think that a good approach to Levinas' thought would characterize it in terms of certain topics that are indeed admissible, but that might justify a cursory reading or might arrest those extreme questions continually being posed to us — would characterize it, for example, as a philosophy of transcendence or as a metaphysical ethics. Such an approach would probably be inadequate, if only because we no longer know how to grasp such words, overcharged as they are with traditional meaning. The word transcendence is either too strong — it quickly reduces us to silence — or, on the other hand, it keeps both itself and us within the limits of what it should open up. In his own unique way, Jean Wahl used to say that the greatest transcendence, the transcendence of transcendence, is ultimately the immanence, or the perpetual referral, of the one to the other. Transcendence within immanence: Levinas is the first to devote himself to this strange structure (sensibility, subjectivity) and not to let himself be satisfied by the shock value of such contrarieties. Yet, one is always struck by one of his typical procedures: to begin, or to follow out, an analysis (most often, phenomenologically inspired) with such rigor and informed understanding that it seems precisely in this way that everything is said and that truth itself is disclosed — right along, that is, until we get to a minor remark, usually introduced by, e.g., an *"unless"* to which we cannot fail to be attentive, which fissures the whole of the preceding text, disturbing the solid order we had been called upon to observe, an order that nonetheless remains important. This is perhaps *the* movement that could properly be called philosophical, not by stroke of force or belabored assertion, but a movement that was already Plato's expedient in his dialogues (his probity, and ruse as well). It is not so much a question of hermeneutics, since in a certain sense Levinas stands out and breaks with a tradition he understands completely, but rather it is that this tradition serves him as a springboard and a frame of reference.

In comparison, and when confronting the unsayable, *philosophical invention* renders our indiscretion concrete — as it does in a quite different way with the call to one who is beyond being, to an *"excess"* that is neither irrational nor romantic. Thus, by a kind of respectful parricide, he enjoins us not to rely on the *presence* and identity of Husserlian *consciousness*, but to substitute for phenomenological (or ontological) rationality a kind of reason understood as vigil, as a ceaseless awakening, as a *vigilance*. This is not meant to be a state of the soul — an ecstasy of drunkenness, a discontent with lucidity — nor to cause excitement about the "Ego" and its decentered interior; rather, it concerns the other in me who is yet ouside of me, that which can no longer be grasped in an experience (it is neither an event nor an advent), since every manifestation (indeed, even the nonmanifest content of the unconscious) always winds up giving itself over to the *presence* that keeps us within being. Thus are we exposed, by way of our own responsibility, to the enigma of the nonphenomenal, the nonrepresentable, within the ambiguity between the trace to be deciphered and the indecipherable.

Likewise (in the same way?), if Levinas pronounces or writes the name of God, he does not pass over into religion or theology, nor does he thereby conceptualize it. In fact, he gives us a presentiment that, without being another name for the Other (always other than the Other, "otherwise other"), the infinite transcendence, the transcendence of the infinite, to which we try to subject God, will always be ready to veer off "to the point of possible confusion with the bustle of the *there is*." But what is there about what Levinas terms the *there is*, aside from all reference to Heidegger's *es gibt*, and even long before the latter had proposed a quite differently structured analysis of it? The *there is* is one of Levinas' most fascinating propositions. It is his temptation, too, since as the reverse of transcendence it is thus not distinct from it either. Indeed, it is describable in terms of being, but as the *impossibility* of not being, as the incessant insistence of the neutral, the nocturnal murmur of the anonymous, as what never begins (thus, as an-archic, since it eternally eludes the determination of a beginning); it is the absolute, but as absolute indetermination.

All this is captivating; that is, it draws us towards the uncertain outside, endlessly talking outside the truth — in the manner of an Other whom we cannot get rid of simply by labelling him deceitful (the evil genius), or because it would be a joking matter, since this speech, which is only a perfidiously maintained laughter, is nonetheless suggestive. At the same time, this speech escapes all interpretation and is neither gratuitous nor playful. In the end it is sober, but as the illusion of seriousness, and is thus what disturbs us most, since this move is also most apt to deny us the very resources of being itself, such as place and light. Perhaps all this is a gift of literature, and we do not know if it intoxicates while sobering, or if its speech, which charms and disgusts, doesn't ultimately attract us because it promises (a promise it both does and does not keep) to clarify what is obscure in all speech — everything in speech that escapes revelation, manifestation: namely, the remaining trace of nonpresence, what is still opaque in the transparent.

That God, by his highest transcendence, the Good beyond being, must give himself over to this inextricable intrigue and that he may not directly (except by the unheard call to rectitude) cancel what Hegel might have termed the "bad infinite," the endlessly repetitive — all this leaves us faced with a demand that is necessarily our own, precisely because it surpasses us. We are confronted by what, within the ambiguity of the sacred and the holy, of the 'temple' and the 'theater' renders us spectators-actors-witnesses of the Divine Comedy, where, if we do happen to laugh about it, "the laughter sticks in our throats."

I would like to add an obsessional touch to these several notes. The book that Emmanuel Levinas has entitled *Otherwise than Being or Beyond Essence* is a philosophical work. It would be difficult not to take it as such, since philosophy, even if it concerns discontinuity and rupture, nonetheless solicits us philosophically. This book begins with a dedication, however, that I here transcribe: "*To the memory of those who were closest among the six million assassinated by the National Socialists, and of the millions on millions of all confessions and all nations, victims of the same hatred of the other man, the same antisemitism.*" How can one philosophize, how can one write within the memory of Auschwitz of those who have said, oftentimes in notes buried near the crematoria: know what has happened, don't forget, and at the same time, you won't be able to.

It is this thought that traverses, that bears, the whole of Levinas' philosophy and that he proposes to us without saying it, beyond and before all obligation.

Note

1. "We are silent about ourselves." Jean-Luc Nancy recalls this for us in his remarkable *Logodaedalus*. (Paris: Aubier-Flammarion, 1976).

Part II

From Ethics to Philosophy

STEVEN G. SMITH

4. Reason as One for Another: Moral and Theoretical Argument in the Philosophy of Levinas

Emmanuel Levinas has represented the divine claim of the moral life, "otherwise than being," by the idea of the absolutely other. His uncompromising treatment of the otherness of God and neighbor seems, however, to negate the minimum conditions of sense and reason, posing a riddle for his interpreters: how can there be a rational argument concerning an infinite that avowedly exceeds any rational totality? How can there be a phenomenological description of something that is not evident, or an ontological analysis of something that is beyond being? If Levinas' analysis is neither phenomenological nor ontological, what is it? Why call it philosophy?[1]

Levinas has often described his thought as a phenomenology.[2] This encourages the formulation of the problem of his method and rationality in phenomenological terms; that is, it may be suggested that there is a (unique) 'object' to which his extraordinary 'descriptions' happen to be 'adequate'.[3] But is it useful or perspicuous to extend the notions of 'object' and 'description' so as to apply them to Levinas' enterprise? I believe not. Consequently, in what follows I will try to show the *sui generis* character of Levinas' nontheoretical yet genuinely philosophical argument, and — because I take 'rationality' to be the conception of last resort governing the demands for justification that may be directed to a philosophy — to elucidate the implications for philosophy of the 'rationality' that Levinas proposes, and that his achievement presupposes.

Levinas' approach to reason is controlled by his understanding of intersubjectivity, which has received two major statements in the last two decades, *Totality and Infinity* (1961) and *Otherwise than Being or Beyond Essence* (1974).[4] These two books are very different, but also complementary; they bring contrasting methods to bear on the common problem of morality. We will attend to these books in turn before weighing Levinas' cumulative argument about the nature and meaning of reason.

I

According to Levinas, the Western philosophical tradition is overwhelmingly devoted to the problem of theoretical truth. Its approach may be epistemological, that is, attentive to the necessary structure of knowing, or ontological, that is, attentive to the necessary structure of being; but there is a root complicity between the two emphases. It is the destiny of knowledge to search out and adhere to being, and it is the destiny of being to disclose itself to be known. The bias towards the 'theoretical', in this inclusive sense, unites such diverse thinkers as Husserl and Heidegger.

Totality and Infinity's main thesis is that justice is prior to truth.[5] 'Justice' is a function of the plural relation between persons. The plurality of human society is ultimately significant in itself and can never be reduced to the unity that is the necessary goal of the search for truth — for example, in the form of the unity of ideally synthesized meaning-objects, in Husserl's phenomenology, or the unity of the one question about 'being' underlying and orienting the many questions about 'beings' in Heidegger's thought. Moreover, the *adaequatio rei et intellectus* brings about a unity between the knower and being, a mutual possession; we 'have' and are had by what we know. In veridical perceptions, for instance, we can "put our fingers on" what we perceive, can traverse these perceptions towards others, and form them into a systematic picture, and so on. The truths of logic refer to possibilities of thought that we possess, in the sense of being able to check and repeat inferences. But the basic and commanding significance of human sociality is that people do not 'have' each other in this sense. Above and beyond the many ways in which the other person is perceivable and thinkable by the self, there is a way in which the other is not disclosed at all, not evident, and beyond the reach of the conclusions that can be drawn from what is evident. Levinas calls the social relation a "nonadequation."[6]

The other person has a different role than to be a known truth. The other is the one *in face of whom* truths are offered and criticized in discourse; he is the judge in the proceedings, never the accused. Nothing that I know or speak *about* could face me in the way that the one *to* whom I speak faces me. Because there is an uncomprehended other, neither my knowledge nor my action justifies itself but can only seek justification in a relationship with the other. This social context, though it is nontheoretical, is the presupposition of the human way of having truth via the public propositions of language. The proper meaning of this context is moral, and we falsify it when we construe or ground it theoretically. But the characteristic faux pas of our philosophy is precisely to carry out such a reduction of goodness to knowing and/or being, to deny the plurality of the order of justice in order to affirm the unity of the order of truth. We abscond from the moral adventure of the "infinitizing" relation with the other as other, in favor of the illicit satisfaction (and eventual violence and cruelty) of unbroken totality. We constrain the other by a conception of his nature, limiting in advance his claim upon us.

The priority of justice to truth is, however, a philosophical thesis. What is Levinas arguing but the *truth* of justice? How can his case be made except as a statement of the case? Further, how can a rational account be given of something that is not a truth?

The meaning of sociality and justice is certainly the "truth" addressed by Levinas' philosophy. In some sense it is impossible to regard it otherwise than as a truth, for just as a well-formed English sentence includes a subject and a verb, it seems that an intelligible philosophy must include a truth and a method of arriving at it. But there are strong reasons for suspecting that Levinas' "truth" is not a truth in the ordinary way. The idea of the infinite is presented in such a way as to make clear that its overflowing, far from fitting into the grammar of ontology or phenomenology, disrupts and subverts the system of disclosures to which the grammar is keyed. The other is a phenomenological nonobject, absolutely nonevident and independent of any intentional correlation. By calling the social relation the "logical plot of being,"[7] and asserting that being is plural, or that "exteriority "is" the essence of being,"[8] Levinas uses the language of ontology to express an anti-ontology; he answers the question of being by displacing it. Thus far, however, he produces only paradox and apparent logical bad faith. Can the relational concept of otherness be absolutized? What could be other than everything? (Does it make sense to introduce moral considerations in antithesis to being or history, rather than as additional desiderata about the meaning of being and history?) Or is the idea of the other a merely verbal proposal of meaning, unfulfillable and untestable, which thus ought to be excluded from philosophical discussion?

This line of criticism is pertinent only on the assumption that Levinas' truth is a theoretical truth after all and not, as Levinas thinks, something fundamentally different. The idea of the absolutely other is incoherent, to be sure, but we still have to ask what this incoherence might betoken, or what purpose it serves. Speaking with a theoretical vocabulary, Levinas registers a nontheoretical exigency, the claim of the moral life; and the paradoxical antiphenomenology and anti-ontology of *Totality and Infinity* are to be taken, not as phenomenological and ontological theses, but as pointers from phenomenology and ontology to that which they fail to express, the transcendence of the moral life. As he writes in "The Trace of the Other":

> If the significance of the trace consists in signifying without making to appear. . . if the trace thus does not belong to phenomenology, to the comprehension of "appearance" and "dissimulation," one could at least approach it in another way, locating its significance from the standpoint of the phenomenology that it interrupts.[9]

We must regard the argument of *Totality and Infinity* primarily as a gesture rather than as a description of an object or state of affairs. We are not being shown an object; in some sense we are being invited to adopt or acknowledge a certain posture that is morally significant. So instead of asking how Levinas' philosophy might or might not be rational according to the theoretical-descriptive idea of rationality, we must ask how his argument revises the meaning of rationality itself, by challenging the assumption that the pursuit of theory simply justifies itself and controls all meaning.

Levinas is a self-designated "phenomenologist," but in explaining his use of the term he makes a transposition from the descriptive to the performative mode. In the preface to *Totality and Infinity*, for example, he refers to a 'break-up' of thought into 'events . . .'

The presentation and the development of the notions employed owe everything to the phenomenological method. Intentional analysis is the search for the concrete. Notions held under the direct gaze of the thought that defines them are nevertheless, unbeknown to this naive thought, revealed to be implanted in horizons unsuspected by this thought; these horizons endow them with meaning — such is the essential teaching of Husserl. What does it matter if in the Husserlian phenomenology taken literally these unsuspected horizons are in their turn interpreted as thoughts aiming at objects! What counts is the idea of the overflowing of objectifying thought by a forgotten experience from which it lives. The break-up of the formal structure of thought (the noema of a noesis) into events which this structure dissimulates, but which sustain it and restore its concrete significance, constitutes a *deduction* — necessary and yet non-analytical.[10]

Just as the idea of the infinite is an 'overflowing' idea, so Levinas' phenomenology is an overflowing phenomenology. It points beyond any possible evidence to the nonevident moral relation between men which, when given a philosophical witness via the perturbation of theoretical truths, "restores the concrete significance" of these truths as human truths offered and received, taught and learned, in the peaceful relation of discourse. Phenomenology's search for the 'concrete' (i.e., the irreducible and underivable) and for 'horizons' of meaning is led, beyond any expectation of Husserl's, to the infinitely abstract *concretissimum* of the other's nonobjective moral claim and to a horizon of justice that belongs neither to consciousness nor the world.

The peculiar character of Levinas' truth produces a corresponding peculiarity in his method, for it is clear now that neither evidence nor logic warrants his 'deduction'. The decisive clue as to what does guide his argument is furnished by his statement that ethics is his optics.[11] The necessity motivating the formulation of the idea of the other or infinite is directly related to the necessity by which men listen to each other and feed and clothe each other. Thus Levinas' deductions are themselves moral events: the book *Totality and Infinity* offers itself to the reader as a generalized prototype of just utterance, focusing on the appropriate deformations of the text of phenomenology and ontology so as to acknowledge the interlocutor's transcendence of the question of his theoretical truth, to distinguish *who* he is from *what* he is. The theoretical content, or noncontent, of *Totality and Infinity* is continuously subordinated to this performative question of one's posture with respect to the horizon of sociality, which includes author and reader.

> And if I set forth, as a final and absolute vision, the separation and transcendence which are the themes of this book, these relations, which I claim form the fabric of being itself, first come together in my discourse presently addressed to my interlocutors: inevitably across my idea of infinity the other faces me — hostile, friend, my master, my student . . . . The face to face remains an ultimate situation. [12]

Since the social relation is known only in the measure that it is effected,[13] how could Levinas convey his thesis otherwise than by rigorously accomplishing the deferral of self before other that is the prime work of justice? The self defers to the other by accepting the breach in the fabric of knowing and being that is created by the transcendence of morality. Ethical "vision" and "optics" are spiritual and personal and are not associated with a subject-object relation. Therefore, the analogy of optics is somewhat dangerous. Ethical transcendence is not a content of experience, although it is sometimes referred to as the experience par excellence.[14] If it were a question of experience, there would be something to describe, instead of something always to be accomplished. In reality we are always given both experience and the moral surplus over experience, and this is reflected in our language, which always retains a reference to knowing and being and yet, because it *is* language, transcends them.

The moral ideas of *Totality and Infinity* often travel in theoretical garb. Even Levinas' negations of the theoretical can be taken as theoretical. For example, the statement *"Being is exteriority"*[15] is both grammatically and semantically an ontological assertion. It is a paradoxical assertion, since the meaning given to 'exteriority' by Levinas is incommensurable with the being of which it is predicated, but it is still ontological in form. There are two primary reasons for venturing this sentence. One is to subvert the ancient privilege of Eleatic unity, the suffocating unity towards which theoretical philosophy drives, by subverting the concept of being itself. The other is to show that justice and being, though incommensurable, are not separate and unrelated. The infinite overflows in being, not elsewhere. Morality is entirely of this world. But can either of these concerns be met by the *via negativa*, pursued throughout *Totality and Infinity*, of denying any commonality between the other and all being and knowing? For if anti-ontology fails to dissociate itself from ontology, what is it but bad ontology? And if it succeeds, what does it show but the distressing fact that morality and reality never come together?

Another side of the same difficulty arises with respect to the rationality of the *via negativa*, to the extent that Levinas accepts a theoretical understanding of 'reason' and thus presents morality as a transcendence of reason. There are frequent indications, however, that the meaning of 'reason' is being revised rather than transcended, as in statements such as these:

> Apology does not blindly affirm the self, but already appeals to the Other. It is the primordial phenomenon of reason . . .[16]

> The other is not for reason a scandal which launches it into dialectical movement, but the first rational teaching, the condition for all teaching.[17]

> The shame for oneself, the presence of and desire for the other are not the negation of knowing: knowing is their very articulation. The essence of reason consists not in securing for man a foundation and powers, but in calling him in question and inviting him to justice.[18]

The two "reasons" in *Totality and Infinity* refer to two philosophical roads. One is a dead end. It leads to the incoherent idea of the absolute otherness of the neighbor and thus discredits every theoretical attempt to deal with intersubjectivity, such as the Husserlian constitution of the alter ego and the Heideggerian ascertainment of the way of being, called *Miteinandersein*, that is presupposed by the events of sociality. A critical No is pronounced against the entire genre of philosophizing that obeys an impersonal reason — and the articulation of this No is, on the whole, the main achievement of *Totality and Infinity*. But even here a second road is indicated, one that leads to a positive claim for the rationality of morality and a positive linkage between justice and being. This is the *via eminentiae* of Levinas' most recent philosophy.

II

In 1964, three years after the publication of *Totality and Infinity*, two important articles appeared. One was Jacques Derrida's essay on Levinas, "Violence and Metaphysics,"[19] which called attention to the theoretical incoherence of the notions of pure infinity and absolute otherness, or exteriority, and on that basis questioned the pretension of this "Jewish" protest against the "Greek" all-mediating logos to be philosophy. The other was "La signification et le sens" by Levinas.[20] Here he followed the struggle of modern philosophy with the theoretical paradigm of language as a representation of the world.

Meaning occurs in events of *signification*, which has the structure of *ceci en tant que cela*, that is, 'this' proposed as, or offered to stand for, 'that.' In Husserl's view, the meaningfulness of language rests on the possibility of intuitively fulfilling the sense that a linguistic indication as such merely proposes. Language fails if we can never be shown what it is 'about'; experience disposes. Unfulfillable, so-called 'empty' significations, such as 'square circle' (or 'absolutely other'!), are senseless even though, like bad checks, they are sometimes passed.[21] Heidegger and Merleau-Ponty depart from Husserl's intuitionism by recognizing that even intuitions depend for their meaning on the context of significations formed by language and culture. Words refer not only to intuitions but to each other and to the whole historical experience of the linguistic community. But for Heidegger and Merleau-Ponty, language is still the house of being, or the poetry that celebrates being. It does not make sense, in their view, to speak of a transcendence of being.[22] Levinas' phrase *otherwise than being* remains an empty signification, even in this enlarged frame of reference.

In order to express a moral meaning that transcends all experience, Levinas must propose a philosophical signification that is not disposed by intuition or by the play of being. It must be the veritable transcendent, namely, the other person in person — or God revealing Himself through the moral claim of the other person — who so disposes. But that means that *ceci* (Levinas' philosophical language) is offered for *cela* in the sense, not of something, but of someone. Ethical signification, the work of language offering a sign for a signified, coincides with the moral event of *substitution* in which one person is responsible for another to the point of bearing his burdens and faults. The self 'stands for' the neighbor as does the sign for the signified, one for another (*l'un-pour-l'autre*).[23] Levinas disputes the standards of rationality and meaningfulness that are implicit in criticisms like Derrida's by showing how language's work of representation is only a mode of its primordial work of opening interlocutors to each other for mutual service. The root structure of reason is, according to *Otherwise than Being*, the 'one-for-another' of substitution and signification.[24] This is a forceful restatement of the message that already appeared in *Totality and Infinity*, that philosophy is morality even before it is theory.

Otherwise than Being tackles the methodic quandary by showing performatively what it is that language can do other than represent objects or paradoxical nonobjects like 'the other.' The problematic of totality and the infinite is now stated as the problematic of *le Dit* (the 'Said', the structurally coherent text created by language) and *le Dire* ('Saying', the primordially generous, nonthematic upsurge of communication). 'Saying' belongs to the horizon of sociality that is incommensurable with the text of the 'Said' but is its origin and presupposition. Levinas' aim in *Otherwise than Being* is to perform a 'reduction' of the said to saying, to 'surprise' saying before it becomes said and thus to resolve the problem of the unsayableness of the good by saying it anyway, in a kind of indiscretion.[25] Levinas calls this move a 'reduction' because it is similar to Husserl's phenomenological reductions in opening a radically new and, in some sense, transcendental field of inquiry.[26]

'Saying', like "the infinite", is conceived as a pure surplus over evidence, theme, and logic; in fact, the saying of 'Saying' is the positive production of the infinite distinct from the negative witness of the gaps created in totality (the phenomenologico-ontological realm) by the theoretical incoherence of the idea of the other. Levinas distinguishes between the *synchronic* meaning of the themes that can be assembled and ordered in one time or system and the *diachronic* meaning of the upsurge of language, which itself never enters into systematically determinable relationships to become an objective theme. In illustration of this distinction he offers the parable of skepticism. The skeptic's assertions can be shown to be self-contradictory, for the apodictic denial of truth presupposes some contact with truth. But the skeptic *himself* eludes ultimate refutation, as is shown historically by the fact that skepticism, though always refuted, always returns with its questions. The skeptic's diachronic performance of doubt is not precluded by the synchronic demonstration of its untenability. Now the ethical surplus of saying is similar to the theoretical minus of skepticism in being essentially refutable, that is, incapable of making a coherent appearance in the text of discourse; but it is also similar in being unquenchable in inspiration, having its own life in its own diachronic way that transcends the synchronic teleology of knowing and being. Language loses its concrete human significance when its synchrony is abstracted from its diachrony. Levinas' philosophy of saying is the event that restores this significance.[27].

Only with the advent of a diachronic philosophy does it become possible to speak of a philosophical *via eminentiae* (the way of superlatives) different from and superior to the *via negativa* of anti-phenomenology and anti-ontology. A good example of the method being practiced while explaining itself is this passage:

> Thus in order that subjectivity signify without reserve, the passivity of its exposure to the other person should not turn immediately back into an activity, but rather should expose itself in turn: there must be a passivity of passivity and, in the glory of the Infinite, a cinder from which the act could not be reborn. This passivity of passivity and this dedication to the Other, this sincerity, is Saying − not as a communication of something Said, which would be immediately recovered and absorbed or extinguished in the Said, but Saying holding its opening open, without excuse, without evasion or alibi, giving itself without saying anything of the Said − "Saying" saying "saying" itself (*Dire disant le dire meme*), without thematizing it, but still expositing it. Saying is thus making a sign of this very significance of exposure (or exposition); it is to expose exposure instead of maintaining oneself as though in an act of exposing: it is to exhaust oneself in exposing oneself . . . (in a) pre-reflexive iteration in saying of Saying itself.[28]

More has changed in *Otherwise than Being* than Levinas' manner of expression. His understanding of subjectivity and intersubjectivity now has a different emphasis. While in *Totality and Infinity* the principal structure of sociality was determined as an absolute *separation* between persons, based on both the 'original atheism' of the self's inner life of enjoyment and the transcendence of the other, in *Other-*

wise than Being the themes are infinite proximity and obsession of the self with the other rather than separation, and prophetic 'possession' by the good, moral inspiration, rather than atheism.[29]

The material implication of all this is that the problem of the apparent *impossibility* of saying the unsayable is not dissolved but made relative to the inner, properly moral *necessity* of saying the unsayable by saying saying itself. Because the self is possessed by the good in an even more original way than the self is separated and 'atheist', there is a positive warrant for saying that is of greater seriousness than the negative warrant, on the level of the said, for rejecting the incoherence of the antitheoretical witness to moral transcendence. Derrida's criticisms are justified, but by a justification that is inferior to the justification of the ethical. The work of language cannot be confined to the theoretical, because life is not so confined. I am in (moral) fact my brother's keeper, and the exegesis of this fact requires the surplus of saying, even in — especially in — philosophy.

The methodological implication is that the only way to reflect the right relation between morality and theory consistently is to derive the theoretical from the ethical. Only thus can theory be shown to be a mode of that which exceeds it: that is, only thus can the claim that justice is prior to truth be philosophically justified. The way of superlation is suited to this task because, given the vocabulary of phenomenology and ontology, it does not point to a privation of knowing and being but rather to that of which knowing and being per se would constitute a privation were they abstracted from it.

Totality and Infinity has a superlative intention, insofar as many of its remarks on sociality are supertheoretical rather than antitheoretical. For example:

> The ethical relation . . . accomplishes the very intention that animates the movement unto truth.[30]

> The face opens the primordial discourse . . . that obliges the entering into discourse, the commencement of discourse rationalism prays for, a "force" that convinces even "the people who do not wish to listen" and thus founds the true universality of reason.[31]

> The face is the evidence that makes evidence possible — like the divine veracity that sustains Cartesian rationalism.[32]

What truth, reason, objectivity, and so on 'really mean' is what *Totality and Infinity* is after, but its expressions remain strictly theoretical. The language of *Otherwise than Being* is more articulate.

It is characteristic of the superlative way to be 'merely verbal'. That which transcends intuition can only be intended emptily, in a venturesome emphasis; the justification of the intention is contingent on something other than an intuition. A favorite example of the superlative method is the emphasis of *se poser* as *s'exposer*:

> In a certain sense, the real world is the world which is posited (*se pose*); its way of being is as a thesis. But to be posited in a truly superlative way — I am not playing with words — is that not to be exposited (*s'exposer*), posited to the point of appearing, *affirmed* to the point of becoming language?[33]

What is the difference between the geometrical or ontological concept of position and the literary or rhetorical concept of exposition? Is there any intuitive object or disclosure of being corresponding to the *ex-* that has been added, and if not, how could the meaning of *position* change or increase merely by adding the *ex-*? The *ex-* refers to saying rather than to any said, to performance rather than to theme. We know what is meant by it, even though a theoretical linguistic science would register no difference between positing and expositing a sense.[34] The crucial difference is moral. It is the difference between the sort of talk that presents its theses as accomplished facts, impervious to critique, and the sort of talk that enters into genuine sociality by opening itself to the critique and justification of others. The mere verbality of Levinas' emphasis reflects the nonthematic overflowing of interlocutors with respect to what they talk about.

III

We have said that the concept of reason is recreated in Levinas' argument as a function of the moral relation rather than of the theoretical relation by which the knowing self comprehends the world, or (as for Heidegger) is comprehended in turn by an impersonal being. Because the question of rationality is inseparable from the question of method, we have examined the methodic innovation of *Otherwise than Being* and the later philosophy, which responds to problems and constructive suggestions already formulated in *Totality and Infinity*. The permutations of Levinas' philosophical approach all serve to emphasize the basic gratuitousness of his appeal; that is, he does not expect to demonstrate or coerce assent in the necessitarian fashion in which intuitions and arguments are typically wielded in our tradition. The moral, unlike the merely skeptical, is a surplus instead of a denial or privation; but it is equally refutable. There is an irreducible possibility of closing one's ears to the moral dimension of life. A pragmatic rule could be adopted to exclude the saying of 'Saying' like the pragmatic rule that forbids the self-refuting utterance of the skeptic. Both moralist and skeptic will sow confusion in the theoretical program if they are allowed to speak. On the other hand, the moral skeptic who is insensitive to his neighbor's claim — let us call him Cain — cannot be shown to contradict himself in the way that the theoretical skeptic is confounded once he submits his assertions to criticism. Cain seems rather to have logic and evidence all on his side, for the evidence is of a universal war from which no one can keep a distance, and logic supports this war by defining everything in terms of everything else (as a matter of identity and contradiction, or genus and species), so that the pluralism demanded by *Totality and Infinity* as the condition of peace is lacking.

Levinas' argument is justified only if Cain is wrong. Only if I acknowledge that I am my brother's keeper am I warranted or constrained to follow the conceptual development of Levinas' philosophy — for example, through the immoderation of responsibility for the other into 'obsession' with the other, the breakup of the theoretical order by the idea of the other, and so on. Only if I acknowledge the surplus of my being toward my neighbor can I grant the appropriateness of the conceptual surplus of the Levinasian emphasis. In other words, only if I acknowledge *substitution* as the normative structure of intersubjectivity, according to which I am hostage to the needs of others, responsible even for their responsibility, need I acknowledge the appropriateness of Levinas' interpretation of *signification* and the corollary interpretation of reason. What sense can I attach to the saying "Reason is the one-for-the-other!"[35] if the appeal of the hungry neighbor does not move me to put myself, as the one, in the place of the other?.

According to Levinas, Cain is wrong; we are elected, prior to any conscious and deliberate assumption of responsibility, to be responsible for our brothers. But it belongs essentially to the goodness of this responsibility that it be gratuitous and independent of coercive demonstration. The personal order is different from the ontological because it rests on appeal and obedience rather than on causation and comprehension. Does this mean that justice is prior to truth only *si vous voulez* and that truth itself is indifferent to the issue? In what way do Levinas' claims about justice impinge on the way we conceive the order of truth? Unless there is some exigent connection between Levinas' ethical metaphysics and our customary assertions about knowing and being, it is difficult to see why his thought should pose as philosophy.

Levinas expressly disavows the transcendentalism that seeks the fixed foundations of things, in the architectural sense.[36] He has even suggested that this sort of transcendentalism originated in pagan wonder at the vault of the heavens, thereby intimating that a fateful choice is to be made between the two objects of Kant's wonder, the starry heavens above and the moral law within.[37] Levinas accepts the designation *"ethical transcendentalism."*[38] What this means is that in an ethical way he claims to find a uniquely significant meaning that is presupposed by all evident meaning, an orienting *sens unique* in being,[39] the hyperpassive gesture of one-for-another. This presuppositional or 'transcendentalist' claim is what makes his discourse an argument and provides his entree into the agenda of philosophical problems. The emphasis of *se poser* to *s'ex-poser* leads to a philosophy of *appearance*, as we have seen. The analysis of moral responsibility as a hostage's condition of substituting for the other so as to bear his suffering leads to a different view of *subjectivity* (thus to a revision of Husserl's philosophy): the uniqueness of the subject is not interpreted as a unity of apperception or horizon of constitution, but as the irreplaceability of Atlas, who is riveted to his spot by the weight of the whole world. Further, Levinas revises and extends Heidegger's attempt to think the difference between *being* and beings, by attempting to think the difference between being and the transcendent good beyond being. The concept of *time* is directly affected here, for Levinas exhibits time as a function of the relation between the self and the other, which ruptures the totality and makes history liable to prophetic, eschatological critique; whereas Heidegger's conception of time as the impersonal play of being merely prolongs the pagan worship of destiny and insensitivity to ethical transcendence.

Being, appearance, subjectivity, and time are all topics about which disagreement is far from trivial. The Levinasian view of these matters must be attended to in order to appreciate the full philosophical weight of his thought. For Levinas, it is a question of opposing the philosophy that produced and underwrote the colonial arrogance of Europe and the totalitarian cruelties of Hitler and Stalin. Philosophy is morality.

IV

There is a definite continuity of intention and achievement between *Totality and Infinity* and *Otherwise than Being*. The great difference between the two works serves the common intention: Levinas confronts us with both alternatives in the issue of the interpretation of reason. The *via negativa* of *Totality and Infinity* — not the whole of that book, but its most impressive part — is premised on theoretical rationality and thus produces the incoherency of the absolutely other in consequence. The *via eminentiae* of *Otherwise than Being*, on the other hand, more persistently attacks the problem of the revision of the concept of reason, superordinating the service of one for another to the disclosures and comprehensions on which theoretical reason is based — even deriving the latter from the former. *Totality and Infinity* had already put theory in its place as a mode of ethical transcendence, but the philosophical gesture by which this was accomplished still employed the language of disclosure (as nondisclosure) and comprehension (as noncomprehension). The later 'emphasis' and reduction of the said to saying open up, however, a realm of nontheoretical yet philosophical argument.

The two versions of reason correspond to two types of necessity by which an argument convinces. Of historically higher dignity in our tradition is the hard necessity of coercive logic or evidence, according to which the structure of thought or being makes it impossible to believe otherwise than has been demonstrated. This is the idea of *episteme*, true knowledge distinct from mere opinion. Of historically lesser dignity, because of the domination of the theoretical ideal of *episteme*, is the soft necessity of the noncoercive 'sweet' reason studied by rhetoricians. Because men do in actual practice argue and come to agreement about matters that cannot be led to the sort of logical or intuitive demonstration that would close discussion once and for all, we acknowledge a kind of reasonableness or moral sense to which these arguments appeal; but when we come to analyze this moral sense, our terms of analysis seem to lead us inevitably to one of two extremes, either to the reduction of moral sense to a moral intuition or logic, conceived on the analogy of theoretical intuition and logic and partaking of the same hard necessity,[40] or else to the reduction of moral sense to the purely psychological question of what in fact moves people to assent and dissent, act and abstain. We either change rhetoric to theoretical demonstration or degrade it to bare manipulation. We lack the capacity of appreciating what the sweet reason of rhetoric might positively mean in its own right.

It is precisely to the problematic appreciation of rhetoric that Levinas makes a great contribution, for his entire philosophy is deliberately and self-consciously 'rhetorical' in the sense we are endeavoring to establish.[41] In the *via eminentiae* an alternative to theoretical reason is enacted. Even the Levinasian *via negativa* is in the end a variant or ploy of the *via eminentiae*, for the theoretically outrageous concept of the Other (with a capital *O*) is achieved emphatically. Indeed the negative way must be ventured first, because only the No of *Totality and Infinity*, establishing the theoretical *nongivenness* of the other, secures the right sense of the Yes of *Otherwise than Being*, establishing the nontheoretical *givenness* of the other in prophetic inspiration. Not by emphasis and not by logic does this philosophy appeal, but by an emphasis of evidence and logic based on the elementary solicitation of every person by every other. We are conditioned to regard this sort of nonbinding appeal as inferior, but Levinas' point is that the appeal if superior because it is genuinely personal and transcendent of the mechanical necessity upon which coercive argument relies. Necessitarian argument per se is less than personal and thus not (per se) reasonable at all. But humanly speaking there is no such thing as purely coercive argument. Nothing that merits the name "argument" is wholly binding; the theoretical skeptic is always permitted to have his say.

The phrase *justice is prior to truth* means that the personal order of appeal and obedience is the horizon that endows the order of being (whose trademarks are unity and necessity) with its concrete meaning. We retain a scandalous freedom to deny or disregard the moral context by participating in being on purely ontological terms, that is, by persevering in our own being in the war of all against all. The goodness and superiority of the ethical argument, otherwise than being, is its very powerlessness to squelch Cain, the moral skeptic. Cain remains on the scene. But because of the divine inspiration of our already-given moral responsibility — an already-givenness more radical than the theoretical nongivenness of the other — *Otherwise than Being*, more than *Totality and Infinity*, makes clear that Cain is not the arbiter of sense and reason. The pluralism of *Totality and Infinity* enforces the hard logic of the other, for the sheer unavailability of the other coerces an absence of significant talk about him. The *presence* of significant talk about or to the other, unleashed as the 'witnessing' and 'prophetism' of *Otherwise than Being*, expresses a position on the sweet side of logic and evidence. Because one does obey the absolutely other, it is no longer necessary or inevitable that one should be constrained by the impossibility of relation with the other, according to the possibilities of the totality. The fact of obedience means that that canon of possibility is no longer canonical. On the other side of the other's incognito is the gracious personal presentation of the speaking other, with whom the self is already engaged in conversation, soliciting assent on the basis of freedom and responsibility.

It is thus not a defect but precisely the glory of purely "rhetorical" argument that it is inconclusive. The coercive demonstration, the winning move that would terminate all argument, is abstained from in order to preserve what argument is primordially expressive of, namely, moral fellowship. For this reason, Levinas' reduction of the said to saying, to a performing that never rounds off into a finished performance (which the idea of transcendence or the infinite also expresses), is a uniquely appropriate philosophical strategy for signifying the moral quality of life which, as the true concrete, is that with which we are more intimately acquainted than anything else.

Notes

1. Levinas' thought is so eccentric with respect to common assumptions about the nature and purpose of philosophy that this question is central to both interpretation and criticism of it; cf. (respectively) de Boer, *Tussen filosofie en profetie* (Baarn: Ambo, 1976), and Derrida, "Violence and Metaphysics," in *Writing and Difference*, trans. A. Bass (Chicago: University of Chicago Press, 1978), 79–153.

2. "In spite of everything, I think what I do is phenomenology, even if it is not according to the rules laid down by Husserl, even if the entire

Husserlian methodology is not observed" (E. Levinas, "Questions et reponses," *Le Nouveau Commerce* 36–37 (Spring 1977), 72.)

3. This is the line taken by de Boer; cf. *Tussen filosofie en profetie*, Chapter V.

4. The Lingis translation of *Totality and Infinity* will be used here; all other translations of Levinas are my own.

5. Cf. TeI, "La métaphysique précède l'ontologie," 12–18/TI, "Metaphysics Precedes Ontology," 42–48.

6. TeI xv/TI 27.

7. TeI 265/TI 289.

8. TeI 268/TI 292.

9. DEHH, "La trace de l'autre," 199.

10. TeI xvi–xvii/TI 28.

11. TeI xvii/TI 29.

12. TeI 53/TI 81.

13. TeI 10/TI 40.

14. If experience is defined as relation with the absolutely other; cf. TeI xii/TI 25.

15. TeI 266/TI 290.

16. TeI 229–230/TI 252.

17. TeI 178/TI 203.

18. TeI 60–61/TI 88.

19. "Violence et métaphysique" first appeared in the *Revue de métaphysique et de morale* 69 (1964): 322–354, 425–473.

20. *Revue de métaphysique et de morale* 69 (1964): 125–156; reprinted in HAH, 17–63.

21. HAH 20f.

22. HAH 28f.

23. AEAE 13–17/OBBE 11–14.

24. AEAE 212/OBBE 167.

25. AEAE 8/OBBE 7.

26. Levinas refers to an *"epoché"* of *"désinteressement"* (disinterestedness being the moral condition that distinguishes truth from ideology, justice from power, etc.), and says that ethics is a movement as radical as the transcendental reduction. Cf. E. Levinas, "Ideology and Idealism," trans. A. Lesley and S. Ames in *Modern Jewish Ethics*, ed. M. Fox (Columbus: Ohio State University Press, 1975), 138 n. 4.

27. AEAE 210-218/OBBE 165-171.

28. AEAE 181f./OBBE 142f.

29. Cf. TeI, "L'Atheisme ou la volonté," 23-31/TI, "Atheism or the Will," 53-60; and AEAE, "La Gloire de l'Infini," 179-194/OBBE, "The Glory of the Infinite," 140-152.

30. TeI 18/TI 47.

31. TeI 175/TI 201.

32. TeI 179/TI 204.

33. Levinas, "Questions et reponses," 74.

34. The difference between positing and expositing would have to be analyzed in terms of felicities and infelicities of response, questioning, counterquestioning — i.e., a pattern of interlocutory behavior. But the irreducibly moral element in this behavior would make a science of its felicities necessarily a moral science.

35. AEAE 212/OBBE 167.

36. Levinas, "Questions et reponses," 73.

37. E. Levinas, "Secularisation et faim," in *Herméneutique de la sécularisation*, ed. E. Castelli (Paris: Aubier-Montaigne, 1976), 101-109.

38. Levinas, "Questions et reponses," 75.

39. HAH 36ff.

40. Some "transcendental" moral arguments, for example, are not clear on the specifically moral nature of the coercion that such an argument may bring to bear and on the undecidability of the issue on purely formal grounds. But such arguments can, precisely by their limitations, help exhibit the logical pecularities of the moral claim.

41. Notwithstanding that in *Totality and Infinity* (TeI, Rhétorique et injustice," 42-44/TI, "Rhetoric and Injustice," 70-72) Levinas takes 'rhetoric' to be manipulation of, rather than sincere appeal to, the listener and on this basis endorses the traditional opposition of true speech to mere rhetoric. But 'rhetoric' means 'public speech', which is surely a paradigm of true speech.

CHARLES WILLIAM REED

5. *Levinas' Question*

"How does he do it?" The question of method continually nags at anyone reading *Totality and Infinity* for the first time. How can Levinas be so aggravatingly profound and yet still retain any semblance of philosophical rigor? Is he merely naive and moralistic? Is there a deep structure concealed within his thought? Or does he prod us into responding to his writings by asking an unheard-of question?

Levinas claims to be simply expanding upon the phenomenological method of Husserl. But his view of philosophical method is quite different from Husserl's:

> That would be my answer concerning method. I would also tell you that I know no more about it. I do not believe that a transparency in method is possible, nor that philosophy is possible as transparency. Those who have spent their lives on methodology have written many books in place of the more interesting books they could have written. What a pity for the walk beneath the noon-day sun that philosophy is said to be.[1]

Intrigued by the possibility of tracking down a method that apparently has to deny its own existence in order to create a positive thought and by the all-too-obvious contradiction between what Levinas claims about his method and the various procedures and stylistic devices he actually adopts, I completed an extensive methodological analysis of Levinas' philosophical writings. And in spite of laboring under that peculiar eclipse of clarity called a Ph. D. dissertation, I did uncover something like a method within Levinas' thought, a way of proceeding that often seemed closer to a style than a method and that was built upon an observation about the structure of all questioning. I named that method "diachronic transcendentalism."[2]

Although I do not doubt the scholarly merit of my endeavor, and while I hope someday to make it available in a more readable and condensed format, I am now firmly convinced that the question of method is simply the wrong entrance into Levinas' thought. Methodology is essentially and unavoidably a quest for transparency about the foundations of thinking; it not only assumes a structure, but it assumes the strict and formal repeatability of certain procedures. As Levinas readily acknowledges, the phenomenological method has deeply influenced his thought. But Levinas' appropriation of Husserl's method is as exorbitant and as indirect as his appropriation of all the rest of the thinkers who have influenced him:

> Do you retain from a philosophy which influences you deeply the truths of an "absolute knowledge," or certain gestures and "vocal inflections" which form for you the face of an interlocutor necessary to all discourse, even internal discourse?[3]

A methodological analysis necessarily misses the gestures and inflections that comprise the original philosophical style Levinas has developed. By considering structure to be primary and procedures to be repeatable, methodology misses the question to which structure is only a response. Methodology can never discover why Levinas induces trembling in those who read him.[4].

The real provocation of Levinas lies in the questions he addresses to us not only as philosophers but also as fellow human beings. These questions are often raised explicitly in his writings, but as with every major thinker it is most difficult to hear them asked for the first time. Levinas aggravates the level of difficulty because of his claims about the nature of his questions: they arise from our relation to what lies outside of ontology, beyond being. Thus his questions also demand an unusual response. Whatever wisdom comes from his philosophizing, whatever he has to teach us, will emerge only after we have heard his questions.

"Everyone will readily agree that it is of the highest importance to know whether we are not duped by morality."[5] Levinas never returns to this sentence, which opens the preface to *Totality and Infinity*. It contains none of the technical expressions he constantly adopts and imbues with new meaning. Yet it provides a convex reflecting

surface by which we can magnify Levinas' indirect, but also indiscreet, manner of confronting the reader with disturbing questions.
By analyzing this sentence and the interactions between its five
elements, I hope to show how Levinas pierces our embedded philosophical expectations and gently forces us not only to hear his questions but to acknowledge the responsibility they provoke.

"Everyone will readily agree . . ." (*On conviendra aisement. . .*).
Socrates taught us why we should mistrust such ready agreements;
a simple process of questioning quickly dissolves their apparently
firm foundations. Thus we begin reading Levinas' major philosophical treatise with the expectation that he will attempt to dismantle our
agreements about various matters. At the very least we expect him
to follow Heidegger and analyze the inauthenticity of the *They* and
its roots in a more authentic ontological relation. But even if we
ignore his problematic relation to Heidegger, we cannot ignore the
fact that so many of Levinas' assertions simply defy skepticism.
Levinas is no skeptic; he is a phenomenologist by training and by
nature and consequently has a phenomenologist's respect for the
errors, delusions, enjoyments, and revelations that constitute such a
part of our everyday experiences and our philosophical analyses. The
skeptical attitude, as an essential aspect of all philosophical questioning, must itself be questioned as to its sources.[6]

Where does this questioning begin? In three words Levinas has
asserted that there is something about which every human being can
agree and that this agreement comes easily, with no need for inflated
rhetoric or complex argument. From a philosophical perspective,
any such agreement demands questioning and criticism, yet Levinas
emphasizes that it is there to be questioned, before the questioning
begins. Skepticism, indeed every sort of critical questioning, is also
a response.

In the following phrase Levinas not only claims that we readily
agree, but that we readily agree about something that is "of the
highest importance" (*"qu'il importe au plus haut point de"*). Philosophers
have always claimed that the issues they address and the questions
they ask are the most important and crucial imaginable. The philosophical enterprise began with this quick ante-raising, which left the
more mundane questions to the scientists and the sophists. Philosophy established itself from the start as *first* philosophy, as an
inquiry into what comes before everything else. Socrates provides a
notable example of the urgency of this firstness: his questions seem

to demand answers before any other sort of discourse can continue.

Already we are alerted to the radical nature of Levinas' question, even though we are still unable to formulate it. Levinas emphasizes the superlative.[7] In fact, the role of the superlative is deeply involved in his "answer concerning method."[8] But rather than asserting the logical or ontological priority of the question as to what is highest, rather than placing it at the beginning of thought and existence as an origin or a foundation, Levinas places it "before the beginning," "on this side of" ontology. Everyone readily agrees about what is highest, yet no one can say it positively. The question as to what is highest possesses an urgency because everything else, including our very freedom to question, seems to depend on it. Thus it invests the entire process of questioning with significance.

Levinas goes still further and asserts that the superlative interrupts and disrupts the mundane; it is an-archic and not originary. Consequently it is entirely opaque to methodology, since no system can be founded upon it. A process of questioning leads back to this pre-originary anarchy, but no response is fully adequate. We can glimpse only the trace of what is highest because it remains absolutely highest only in its continuous withdrawal from manifestation.[9]

The history of philosophy provides a long list of names for what is highest: the good, reason, spirit, God, mind, being. From the titles of his books we may expect Levinas to add still more names: infinity, otherwise than being, beyond essence. However, Levinas is not simply renaming a familiar concept. The idea of infinity, and its later refinement into the otherwise than being, redefines the operation of the superlative. More precisely, in the idea of infinity the superlative functions as an aggravating interruption rather than as an ideal limit. We always already have an idea of infinity, and it always exceeds our having. Levinas awakens us to the exorbitant significance of the superlative, and we now tentatively formulate his question: What is infinity? How can we think something that by definition exceeds the idea we have of it? Is there a positive relation to an absolutely other, to an otherwise that lies entirely elsewhere? And why must such a relation be described in ethical terms, as Levinas believes?

The third phrase apparently provides an answer these questions: Everyone readily agrees that it is of the highest importance *to know* (*savoir*). But before asking the obvious question, to know *what*?, I want to consider this all-too-ready agreement about the importance of knowledge. First, Levinas is much more closely related to the philosophers who claim that knowledge is not of the highest importance. Much of *Totality and Infinity* in particular is devoted to a critique of the general conception of knowledge as comprehension or possession and of the phenomenological conception that consciousness is always consciousness *of* something. Levinas criticizes intentionality because it cannot account for the absolute transcendence that the idea of infinity requires. In the attempt to know what is highest, the superlative disrupts the very way in which knowledge is conceived; we do not have the idea of infinity in the same way that we have the idea of an elephant. Second, another blatant contradiction has emerged from the sentence as analyzed thus far. Everyone *agrees* that it is important *to know*. Knowledge is under the sway of opinion, and we suspect that Levinas has no intention of replacing our ready agreement with a certain knowledge. The agreement remains prior to knowledge; it is never superseded.

Now, *what* is of the highest importance that we know? Above all else we must know "whether we are not duped" (*"si l'on n'est pas le dupe de . . ."*). Levinas' question now seems to be, "Have we been duped?" Descartes took the notion of philosophical dupery to its hyperbolic extreme by positing an evil genius who could distort even the simplest of our perceptions. An apodictic moment of self-certainty is required to avoid every possible dupery and found all knowledge. Thus Descartes could claim positively that we are not duped as long as we retreat to apodicticity and depend on God and the principles of the geometric method for the rest of our knowledge.

Since Descartes, many thinkers have shown that all the thickness of historical existence, as well as the unavoidable structures of language, permeate the apparently lucid transparency of Descartes' founding philosophical moment. The simple act of attending to oneself thinking is no longer sufficient to guarantee one's existence independent from all possible means of dupery: capitalism, repressed desires, the fiction of the subject, the death of God, the primacy of writing have all made the evil genius look rather amateurish. We modernists and post-modernists are no longer comforted by the haven Descartes discovered. We will always suspect we have been duped, and the overriding philosophical issue of our time has been to determine precisely how an opacity arises in the midst of transparency; we want to know how the fraud operates even though we cannot be rid of it entirely. We *are* duped; above all we are duped by our own demand for absolute transparency. Therefore we must continue to philosophize. Only within this oscillating interrogation can we still seek to understand and describe human existence.

By adding the crucial last word to our sentence, we leave the Cartesian quest for apodictic knowledge behind and move closer to Levinas' own question: have we been duped by *morality* (*la morale*)? In Descartes' system, morality was at the furthest extremity from the founding moment; morality was the fruit of the tree of knowledge, and by following his method, under the guarantee of God's omnipotent guidance, we could arrive at the universal precepts of morality. Levinas certainly does not mean to furnish a corrected version of Cartesian morality.

However, he has learned from Descartes how to describe a relation to infinity. In Descartes' effusive glorification of God at the end of the third *Meditation*, Levinas recognizes an important linguistic device. If superlatives are emphasized to the point of hyperbole, they are enabled to describe something that absolutely exceeds their grasp: in this case the relation to God.[10] Of course this emphatic excess quickly evaporates under the keen eye of the critic. But the significance of the superlative and the transcendence it requires always reemerge. This rhythm of transcendent excess and its counterbalancing analysis is what Levinas has called *diachrony*. Both are necessary to the philosophical project, but neither can predominate without losing precisely what philosophy claims to teach: wisdom.

What then does it mean to be duped by morality? And how would we know if we were? By examining two apparently contradictory possibilities, we can approach Levinas' question in a more appropriate way. First: we have been duped by morality. We remain convinced that an absolute moral precept is available and transparent to our knowledge. Moreover, we believe that the assertion and recognition of such a precept will lead all our actions towards the good: perfect transparency between human beings, a state of harmony produced through the universality of our agreement. We have been duped by morality to the extent that we expect some new knowledge to alter the agreements under which we live. Structurally the dupery is even more explicit, for by assuming that some form of knowledge will alter our behavior, we place the ego at the center of the moral universe, thus excluding the others whom morality supposedly involves. We have been duped by morality to the extent to which we place the ego before and above the other person.

As I suggested earlier, Levinas does not believe that any knowledge will alter our agreement as to what is of the highest importance. And so, second: we have not been duped by morality. Morality demands that we preserve some trace of infinity in our construction of a scientific totality; morality, by preserving the position of the other person above the ego, preserves the absolute transcendence that invests experience with meaning. We are all vaguely aware of the agreements by which we can live peaceably. We all live with the awareness that it is absolutely wrong to look another person in the face and then kill him in cold blood. One of Levinas' philosophical tasks, then, is to reawaken us to this traditional wisdom, to remind us of what we have always known. We have not been duped by morality to the extent that this reawakening remains a possibility.

Where do these apparently opposing paths lead? Stated negatively, Levinas' question now seems to be: What prevents me from killing the person next to me? If this were all he asked, Levinas would be considered a most interesting social thinker. If he were able to answer it, he would be considered a major social thinker. But the weight of Levinas' philosophy consists in his attempt to state his question radically and positively. For example: What is my relation to the other person such that we could agree about what is highest? Yet even this formulation still places the ego at the center of the interrogation, and we have not moved all that far from Descartes. How then does Levinas himself formulate his question?

What is being's other? Would anyone even agree that this is a meaningful question? The distance between this most philosophically abstract formulation and the one I have just suggested seems impossible to overcome. Yet by examining the nature and the structure of this question, we will be able to hear the question that provokes the deepest response, the question from which philosophers must always begin.

Levinas raises the question of being's other at the beginning of his second major work, *Otherwise than Being.* He admits the contradiction involved in attempting to ask what lies outside ontology in an ontological format. But implicit in all his philosophical analyses is an observation about the structure of the question that Heidegger simply neglected, which will enable Levinas to ask about what lies beyond ontology. In addition to what is asked about in the question — that which is interrogated, and that which is to be found out by the asking — there still remains: To whom is the question addressed? The structure of interrogation itself reveals a relation that exceeds the totality the question seeks to establish. "The Other to whom the petition of the question is addressed does not belong to the intelligible sphere to be explored. He stands in proximity."[11] The other person stands in proximity; that is, he stands on this side of any ontological structure in terms of which I might attempt to explain him. The other person is closer to me than is knowledge or ontology.

Thus, *Who is the other to whom the question is addressed?* is implicit in every question. Even the question of being is put to someone; even the question of being acknowledges the face of the other.[12] My very freedom to question is itself called into question by the necessary presence of an other to whom the question is put. This calling into question of my spontaneity is precisely what Levinas names *ethics*.[13] Much of *Otherwise than Being* is concerned with showing how an ethical language can describe, albeit indirectly or 'diachronically', a relation to what lies beyond being.

We can now state a positive form of Levinas' question: "Who is the other?" In this formulation we have reached the deepest level of Levinas' *teaching* because this question can only be put to the other person himself. With this realization comes Levinas' teaching about the idea of infinity:

> To approach the other in conversation is to welcome his expression, in which at each instant he overflows the idea a thought would carry away from it. It is therefore to *receive* from the Other beyond the capacity of the I, which means exactly: to have the idea of infinity. But this also means: to be taught.[14]

But we still have not arrived at the most radically indiscreet form of Levinas' question; we still have not arrived at the question that philosophers must raise if philosophy is truly to be an inquiry into what is first.

> The question par excellence, or the first question, is not "Why is there being rather than nothing?" but "Have I the right to be?" It is a question of meaning directed toward no natural finality, but

it is perpetuated in our strange human conversations about the meaning of life in which life awakens to humanity.[15]

The response to this question is frightening in its exorbitance, for it calls for nothing less than a continuous self-questioning and an infinite responsibility. The very fact that a question is put awakens me to the realization that my entire self may be nothing but a response to another's question, and thus infinitely responsible. I am responsible not simply for my own intentions, which I can account for and thus be held accountable for, but for everything and for everyone. I am responsible not because I cannot hide my face, but because the other person does not hide his. "The new transcendence . . . is the certitude that nothing can mask the hunger of the other man."[16] It is on this level that the questions Levinas raises cause us to tremble.

Notes

1. E. Levinas, "Questions et reponses," *Le Nouveau Commerce* 36–37 (Spring 1977), 75.

2. C. W. Reed, "The Problem of Method in the Philosophy of Emmanuel Levinas," Ph.D. Dissertation, Yale, 1983.

3. DEHH, "La ruine de la representation," 126.

4. Cf. J. Derrida, "Violence and Metaphysics," in *Writing and Difference* trans. A. Bass (Chicago: University of Chicago Press, 1978), 82.

5. TeI ix/TI 21.

6. "Skepticism, which traverses the rationality or logic of knowledge, is a refusal to synchronize the implicit affirmation contained in saying and the negation which this affirmation states in the said. The contradiction is visible to reflection, which refutes it, but skepticism is insensitive to the refutation, as though the affirmation and negation did not resound in the same time" AEAE 213/OBBE 167–168.

7. 'Emphasis' is a technical term Levinas uses to signify the operation of transcendence within the superlative. Cf. "It is . . . in the hyperbole, the superlative, the excellence of signification from which [notions] derive, the transcendency that passes in them or surpasses itself in them, and which is not a mode of being showing itself in a theme, that notions and

the essence they articulate break up and get woven into a human plot. The emphasis of exteriority is excellency" AEAE 231/OBBE 183.

8. Cf. Levinas, "Questions et reponses," 74–75.

9. The *trace* is another technical term Levinas adopts, which bears little resemblance to its usage in ordinary language. Cf. DEHH, 'La trace de l'autre," 187–202.

10. Cf. TeI 186–187/TI 211–212.

11. AEAE 31/OBBE 25.

12. Cf. "The question *who?* envisages a face [*vise un visage*] . . . . To aim at a face is to put the question *who* to the very face that is the answer to this question; the answerer and the answered coincide." TeI 152/TI 177–178.

13. "A calling into question of the same — which cannot occur within the egoist spontaneity of the same — is brought about by the other. We name this calling into question of my spontaneity by the presence of the Other ethics. The strangeness of the Other, his irreducibility to the I, to my thoughts and possessions, is precisely accomplished as a calling into question of my spontaneity, as ethics" TeI 13/TI 43.

14. TeI 22/TI 51.

15. E. Levinas, "Notes sur le sens," *Le Nouveau Commerce* 39 (Spring 1981), 126–127.

16. E. Levinas, 'Secularization et faim," in *Hermeneutique de la sécularisation*, ed. E. Castelli (Paris: Aubier-Montaigne, 1976), 109.

THEODORE DE BOER

6. An Ethical Transcendental Philosophy

To speak of the philosophy of Levinas as a transcendental philosophy
seems paradoxical — indeed, a form of imperialism against a thinker
who rejects any and every transcendental philosophy. Doesn't the
transcendental method imply that philosophy is based upon the
indubitable certainty of the *ego cogito*? Didn't Husserl characterize his
transcendental philosophy as egology? But Levinas rejects such
thinking as egoism and the predominance of the same. His starting
point is the primacy of the other. In the great work on intersubjectivity written by the German philosopher Michael Theunissen,
transcendental philosophy is the opposite of dialogical philosophy.[1]
Levinas undoubtedly takes the side of the latter, although he does say
in his later work that dialogue is not enough.[2]

On the other hand, there are a number of passages in the writings of Levinas in which we find him coming out in favor of a phenomenological and transcendental method. How is it possible to
combine such seemingly antithetical manners of thinking — the
transcendental-phenomenological method of Husserl and the
dialogical method of Buber and Rosenzweig? In this article I will
defend the thesis that the originality of Levinas' thinking lies in his
integration of these two philosophical traditions to form an inner
unity. His synthesis is not obtained, however, via a blurring of different standpoints. Levinas is too original a thinker to fall prey to
such 'syncretism'. In his radicalism — that is, his thinking out of an
origin or *radix* — Levinas can measure himself against his master
Husserl. I will endeavor to demonstrate that Levinas integrates
phenomenological ontology into dialogical thinking. Only the philosophy of the other, only "metaphysics", is able to provide a foundation for this ontology. Dialogue is the transcendental framework for

the intentional relation to the world — or, to formulate the same point in terms drawn from Buber, the I-Thou relationship is the transcendental condition for the I-It relationship. This new function of the I-Thou relationship also has consequences for dialogical thinking itself, which now takes on a specific philosophical task. Is this a degradation and weakening of the originally prophetic thought that Levinas himself opposes to the evidences of philosophy?[3] Or could we say, to the contrary, that Levinas is the emancipator of dialogical philosophy, the one who has given philosophical significance to its inspiration?

I. Ontology

It is evident that the philosophy of Levinas has developed out of a confrontation with phenomenology. Therefore, a study of the place of phenomenology in his writings will at the same time deal with the genesis and structure of his thought. His dissertation of 1930 dealt with the concept of 'intuition' in Husserl's phenomenology. In the same period of time he was working on a translation of Husserl's *Cartesian Meditations*. His articles on Husserl and Heidegger were published in 1949 under the title *En découvrant l'existence avec Husserl et Heidegger*. In the preface to this book Levinas says that these articles reflect his first encounter with phenomenology and the expectations raised by this discovery. Two years before this, in 1947, he had already published a small book entitled *Existence and Existents*; as the title indicates, this work was an initial proof that Levinas was an independent thinker. In the introduction to the book Levinas wrote that his thought was at the same time determined by the renewal of ontology undertaken by Heidegger, and he spoke of a deeply felt desire to distance himself from the climate of Heidegger's philosophy.[4] This philosophy, he observed, is dominated by the distinction between existents and existence and is concentrated on the thinking of existence (*Seinsdenken*). Levinas was moving in the opposite direction — "from existence to the existent (*de l'existence à l'existant*) and from the existent to the other."[5] This path from existence to the existent is the path that leads from ontology to metaphysics, or from totality to infinity. But what does it mean that Levinas distances himself from phenomenological ontology? Is it a dismissal or denial of his past, or is it to be understood in the sense in which it might be said that to understand Husserl is to go beyond him? Dondeyne has correctly underscored the fact that Levinas entitled his main work "Totality *and* Infinity" — not "Totality *or* Infinity."[6] What does the little word *and* in this title mean? If we are to find an answer to this question, we must first delineate more sharply Levinas' conception of ontology and metaphysics.

Levinas' dissertation is still one of the best books on Husserl. Husserl's first students generally understood his transcendental idealism as a denial of the concept of intentionality and of the so-called turn to the object (interpreted in a realistic sense). That Levinas understood Husserl's real intentions precisely was already evident from the titles he gave to the first chapters of the dissertation: "The Naturalist Theory of Being" and "The Phenomenological Theory of Being." In the former chapter he described the naturalistic ontology that the transcendental-phenomenological reduction places between brackets: the naturalistic interpretation of consciousness, which is based on an absolutizing of the physical thing. Husserl develops his phenomenological ontology in opposition to this. Instead of placing the world as object in an antithetical way over against subjective consciousness, which would leave us with the insoluble problem of the relation between them, Husserl is interested in the first place in the mode of being of the world and of consciousness. In the traditional theory of knowledge, the meaning of these terms is supposed to be known. The way of being of a substance is implicitly attributed to consciousness and to the thing. Husserl takes a decisive step beyond the Cartesian problematics when he defines the thing as something that unfolds its existence *in* its modes of appearing.[7] On the other hand, consciousness is not a substance with intentionality as a property. Intentionality is the subject's subjectivity itself. "Its substantiality consists in transcending itself."[8] Transcendental phenomenology, which places being between brackets, is to be understood as a new form of ontology.[9] What is suspended in the well-known epoché is not being, but an aprioristic, realistic interpretation of being.

In Husserl, the thesis that the existence of the thing is to be defined as a function of its appearances results in an idealistic philosophy. Not one of Husserl's students followed him in this respect — nor did Levinas. The 'renewal of ontology' is in fact an achievement of Heidegger's, as Levinas already indicated at the end of his dissertation. Heidegger's philosophy is not a philosophy of freedom, in the sense that subjectivity is the constituting origin of the world.[10] From the outset the human being is determined by his history, which he can take over at every moment but cannot control. According to Levinas, Heidegger's originality lies in the fact that the relation of consciousness to the world is not primarily one of objectifying intentionality, or 'representation.' Objectifying knowledge is a derived mode of existence and is based on prereflexive being-in-the-world. All activities — labor, play, art, and even the life of the emotions — are modes of 'understanding of being' (*Seinsverständnis*).[11] In each form of human behavior the world is disclosed in a specific manner. Levinas expresses this point as follows: the verb *to be* is to be conceived of as a transitive verb. It is just as transitive as is the verb *to think*.[12] It is philosophy's task to make explicit the implicit 'understanding of being' in the different modes of existence. An example is Heidegger's analysis of 'the world of tools' (*Zeugwelt*).

Levinas explains the idealist character of Husserl's philosophy by pointing to the primacy of the objectifying act, or representation. His attachment to cognitive consciousness leads to the affirmation that the object of consciousness is a product of consciousness, a meaning or 'noema'. In representation the human mind thinks itself autonomous — a source of being. But this is true only of the representation that is detached from the conditions of its latent birth.[13] Cognitive knowledge is absolved from its prereflexive background. In later articles Levinas contends that Husserl has surmounted this idealism by his discovery of the preobjective roots of the objectifying acts. In his article "The Ruin of Representation" he maintains that the proper task of the phenomenological reduction is to reveal the anonymous latent life behind every (re)presentation. This would put an end to the illusion of sovereign and creative thinking.[14]

Levinas' repudiation of Husserl's doctrine of absolute consciousness is apparent from his assertion that consciousness may be the condition for the appearance of the world but that this condition is itself conditioned. The fact of human consciousness itself means a 'revolution in being', inasmuch as consciousness can think its own conditions of existence — insofar as it transforms the anterior into a posterior — but this does not mean that consciousness is the only origin of the world. The consciousness that makes the world appear is itself a product of being. This paradoxical situation is formulated by Levinas in the following words:

> This turning where being is the foundation of the act which pro-
> jects being . . . but, where, immediately, the being of the object is
> *completed* in the attitude of consciousness to it and where the anter-
> iority of being is posed again in the future . . . this is phenomen-
> ology itself.[15]

This is indeed the kernel of existential-phenomenological ontology. It is not difficult to find parallels to this statement in the writings
of Merleau-Ponty.[16] Beneath objectifying knowledge, the latter
uncovers the constituting activity of perception and of the body.
Levinas tries to demonstrate that our primary relation to the world
is enjoyment — bathing in the elements. This enjoyment has an
intentionality of its own which, while dependent, at the same time
experiences its independence. The content of enjoyment, of labor, of
nourishment, is not present in the manner of a represented object.
If it is still permitted to speak of constitution, we would have to say
that the constituted becomes the condition for the constituting. "The
ailment conditions the very thought that would think it as a condition".[17] Levinas is opposed to Heidegger's degradation of such living
as inauthentic on the grounds that it is not founded in 'care for existence' and does not anticipate the ultimate horizon of existence,
which is death. Life is not lived under such a permanent quasi-
heroic tension. To work is to enjoy work; we eat for the sake of
eating, and not out of a concern for self-preservation; to live is to
warm oneself in the sun; life is the love of life. Most people are more
concerned about their daily bread than they are worried about the
authenticity of their existence — and rightly so. It is the strength of
Marxist philosophy that it departs from the sincerity of hunger and
thirst and avoids the hypocrisy of sermons.[18] As we shall see, Levinas
is more concerned about justice than about the authenticity of existence, which is an existence in view of the whole of existence.[19] This
care for the whole can be characterized as a typical ethics of a philosophy of totality.

It is interesting to note that Levinas' repudiation of idealism is
also based on an experiment of world-annihilation — the same
experiment that was a decisive argument in favor of idealism in
Husserl's *Ideas I*.[20] The experiment involves a destruction in thought;
it is an experiment in imagination, which can lead to the discovery
of the independence or nonindependence of the contents of consciousness. In this case it is applied to the relationship between

consciousness and the world. The outcome is that when we think consciousness away, the world disappears because it is a correlate of acts of consciousness. When the world is eliminated in thought, however, consciousness is only modified. All it means is that certain ordered, experiential connections are lacking, experiences that fit together harmoniously. Husserl concludes from this that the world has a mode of existence that depends on consciousness; it has a merely phenomenal, relative existence, "and beyond this nothing." In a comment Husserl made on his own formulation, the latter phrase was altered to "and beyond this an absurdity." There is an important difference between these two wordings. It is true that the phenomenal world is dependent on the human mind and that the appearance of a world without a constituting consciousness is inconceivable; yet does this mean that there is nothing left? It is clear that we can have no idea, no 'representation', of something existing beyond or outside the (re)presented world, but isn't this an indication that we are approaching the limits of representational or objectifying consciousness? In my opinion, this is the conclusion that follows from Levinas' thought-experiment. When we make things and persons disappear in imagination, what remains is not "nothing" but is existence itself, an anonymous existence from which things and persons raise themselves by a hypostasis. You can neither affirm nor deny something of this being. It reveals itself in the sleepless nights in which the eternal silence of infinite space frightens us (Pascal). Levinas call this existence "*il y a.*" He describes it in a suggestive way by drawing on quotations from Racine, Shakespeare, and Blanchot. Here the thinker must make room for the poet.

It is not my intention to give a detailed analysis of Levinas' contributions to ontology, which we can find in the second section of *Totality and Infinity*, entitled "Interiority and Economy." I will conclude my sketch of his phenomenological ontology by touching on those characteristics of phenomenology that illustrate the totalitarian tendencies inherent in all of Western philosophy — primacy of the ego and the reduction of everything to the same. The egological character of phenomenology (not just Husserl's idealist variety but also existential phenomenology) can be elucidated by means of a brief analysis of three concepts — truth, exteriority, and totality.

When the thing is defined as a function of its modes of appearance, it follows that it is impossible to define the concept of truth as correspondence (*adequatio*) between thought and being, on the assumption that consciousness can reflect the established order of things in a passive way. As De Waelhens argues in his essay on the phenomenological concept of truth, the term *adequacy* must be replaced by the term *promotion*.[21] It is true that intentionality is a directedness of consciousness to the other — insofar as this concept is justly considered to be a protest against an idealism that dissolves the world into contents of consciousness — but this other is a product of the constituting, or sense-giving, capacity of the ego. "The exteriority of the objects results from absolute respect for the interiority of their constitution."[22] This sentence is drawn from a review article on the writings of Husserl, but it also holds true for his existentialistic followers. Here human existence, or the lived body, substitutes for the transcendental ego. Exteriority can only appear within the circle of this sense-giving center. This is the reason why Levinas can also characterize existential phenomenology as a philosophy of the same. It is at the same time a philosophy of totality, because existence is the perspectivistic point from which the world of experience is 'totalized' (Sartre). In his analysis of the world of tools, Heidegger demonstrates that all object-implements refer to each other and, in their totality, to the handler of the utensils. They form a system of references that is "in view of" the user of the instruments and the 'understanding of being' implicit in how he uses them.[23] The subtitle of Levinas' *magnum opus* is "An Essay on Exteriority." This subtitle reflects his concern with thinking an exteriority that is not an object, a theme, a noema, a result of sense-giving by a subject. The subtitle testifies to "an aspiration to a radical exteriority" — not the exteriority of ontology, but of metaphysics.[24]

II. Metaphysics

The first section of *Totality and Infinity* is entitled "The Same and the Other." This reminds us of the famous opposition in Plato's dialogues between *to auto* and *to heteron*. Levinas summarizes his entire philosophy in these two key terms. Everything written above about ontology can be subsumed under the heading "The Same." To the same belongs not just the self in a strict sense (the *ego cogito*) but also, as we have seen, the intentional correlates, the *cogitata qua cogitata*, the objects of consciousness (Husserl), or the world appropriated by the incarnated existing subject (existentialism). Using a

Hegelian term, Levinas calls the incorporation of things "negation."[25] What is denied is the independence of the existents. Levinas speaks of cognition as suppression, an exertion of violence.

> The act of knowing by which we leave ourself is a sort of slow reabsorbing and consuming of reality. The resistance of reality against our acts turns into an *experience* of that resistance: as such it is already absorbed by knowledge and leaves us alone with ourselves.[26]

The correlation of I and the same is an 'identification', but not a monotonous, formal tautology.[27] It would be a formal tautology if the return to the same were a returning of the ego to an unaltered ego; but the ego is involved in the world, and reflection is a coming back after experience and history. So the "I am I is not an "A is A" formalism. According to Derrida, this is the reason why history cannot be called a process within the same. History presupposes resistance and conflict. In a closed totality and in actual infinity, a historical process would be impossible. History is accomplished as the difference between totality and infinity.[28] In Levinas, however, totality is not a closed totality. It encompasses history, because this concept is taken in the Kantian sense. It is the totality of an infinite process, a *progressio ad infinitum*. This is a *horizontal* concept of infinity, which Husserl introduces in *Ideas I* when he analyzes the experience of things. The perception of many-sided things moves to the limit of complete knowledge without ever arriving there. This form of infinity as "infinite task" is also characteristic for culture as a never-ending process of giving form to reality (which is called "essence" in the later writings of Levinas and is his equivalent of the Heideggerian *Wesen* as *nomen actionis*). The *vertical* concept of infinity, which Levinas opposes to totality, is like a perpendicular on this infinite, horizontal process of disclosing and cultivating. As we shall see, this concept of infinity is related to the infinite of the ontological proof for God's existence; it is an infinity that is presupposed by every finite link in the endless chain of horizontal infinity, inasmuch as it can only be recognized *as finite* in relation to the vertical infinity.

Does the same also encompass the other (as distinct from the Other)? In answering this question, we can distinguish the philosophy of Levinas from phenomenology on the one hand and from dialogical thinking on the other. According to Levinas, the phenomenological doctrine of the other mind is also a philosophy of the same. This already seems unjust with regard to Husserl, who explicitly refuses to reduce the alter ego to an appearance of my consciousness and who calls the other ego a "transcendence." The other is really "outside" me. The ego is not solitary but is a member of a community of monads. In Heidegger, being-together (*Mitsein*) is an original mode of being of its own. In phenomenology, the other person is not reduced to a moment, or element, of a supra individual spirit. The other seems to be a resistance that cannot be encapsulated, because it is itself a center of activity and sense-giving.

Levinas takes distance from the phenomenology of the other in two steps.

1. He joins with the dialogical thinkers, arguing that the relation to the other is a *face-to-face* relation. In phenomenology, the relation to the other is a being-present to the world together; it is accomplishing a task together, a looking in the same direction.[29] A community is built in this way, as we inhabit and cultivate a common world. Levinas' position is that the *direct* relation is primary and that it is not mediated by (an intentional relation to) the world. This relation is expressed in the vocative: to know a fellow man is not to thematize him as an object but to greet him. It is not mentioning but addressing. The other is an ally rather than an object of perception and thinking. Since I invoke him, dialogical thinkers call him a "thou."[30]

More precisely, the relation to the other is mediated in two ways, according to phenomenology. In the first place he is a directedness *to* the world, the same world that I am perceiving or inhabiting. The world is the link between the egos, or existing subjects; it is their common field of knowing and acting. Like me, the other is a world-constituting ego, a cosubject. In the second place he is also an object *within* the world, within my field of perception and action. We meet him as a being-within-the-world (*innerweltlich seiendes*), to use Heidegger's terminology. The difference between Husserl and Heidegger in this regard is that, according to Husserl, I perceive only the material body of the other and can only "ap-present" his mind (not by an analogy-argument but by analogy-perception), whereas in Heidgger as in Scheler there is an original, underivable relation to the other. For Heidegger, I do not know the other by a projection of my own mind onto his body. But the difference between Husserl and Heidegger on this point should not be exaggerated, as

Theunissen has argued convincingly in his book on intersubjectivity. According to Theunissen, Heidegger's thinking in this area is not a renewal of the transcendental approach taken by Husserl but a modification of it. What Husserl and Heidegger have in common is that the other is exclusively considered a cosubject, a coinhabitant of the world. He is indeed an *alter ego*, a reedition of myself, but not a *partner*.

This affirmation has the important consequence that the existence of the other is not determinative for my own being. The subject that constitutes the world is not influenced in his being by the other (he is only determined by his contribution to the common world). As in Descartes, the starting point of philosophy remains a monadic, solitary ego. Hence Levinas characterizes the phenomenological theory of the other as the "return to oneself."[31] In Husserl's theory of intersubjectivity, this self is the "primordial ego", which is disclosed by the egological reduction as the final foundation of the intersubjective world. In Heidegger, the self is revealed in the solitude (*Vereinzelung*) of authentic existence. It was in opposition to this viewpoint that Buber formulated his famous adage "*Ich werde am Du*" ("I am becoming through you").

In the phenomenological theory, the other, as only a coconstituting subject, has no quality or intrinsic value. He is absorbed in his sense-giving activities. The issue at stake here in the controversy between the phenomenological (transcendental) and dialogical philosophies of the other is nothing other than the true condition, or predicament, of man. Is man primarily present to himself (*pour soi*) and secondarily directed towards the other (mediated by the world), or is he face to face with the other from the very beginning (in conversation, hospitality, and desire) and only in the second place (by abstraction) a self-consciousness?[32]

2. From the very outset, the dialogical theory of the I-Thou relationship is deepened and radicalized by Levinas. When he received his honorary doctoral degree from Leiden in 1975, Levinas declared that he had never considered Buber's vocative to be sufficient.[33] What is important in the relation to the other is responsibility, which involves more than simply saying "Thou." For Levinas, to see a face is to be interpreted as hearing a voice that says, "You shall not commit murder." And in the words "You shall not commit murder" we hear the words "social justice." Since God is invisible, his voice reaches me only in and through the voice of the other.[34]

According to Levinas, to stand before the face of the other is to be cited. The other is not only met by me but summons me to responsibility and accuses me. The dimension of height from which he makes his appeal to me is at the same time the dimension of transcendence. The alterity of the other cannot be absorbed into my own identity; it is an absolute alterity, an alterity that calls my freedom into question. The other derives this alterity, which unseats me, from the trace of God that he leaves behind in passing me.[35]

The absolute exteriority that cannot be interiorized, the true alterity that is not reducible to the same (neither by predictive calculation nor by an encapsulating interpretation, is the entrance of the other. "The absolutely new is the Other."[36] His presence as visage and visitation is unexpected, passing a sentence on the same. The free subject, out of itself, has the naiveté of a direct impulse, of a "force on the move," to use the words of Victor Hugo in his *Hernani*. Nevertheless, this force can encounter limits. This limit is neither a physical resistance nor a mathematical limit. Resistance and limit are themselves concepts of ontology. Heidegger argues — correctly — that the phenomenon of resistance can only manifest itself in the openness of human experience, and Parmenides was already aware that a limit does not separate but connects. What does make freedom ashamed and limits its unlimitedness is the defenseless resistance in the eyes of the other that teaches us "you shall not commit murder." This resistance cannot be denied or appropriated. There are only two possibilities — acknowledgment or total negation, that is, murder.[37] Therefore the other does not limit our freedom in a physical or mathematical sense. Freedom is unmasked as injustice and summoned to change the exercise of violence into goodness and hospitality.

As we try to achieve a correct understanding of Levinas' effort to express the relation to the other, we must bear in mind that the terms used are to be taken in an ethical sense. In platonic fashion, this relation is called "desire." Desire is not the same thing as need. Need can be satisfied; it is a phenomenon within the same. The metaphysical desire goes beyond anything that might be expected to satisfy it; it can only be deepened, for it nourishes itself by its own hunger. This is an expression of the ethical experience that responsibility increases in the measure that it is assumed. To the extent that they are accomplished, duties become greater. The more just I am, the guiltier I am.[38] Is it not the experience of those who hunger and thirst for justice that ever more injustice is discovered? The distance that separates us from the other cannot be bridged. For this reason, the relation to the other is a metaphysical relation. It is accomplished concretely as "discourse." The essence of language, as we shall see, is hospitality, goodness.[39]

Levinas makes several different attempts to clarify this relation philosophically. I will only describe in detail his use of the Cartesian idea of infinity.[40]

In Descartes, the relation to the infinite has a formal structure that is analogous to the ethical relation to the other. In the first place, this idea is not a concept. The infinite is not a theme of our thinking: by definition, we cannot comprehend the infinite by means of our concepts. It is a property of the infinite that it overflows the thought that thinks it; in other words, the idea of the infinite is overflowed by its own content. It "thinks more than it thinks." The infinity of the ideatum consists precisely in this overflowing, in the disproportion between idea and ideatum, in this "infinition." The distance that separates ideatum and idea constitutes the content of the ideatum itself. Therefore the infinite is the true exteriority, the absolutely other, the Other.

In opposition to Descartes/Levinas, one might argue along Kantian lines that the existence of the infinite is uncertain because there is no guarantee that there is a reality corresponding to the idea of the infinite. This would be a misunderstanding, however, of the true nature of the ontological argument. The idea of the infinite is not a concept, and the infinite is not an object. When it comes to the infinite, doubt, which is always possible in the case of intentional objects, is excluded. The idea of the infinite is not a concept but the way of being of the infinite itself; it is a manifestation or epiphany, with the infinity, as argued above, consisting in the disproportion between idea and ideatum. The existence of the infinite cannot be put between brackets in a phenomenological epoché. The idea of the infinite is the revelation, the "infinition" of the infinite.

This comparison with the ontological argument can also clarify another paradoxical definition. Levinas says of the other that its otherness is not a formal characteristic but makes up its content. Thus alterity is constitutive of the very content of the other.[41] Here again one might raise an objection along Kantian lines by arguing that alterity, like existence, cannot be a material predicate. Such an objection, however, would testify to a misunderstanding of the for-

mal structure of the argument. The question is not whether one
accepts existence or alterity as a predicate, but whether one accepts
the phenomenon — or better, the revelation — of absolute exteriority as an experience *sui generis* that is conceptualized in the ontological argument.

I will argue below that this relation to the infinite is the model
for the "transcendental" relation of the same to the other. As Descartes argued, the perception of the infinite precedes the perception
of the finite. Translating this into Levinas' terms, we could say that
metaphysics precedes ontology. In other words:

> Intentionality , where thought remains an *adequation* with the
> object, does not define consciousness at its fundamental level. All
> knowing qua intentionality already presupposes the idea of infin-
> ity, which is preeminently *nonadequation*.[42]

In the meantime it should not be forgotten that this train of thought
must also be translated into ethical categories. Descartes makes this
suggestion himself. We could not have an idea of our imperfection,
he contends, if we had no idea of a perfect being. According to
Levinas, that the other overflows my capacity for comprehending
means that he places the power of my liberty in question. The other
is not infinite in a quantitative or ontological sense; he is an ethical
authority.[43]

III. The Founding of Ontology by Metaphysics

Before I discuss in more detail the specific form of transcendental philosophy found in Levinas, I will demonstrate how the other,
in his concrete analysis, functions as the transcendental foundation
of the same. Let us concentrate our attention on three fields of
ontology — knowledge, labor, and society.

Knowledge

The passages dealing with the founding of the theory of cognition are among the most fascinating in all of *Totality and Infinity*. The
freedom that men enjoy is of itself an uninhibited power, a "joyous
force on the move." To know is to exert this power of freedom. Why
should this freedom worry about objectivity? Why should it let itself

be held up by the difficult, inconvenient truth? According to
Levinas, there would be no objectivity if it were not for the other
watching me, for he troubles my naive spontaneity and awakens a
critical attitude. This breach with natural dogmatism would not be
possible without his presence, in the face of which arbitrariness
shrinks back and is ashamed. The shock that comes about when the
violence and injustice of my spontaneous activity is revealed is the
origin of critical consciousness.[44] You may think, for example, of love
for the truth in daily life, or for the ideal of objectivity in science and
critical reflection in philosophy. It is because of an attitude of mind
that is ethical in nature that all of this is possible. (We are reminded
here of the decision that, according to Popper, commits us to rationality but cannot be rationally justified itself. The neodialectical
philosophers accordingly accuse Popper of "decisionism", of forsaking
rationalism or cutting it in half, yet they themselves are not able to
found this decision rationally either.[45].)

According to Levinas, this commitment finds its origin in the
"gentle force" originating from the face of the other. This denial of
the possibility of self-founding is opposed to the whole Western tradition of the autonomy of thought. There is no better way to illustrate
this than by way of the philosophy of Husserl, Levinas' master. In
Ideas, Husserl sets out to unmask the dogmatism of the natural attitude and to disclose the foundations of a critical philosophy. For
Husserl, thought elevates itself solely through its own power to this
critical level. Characteristic is the expression he uses to introduce the
transcendental reduction. After a description of the natural attitude,
we read: "Instead of remaining in this attitude, we *propose* to alter it
radically." When the natural world is placed between brackets, this
is a matter of the realm of our "complete freedom."[46] If we follow
Levinas, we must say that this is a form of self-deception. In an
egological world in which the other had not yet made an appearance
— and this is ex hypothesi the case for Husserl — it would never
occur to me to criticize my natural concept of reality. Husserl
believes he has an infallible and self-sufficient instrument at his
disposal to execute this critique — the apodictic critique of experience, with the concept of evidence defined as self-givenness (*Selbstge-
gebenheit*) as the only standard.[47] According to Levinas, this Cartesian
clarity and distinctness is not sufficient to make the mind yield to the
authority of truth. For this to come about, respect originating in the
confrontation with the other is needed.

As I indicated earlier, the relation to the other is enacted concretely in discourse. This can be illustrated by means of the well-known triangle of Karl Buehler, in which the linguistic sign has a relation to the referent (or 'theme', to use Levinas' term), to the sender (expression), and to the receiver (appeal). Levinas is interested especially in the latter function. When I am talking with someone, this relation is primarily an appeal, an invoking of the conversation partner. This appeal is the foundation of the discussion, which is focused on a theme. What is asserted is said against the background of the person to whom I am talking. The saying *of* something is always a talking *to* somebody. Thematizing means that a subject matter is being appropriated; the other never becomes the theme. I can indeed talk about him, but in that case, too, the person being addressed rises up behind the theme. I speak *to* him if I speak about him. The addressee is always withdrawing himself from objectification and at the same time making it possible. That which is invoked is not comprehended but presupposed in every comprehension. The essence of language is interpellation.[48] The vocative lays the foundation for the indicative. What Levinas means to say, in my view, is that if I speak without the presence of the other to commit me to truth, I will fall prey to confusion and ambiguity.

The primacy of invocation also comes to expression when Levinas says, "The first content of expression is expression itself," or, "The first teaching the other gives me is the fact of his teaching."[49] This teaching is the presence of the other, which makes possible every teaching. It is not true or false in itself but is the condition for all truth and falsehood. Levinas calls it the *primum intelligible*, the first intelligible, the first rationality, or the "first signification." It can be compared to the function of being in Heidegger: being makes beings appear, but it does not appear itself. In Levinas, however, this transcendental condition is an ethical experience enacted in discourse. This event calls me to responsibility. Levinas' philosophy of language reveals a metaphysical depth-dimension of language. The semantic concept of meaning (reference) and the semiological concept (immanent relation to other meanings in a system of linguistic signs), which correspond to 'signification' and 'value' (*valeur*) in De Saussure's terms, have a metaphysical background. The metaphysical meaning of signification is responsibility, which is the condition that makes every true communication possible. Every language presupposes a relation to a face, which is somehow a word of honor.[50] The exchange of verbal signs refers to this primordial word of honor as the transcendental condition of discourse. In other words, the relation to a face is a primordial discourse "whose first word is obligation." It is this discourse that obliges one to enter into discourse. This metaphysical founding of meaning, this signification prior to any signification in the strictly linguistic (ontological) sense, is what is meant by the expression *first signification*.[51]

The face of the other is also the basis for objectivity in the sense of universality. In this regard Levinas can join with Husserl, who in the fifth of his *Cartesian Meditations* demonstrates that the alter ego is necessary for the constitution of an intersubjectively identical world. It is because of the other that a world-for-everybody is constituted. But this argument also undergoes an ethical turn in Levinas. The presence of the other represents in the first place a calling into question of my "joyous possession" of the world; it is an abolition of inalienable property. The thing becomes an object when it is offered, when we have welcomed an interlocutor. Language universalizes. "To speak is to make the world common, to create commonplaces."[52] This is an ethical event, an original dispossession. The thing becomes a thing-for-everybody, a possession of the community. Thus the objectivity of the object is not a performance of an unmoved, disinterested spectator, "The generality of the Object is correlative with the generosity of the subject going to the Other."[53] The data are objective when they are given in a literal sense.

Levinas criticizes the manner in which Heidegger derives theoretical knowledge from pretheoretical concern (*Sorge*). What occurs "before our hands" (*vorhanden*) as object occurs only when the primary relation to the "handy," or "at hand" (*zuhanden*), usable things of the practical world is broken. Levinas interprets this to mean that the happy world of enjoyment is shattered by the disturbing visitation of the other. It is his presence that makes me consider my subject matter from two sides, that is to say, objectively. In the pro-position, language poses the objectivity of the object.[54]

Language is also a disenchantment of the world. It introduces a principle in the anarchy of appearances. Without the other, the silent world would be without substance — a pure spectacle. It would remain in equivocation, and our suspicions about an evil genius would not be dispelled. Are the things before us really as they seem to be? Without the other who supports the things with his language, my doubts would never be set at rest. A pilot in a plane who observes an unidentified flying object might well distrust his own eyes, until his observation is confirmed by a ground station. Why is he then set at ease? The silent world is bewitched. Every phenomenon masks; it mystifies *ad infinitum.* Mystification interlocks in mystification. This ambiguity can be halted only when there is an other who supports the phenomena with his teaching, with his "first signification." The authority that can call a halt to my arbitrariness is the only master that can give solidity and substance to the spectacle of the world.[55]

In philosophy there has been much ado about the so-called reality of the external world. Since Descartes, philosophy has been haunted by the idea that the world is a dream and that one's fellow men are a mirage. This is apparently an authentic experience, which cannot be exorcized by Heidegger's remark that the real scandal is not that this question has not yet been answered but that it is still being posed. According to Levinas, the only resistance firm enough to convince us of real exteriority is the face of the other. His countenance is the light in which everything appears; it is Plato's intelligible sun, the idea of the good. The spendor of this security shines on all things. Quoting Buber, Levinas writes: "Everything lives in his light. You can have confidence — confidence in the world because this person exists".[56]

Labor

When criticizing Heidegger's concept of authenticity, I indicated that economy is of great importance for Levinas. It is surely not the case that the relation to the other happens in some ethereal place hovering above daily life, as in Buber's I-Thou relationship. The acknowledgment of the other has to be made real on earth, in economic existence. No interhuman relationships can be enacted apart from economic life; no face can be approached with empty hands and a closed home.[57] We have seen that language creates a common world. The face does not disclose an inward world, and conversation is not "a pathetic confrontation of two beings absenting themselves from the things and from the others. Discourse is not love."[58] It is not permitted to absolve the vocative from the indicative — indeed, it is impossible. Speech is thematizing the object before the face of the other.

But speech is easier than doing. And knowledge is more easily shared than money. Could it be argued, regarding the economic

process and the polity of labor, that the other has a constituting function here? Is labor not a manifestation of our egoism, of our attempt
to secure our own joyous existence? As such, does it not testify to the
absence of the other? In the course of his argument, Levinas sometimes says that the other is also the "condition" of labor.[59] When we
look more closely, it appears that what he is thinking of is the
presence of the "discreet" other, that is, the woman who plays a domi-
nant part in the dwelling.[60] Dwelling is the condition for the possibility of work. It is by no means fortuitous that the other is here called
"discreet." The discreetness consists in not calling the possession into
question. Love is a dual egoism. "It excludes the third party and
remains intimacy, dual solitude."[61] This seems to be an affirmation
that economic life is primarily egoistic in character. But in that case,
what does it mean that the other is the "condition of possibility" for
economic life? Economic life is seemingly in no need of the presence
of the other. In this regard it is remarkably different from the dimension of knowledge. In our previous paragraph, it seemed almost self-
evident that an ethical attitude plays a founding role in the process
of cognition. Seldom does a person withdraw himself from a conversation. This is true particularly if the conversation is an academic
discussion; here the refusal to communicate would be an exception.
Can this phenomenon not be explained by the relatively noncommit-
tal character of knowledge? Cognition is a non-violent process, as
Aristotle already realized; it does not change the world physically.[62]
When it comes to knowledge, then, considering or reckoning with
the interests of others is not so difficult. If information is not linked
up with material interests, it is cheap. But if the other has any
"power" in the world, he has to prove himself in the economic sphere.
Does his critical presence have any influence here? What does it
mean when we call him the transcendental presupposition of economic life? One thing is certain: when we speak of an ethical transcendental philosophy, this cannot mean (as traditional transcendental philosophy would have it) that this presupposition is a universal,
impersonal, and necessary structure, which can be reconstructed out
of the phenomena. It is not a condition operative behind our backs,
like transcendental apperception in Kant or the clearing (*Lichtung*)
of being in Heidegger.

Society

   The other manifests himself in knowledge as an operative ferment and in labor as a valid command, while in social philosophy both of these apply.

In his philosophy of society, just as in his theory of cognition, Levinas disputes the thesis that human freedom must be the self-evident point of departure, as is found, for example, in the doctrine of natural rights of Hobbes and his followers. The problem with this theory lies in how to justify the claim that man, who is originally free, enters into a community in which he is not free. What needs explaining are the limitations that freedom imposes on itself. Those limitations can only be justified if they are in the interests of freedom itself. The latter is not called into question as such. What is problematic is not freedom, or its injustice, but the limits of freedom. If freedom were infinite, there would be no problem. According to Levinas, the scandal lies not in the *exercise* of liberty but in its finiteness. (In making this statement he is offering a characterization of the history of Western philosophy from Plotinus to Heidegger.) The point of departure is simply "the naive right of my powers, of my glorious spontaneity of living being." In opposition to such thinking, Levinas maintains that the irrationality lies not in the obstacles to freedom but in its violence and unjustified egoism.[63]

In traditional political theory, what is the free man's reason for accepting the obligations of society? He is forced to take this step by dire necessity. The failure of freedom forces him to agree to the laws of the community. Suffering is the mother of wisdom. This is the enlightened, well-understood — or better, well-calculated — self-interest of liberalism. Is it possible, however, that the painful experience of failure can convert, or transform, the savage will into a rationality that is more than slyness? Are we not appealing to magic when we suppose that the simple addition of free wills can produce the coherence and harmony of reason?[64] Rationality presupposes self-criticism. But critique does not arise spontaneously; rather, it emerges in confrontation with the other, when freedom discovers its own murderousness and is ashamed of itself. The origin of community lies in a "reason before reason" or in a "discourse before discourse," that is, in the decision to enter into discourse. According to Levinas, that which Buber calls dialogue precedes the political dialogue; it is the dialogue that obliges us to enter into dialogue.[65]

This quest for a metaphysical foundation of the social contract is a search for an origin deeper than the agreement of free wills that serves as the final foundation in ontology. One might speak of this

quest as a "transcendental reduction," a descent to the sources. Thus
it is a "way down." But in the later writings of Levinas, as in Heraclitus (and in Eliot,[66]) there is also a "way up" — not a reductive way
or method but a productive one. Here the metaphysical relation to
the other (which is the terminus of the first way) is the point of
departure, and the region of ontology is developed productively —
theory (science and philosophy), praxis (law, the institutions, the
state), and finally labor (and technology).[67] One might speak of the
way up as a sort of "onto-dicy," for it gives Levinas an answer to the
question why is there something and not nothing? The argument is
this: the point of departure is the dual relation of the one-for-the-
other. My fellow man is not the only one around, however; he in turn
has a fellow man, who is also my neighbor. The entrance onto the
scene of the *third man* makes a comparison and weighing of responsibility necessary — and thereby also a thematizing and theorizing.
This implies a certain correction, as Levinas puts it leniently, of the
infinite demands that the other imposes upon me. I am also a
neighbor to others; because I am part of a community of fellow men,
I incur various other obligations. This is the origin of the society in
which I am a citizen, with certain rights and duties. My infinite
responsibility is translated into social and political justice. Justice
calls for weighing and measuring and this requires the presenting
and collecting of givens. This means the genesis of consciousness and
research in order to attain truth. In his later writings, Levinas speaks
of the "wisdom of love," thereby rehabilitating the term *love*. It is part
of love's prudence that it accepts rationality as a guide. These two
ways (the way up and the way down) each underscore the fact that
the metaphysical realm is not a realm on its own, hovering above
reality somehow. The relation to the other is the depth dimension
and the spirit that blows through ontology.

The philosophy of Levinas is sometimes reproached for paying
too little attention to social structures. It is true that one does not
find prescriptions for revolution in his philosophy. His concern could
better be characterized through the term *revolt* than through the term
revolution. Revolution establishes new institutions, while revolt inspires insurrection against unjust societal structures and is a permanent source of critique. But it is not the case that institutions are of
no importance for Levinas: they are necessary to protect freedom.
In the years 1933–1945 we experienced concretely what it means
when institutions forsake justice. Man was left to the guidance of his

own conscience. This was the predicament of the Jews.[68] Law is an objective guarantee of freedom. But law itself is in need of a foundation, and it is not to be sought in the well-known principle of self-interest. The philosophy of Rousseau serves to illustrate this thesis of Levinas. One might say that when man abandons freedom, in the name of freedom, he is in a bad way; he becomes the slave of the general will, which can do him no harm because it is his own will in its objective appearance: *volenti non fit iniuria*. This is the consequence of thinking in totality concepts that allow each individual to coincide with his place in the whole.[69] For Levinas, the problem is not the limitation of freedom but freedom itself, that is, its injustice. What must be abandoned in the social contract — or better; in the dialogue that makes us enter into community — is not freedom but its arbitrariness. When I agree to the social contract, I do not give up the yardstick of critique; on the contrary, I discover it. The dialogue that institutes society is also a standard of permanent critique. Levinas lays a foundation — and at the same time some dynamite — under institutions. Dialogue is not practiced beyond political structures, in a realm of friendship and existential communication. It originates in a dimension beyond or beneath the level of politics. Only by "breaching" the level of ontology and totality can it protect politics against totalitarianism. According to Levinas, Western philosophy can offer no principial resistance against the universal pretensions of the state because it is a philosophy of the same. If there is no transcendence or "ex-cendence," the individual becomes the victim.

The philosophy of Levinas has political implications that are not added to it externally and artificially but come from within. Totality is both a theoretical-philosophical concept and a political concept. Theory and practice can be called "two modes of the metaphysical relation,"[70] since the metaphysical dimension transcends and founds the whole sphere of the same. It is not a noncommital friendship hovering above the terrestrial necessities. It is sometimes called a "surplus"; yet, far from being superflous, it is a condition of possibility. "It is the surplus possible in a society of equals, that of glorious humility, responsibility, and sacrifice, which are the condition of equality itself."[71] It is true that charity without social justice is void, but social justice without this dimension of goodness and hospitality may be blind.

IV. The Transcendental Method

I will now come back to the problems raised in the introduction and try to answer the following questions: (1) To which type of transcendental philosophy does the philosophy of Levinas correspond? (2) What is the difference between Levinas' thinking and dialogical philosophy?

Question 1. We cannot say that Levinas pays much attention to method. I asked him a question about method when he received an honorary doctorate in 1975, and he replied: "I do not believe that transparency is possible in method, or that philosophy is possible as transparency. Those who have devoted their entire life to methodology have written many books, but those books take the place of the more interesting books that they could have written."[72] Levinas is certainly right here: philosophy is more important than worrying about method. But if it is true that prophetic philosophy has the task of "translating Jewish wisdom into Greek,"[73] the concern for methodology is legitimate. Rationality, which is a Greek invention, implies the ambition to justify our rational thinking rationally. Phenomenology implies a phenomenology of phenomenology, as Husserl understood so well.

Reflection on method is by no means absent in the work of Levinas. In the second edition of *En découvrant l'existence* (1967), we find four new articles on Husserl, called "New Commentaries." In these articles Levinas clarifies his relationship to Husserl. He makes it clear that he finds inspiration in Husserl, even when he is taking distance from him. It is Levinas' opinion that if certain concepts of Husserl's are radicalized, the idealistic character of Husserl's philosophy can be overcome; then, by a second step, we can arrive at the metaphysical level. As we have seen, the starting point of Husserl's philosophy is objectifying representation. But in Husserl's own philosophy we already find indications that this representative consciousness has a horizon. If we explore this horizon by intentional analysis, that is, by penetrating the implications of the object of representation, we discover that it is embedded in a nonobjectifying consciousness. Levinas writes that the strictly cognitive relation has "transcendental conditions." These conditions lie beneath and beyond representation — in corporate and cultural existence. The object of perception is determined not only by the objectifying act but also by the attitudes of the body — in walking, for instance, and also by language and history.[74] Moreover, in "Signature," his brief autobiography, Levinas mentions culture and the body as transcendental conditions of representative consciousness.[75]

The method for detecting these conditions is intentional analysis, for this method restores the concrete horizon to which every phenomenon implicitly refers but which is forgotten in ordinary, "straight" consciousness. Ordinarily we are directed to, or focused on, the object, neglecting its modes of appearance. Levinas regards this disclosing of contexts as Husserl's most important discovery, from a methodological point of view. Husserl's greatest achievement in this respect is his analysis of the roots of the intentional act in inner time-consciousness. Through this analysis of the conditions of the objectifying act, we can surmount the primacy of this act and also the seduction inherent in it — idealism.

This inquiry into the conditions for the possibility of strict cognitive knowledge *beneath* objectifying consciousness is also to be found in Merleau-Ponty, who roots the transcendental ego in the body-subject (*corps-sujet*). It is obvious from the earlier discussion of Levinas' interpretation of Heidegger that he believes the significance of Heidegger is to be sought in his exploration of the preobjective areas of human experience and their implicit understanding of being. Moreover, theoretical thought is for Heidegger only a derived, unoriginal mode of approaching the world. Especially in the later works of Ricoeur dealing with symbolism, interpretation, and narration, the conditions of knowledge *beyond* objectifying consciousness are analyzed in a more detailed manner.

Levinas, however, takes a second step beyond Husserl: he also distances himself from existential phenomenology (as we saw earlier). I argued that Levinas digs more deeply and discloses a metaphysical depth dimension. Is this still phenomenology? In any case, there is at least one fundamental objection to be raised against the use of the term *phenomenology* here: the transcendental condition is not a phenomenon! The face of the other is not disclosed by a phenomenological unveiling (*dévoilement*), which would restore the all-embracing comprehension of the same. It is disclosed by revelation (*révélation*). The condition for the possibility of experience is not experience itself. In this respect Levinas' transcendental method is closer to Kant than to Husserl. Husserl was convinced that nothing in the universe could escape the grasp of intuiting evidence. Every statement had to justify itself by means of intuition: no exception could be made for philosophy or the philosophy of philosophy. This is the well-known "definitively founding justification" (*letzt begruendende Rechtfertigung*) on which the scientific character of phenomenology depends. Levinas' method is not the intuitive, explicating disclosure of the phenomenologists. Are there other philosophical instruments available when this mode of analysis fails?

In the preface to *Totality and Infinity*, Levinas gives us an indication of what this method of thinking beyond phenomenology is. We read that it is essential for philosophy to oppose opinions and illusions in the name of experience and evidence. Does the endeavor to transcend this realm of experience, to think outside this evidence, amount to falling back into prephilosophical opinions and beliefs? This would be the case "unless philosophical evidence refers from itself to a situation that can no longer be stated in terms of totality . . . . We can proceed from the experience of totality back to a situation where totality breaks up, a situation that conditions the totality itself." This means that in certain situations where it "breaks," ontology itself refers to transcendental conditions. "Such a situation is the gleam of exteriority or of transcendence in the face of the Other. The rigorously developed concept of this transcendence is expressed by the term infinity." Levinas calls this way of working back from the objective certitude of objectifying knowledge (the way down) "the transcendental method."[76] I have already shown that the same procedure could be called "intentional analysis," for it is a revealing of the horizons within which every object of thought is implanted and that are unsuspected by the naive, direct gaze of that thought. It is true that these horizons of objects were interpreted by Husserl himself in turn as objects. What counts is the idea "of the overflowing of objectifying thought by a forgotten experience from which it lives."[77] It is now clear why Levinas still calls his method "phenomenological." He shares with all of Husserl's existentialist followers the idea of the overflowing of representational thought — interpreted in a sense more radical than Husserl's own. This exposition in the preface to *Totality and Infinity* was repeated by Levinas in 1975 when he answered my question about his method.[78]

There are important differences, however, between Levinas' intentional analyses and those of the other phenomenologists. Levinas does not deny this, for his analysis is not based on intuition. The difference here is not only one of method; it is internally bound up with the content of his philosophy. We may speak of it as a radical difference, because it concerns the radix, or root, of his thought. This becomes obvious when we compare Levinas with Husserl. Husserl views his transcendental reduction as a return to the absolute bottom or ground of the existent, to "the roots of all things," as he puts it, borrowing an expression from Empedocles.[79] This ground is absolute consciousness — and in particular, the original source (*Urquelle*) of immanent time. To go beyond this "makes no sense," Husserl often declares.[80] But Levinas wants to pose this "senseless" question, for he is looking for a source beyond the source. When knowledge becomes critical, when it is unsettled, it moves back to what precedes its origin. It is a "tracing back from its condition to what precedes that condition." "To philosophize is to trace freedom back to what lies before it." The origin prior to the origin, which lies on this side of the origin (or "higher than the origin"), is the other. This shocking of the condition, this awakening, comes from the other. Levinas calls it an "unnatural movement."[81] In other words, it is really the surmounting of the natural attitude! The hypercritical philosophy of Husserl, which opposes every form of dogmatism, is itself dogmatic. It belongs to the old tradition of philosophy that seeks a foundation in the self, in immanent perception, in the "for itself" (*pour soi*) of consciousness. Levinas calls this "egoism" or "narcissism." If the essence of philosophy is critique, it enjoys the prerogative of calling itself into question. The face of the other is the principle, and the commencement, of philosophy.[82]

This critique of Husserl also applies to his existentialist followers. In existential phenomenology, the idealist point of departure is abandoned as presumptuous. However, autonomy is only limited; it is not called into question. The philosophies of Heidegger and Merleau-Ponty penetrate beneath the level of representational thinking to prereflexive areas of experience but do not call these areas of experience themselves into question.[83]

At this point, one might ask about the relationship of Levinas to the later Heidegger, for there seem to be some affinities. First of all, there is a formal similarity in that both these thinkers take their point of departure in a dimension that, while not experienced itself, is the foundation of experience. One could formally compare the function of being in Heidegger to that of the face in Levinas: both are the "first signification," the *primum intelligible*, the light in which every being appears, even though it does not appear directly itself and can only be approached indirectly. Secondly, the later Heidegger rejects the autonomy of thought. To think is to thank, and being is a gift. Man is not the master of being but its shepherd or guardian. Despite these changes in the thought of Heidegger, however, there is one important trait that remains constant — the ethical indifference of his philosophy. Being is neutral, anonymous. It does not accuse freedom. Man receives a place (*Ort*) in the clearing of being, but this place in the sun is never called into question. The exercise of freedom is never unmasked as injustice. Heidegger's thinking of being is "on the other side of good and evil," while Levinas' ethics is, on the contrary, "on the other side of essence."[84] The distance between Heidegger and Levinas is as great as the distance between Nietzsche and Plato. Therefore, I believe that Levinas is correct when he writes that the philosophy of Heidegger is based on the primacy of ontology over ethics.

In formulating a conclusion regarding the question of method, we can ascertain that Levinas uses a transcendental method, which is also called "intentional analysis." In the final analysis, however, this analysis is not based on experience or self-evidence but on a tracing back from every intuition or reason to an ethical condition that cannot be thematized. This condition reveals itself when thought "breaks" in theoretical and practical respects, when the appeal of the other disturbs the self-sufficient existence of the self. This method of working back is indeed akin to that of Kant, the father of transcendental philosophy. This is probably the reason why Levinas does not use the phenomenological term *reduction* here but the Kantian term *deduction*.[85] The argument he offers is analogous to that of the *Critique of Pure Reason*. The contingency of experience and the fact of science together justify the validity of the Kantian categories. In the same way, human egoism together with the fact that (self-) critical knowledge and community are possible (as situations where the totality "breaks") are indications pointing to the epiphany of the face of the other.

If we call this philosophy an ethical transcendentalism, the adjective *ethical* must be stressed. I have already suggested, at the end of the section on labor, that it is not a transcendental philosophy in the traditional sense. The transcendental condition is not a necessary ontological structure that can be reconstructed from the empirical phenomena; it is rather an unrecoverable contingent or ontic incidence that intersects the ontological order. In the words of Levinas, this dimension is "more ontological than ontology, more *sublime* than ontology." When Levinas was asked whether "ethical transcendentalism" is a correct way to characterize his thought, he replied: "I agree absolutely to the formula in that transcendental means a certain priority — that ethics is prior to ontology . . . . It is therefore a transcendentalism which starts with ethics."[86] I believe my exposition of Levinas is in agreement with this statement.

Question 2. We come now to the final question — the significance of Levinas' thought for dialogical philosophy. What are the consequences when dialogue is no longer an event above ontology in an ethereal sphere but is placed at the bottom of ontology? The answer can be summarized in three points.

(a) Levinas criticizes the spiritualism of Buber. Because of the transcendental turn, dialogue is bereft of its own territory above ontology and has to prove itself in economic life. To clothe the naked and feed the hungry is the true and concrete approach to the other — and not the ethereal space of friendship.[87]

(b) Levinas accuses dialogical thought of formalism. In the I-Thou relationship he finds the ethical aspect missing. According to Levinas, there is no reciprocity in the relation to the other, but rather a-symmetry. The other speaks out of the dimension of height: he calls me to responsibility. But Buber also speaks of an I-Thou relationship in connection with nature. This second objection is inwardly bound up with the first: when dialogue becomes an independent realm on top of ontology, it loses its critical function.

(c) Levinas also takes a wholly different stand when it comes to the problematics of alienation and becoming oneself. This can be illustrated by means of Buber's well-known adage, "I am becoming (myself) through you" ("*Ich werde am Du*"), which is directed against the primacy of the ego in traditional transcendental philosophy.[88] The interpretation of this adage leads to insoluble problems. It cannot be said that the ego is already there before it comes into contact with a thou: it becomes itself after such contact. But neither could one say that the I becomes the I through the encounter, for a real confrontation presupposes the subsistent existence of the partners. Theunissen chooses a middle way by assuming that the I in the encounter is in the process of becoming a *true* self. But insofar as he presupposes a solitary ego at the outset, he in principle falls back into the transcendental position. A third possibility, namely, that the two partners constitute each other reciprocally, also leads us into a blind alley: how am I to conceive of this reciprocal constitution? If the I constitutes a thou, the I must be there from the start — yet the I cannot exist without being constituted by the thou. The thou, in turn, has to be constituted by the I, the same I that is dependent for its existence on the thou. In my opinion, this paradox is caused by the confusion of an ontological domain of discourse with an ethical (or metaphysical) one.

Levinas is very clear in this respect. Becoming oneself by means of the other represents an investiture. What happens in the confrontation is that there is a transformation from egoism to being-for-the-other, to goodness and hospitality. I am not "constituted" by the other, for in my joyous existence I was already an independent being;[89] rather, I am judged by the other and called to a new existence. The encounter with the other does not mean the limitation of my freedom but an awakening to responsibility. The dialogical philosophers try to formulate a "metaphysical" problem in ontological terms. According to Levinas, the scandal lies not in the independent existence of freedom but in its arbitrariness. Every discourse presupposes an independent partner's "deriving its existence from itself." Levinas opposes the idea that I owe my existence to the acknowledgment of the other.[90] The face-to-face relationship means a dependence but at the same time maintains independence.[91] I owe to the other my responsibility.

In the preface to *Totality and Infinity*, Levinas says that his book is a defense of subjectivity. The awakening to responsibility is an exaltation of singularity, a deepening of interiority, a surplus of consciousness.[92] The investiture does not deny my freedom but founds and justifies it. The other "promotes my freedom by arousing my goodness."[93] The ontological problem, how is it possible for me to be constituted by a thou? is solved practically in every act of hospitality. Thus the inspiration of dialogical philosophy is not forsaken by Levinas but liberated from an inadequate conceptual apparatus. It obtains a critical significance for cognition, labor, and society.

On the other hand the other is the eye-opener of the same, while on the other hand the same is the concrete content of the relation to the other. Ontology without metaphysics is blind; metaphysics without ontology is void.

Notes

1. Michael Theunissen, *Der Andere: Studien zur Sozialontologie der Gegenwart* (Berlin: de Gruyter, 1965).

2. See note 33 below.

3. TeI xii/TI 24.

4. DEE 19/EE 19.

5. DL 324.

6. A. Dondeyne, "Inleiding tot het denken van E. Levinas" "(Introduction to the Thought of E. Levinas)," *Tijdschrift voor Philosophie* 25 (1963), 555.

7. E. Levinas, *La Théorie de l'intuition dans la phénoménologie de Husserl* (Paris: Vrin, 1930), 59/ *The Theory of Intuition in Husserl's Phenomenology*, trans. A. Orianne (Evanston, Illinois: Northwestern University Press, 1973), 32.

8. Levinas, *La Théorie de l'intuition*, 79/*The Theory of Intuition*, 41; also DEHH 60.

9. Levinas, *La Théorie de l'intuition*, 15/*The Theory of Intuition*, xxxiv.

10. DEHH 49f., 95f., 143.

11. DEHH 57, 60, 65ff., 77f., 94, 101; TeI 83/TI 111.

12. DEHH 99, 101.

13. TeI 95, 99, 102/TI 123, 126, 129; DEHH 141, 159.

14. DEHH 131.

15. DEHH 133ff.; TeI 25, 144/TI 54, 170.

16. Maurice Merleau-Ponty, *Phénoménologie de la perception* (Paris: Gallimard 1945), 305/ *The Phenomenology of Perception*, trans. C. Smith (London: Routledge, 1962), 264; M. Merleau-Ponty, *Eloge de la Philosophie* (Paris: Gallimard, 1953), 27/ In *Praise of Philosophy*, trans. J. Wild and J. M. Edie (Evanston, Illinois: Northwestern University Press, 1963), 20.

17. TeI 101/TI 128.

18. DEE 69ff./EE 45ff.; E. Levinas, "Le temps et l'autre," in J. Wahl et al., *Le Choix, le Monde, l'Existence* (Grenoble–Paris: Arthaud, 1947), 141; 2nd ed. (Montpellier: Fata Morgana, 1979), 42. Henceforth "TA" and TA respectively.

19. TeI 106f/TI 133f; Martin Heidegger, *Sein und Zeit* (Tuebingen: Niemeyer, 8th ed. 1957), 235/*Being and Time*, trans. J. Macquarrie and E. Robinson (New York: Harper & Row, 1962), 278–279.

20. Theodore de Boer, *The Development of Husserl's Thought*, trans. T. Plantinga (The Hague: Nijhoff, 1978) 338; DL 324; DEE 25, 93, 103, 111/EE 21, 57, 63, 66; "TA" 134f., 167; TA 25ff., 60; TeI 115, 117, 120, 124, 165, 236, 257/TI 141, 143, 146, 150, 190, 258, 281; E. Levinas, *De l'evasion* (Montpellier: Fata Morgana, 1982), 15f., 70.

21. Alphonse de Waelhens, *Phénoménologie et verité* (Paris: PUF, 1953), 59.

22. DEHH 50; see also 59, 93; DEE 75/EE 48.

23. DEE 76/EE 49f.; DEHH 63ff., 168; TeI 91, 106/TI 118, 133.

24. TeI xvii, 18, 20, 271/TI 29, 47, 49, 295.

25. DL 20.

26. DL 18, 22; TeI 3, 16/TI 33, 46.

27. TeI 6ff./TI 36ff.

28. J. Derrida, *L'écriture et la différence* (Paris: Sevil, 1967), 139, 168, 173, 186; also 153, 191/*Writing and Difference*, trans. A. Bass (Chicago: University of Chicago Press, 1978), 93, 114, 117, 126f.; also 103f., 130.

29. DEE 162/EE 94f.; "TA" 128, 195: TA 19, 89; TeI 18, 61/TI 47, 89.

30. DL 19f.

31. DEE 145, 172/EE 85, 100.

32. QLT 175, 181; DL. 33.

33. E. Levinas, *De Dieu qui vient a l'idée* (Paris: Vrin, 1982), 129, 156. Henceforth DVI.

34. DL 21.

35. DEHH 199, 201; HAH 63, 65; AEAE 14, 155/OBBE 12, 121.

36. TeI 194/TI 219; DEHH 193f.

37. DEHH 173; TeI 168, 172, 174/TI 194, 198, 199f.

38. DEHH 176, 197; DL 39; HAH 51; TeI 222f./TI 244f.

39. TeI 149, 282/TI 174, 305.

40. DEHH 165–178, 196; TeI xiv, 19, 140, 186/TI 25f., 48f., 196, 211.

41. TeI 5, 9, 20, 170/TI 35, 39, 49, 196; DEE 161/EE 94; "TA" 170, 183, 187: TA 63, 77, 80.

42. TeI xv/TI 27.

43. TeI 33, 170/TI 61f., 196.

44. TeI 13, 53f/TI 40, 80f.; HAH 53.

45. *Der Positivismusstreit in der deutschen Soziologie*, T. Adorno, J. Habermas, K. Popper, et al. (Berlin: Luchterhand, 1969), 174, 227, 252, 291.

46. E. Husserl, *Ideen zu einer reiner Phaenomenologie und phaenomenologischen Philosophie* I, Husserliana III (The Hague: Nijhoff, 1950), 53, 56, our italics/*Ideas Pertaining to a Pure Phenomenology and to a Phenomenological Philosophy*, first book, trans. F. Kersten (The Hague: Nijhoff, 1982), 57, 61; DEHH 40ff., 48.

47. de Boer, *The Development of Husserl's Thought*, 366ff., 377f.

48. TeI 18, 41/TI 47f., 67.

49. TeI 22, 146, 175/TI 51, 169, 200; DEHH 231, 236.

50. TeI 175, 177/TI 200, 202.

51. TeI 47, 69, 182f., 194, 273/TI 74, 94f., 207f., 218f., 296f.; DEHH 224, 229.

52. TeI 41, 48, 184f./TI 69, 76, 209; DEH 224.

53. TeI 48f., 148/TI 76, 173f.

54. TeI 67, 143/TI 93f., 168f.; DEHH 193.

55. TeI 63ff., 72, 154/TI 90f, 99, 179; "TA" 159: TA 49.

56. E. Levinas, "Martin Buber und die Erkenntnistheorie," in *Martin Buber: Philosophen des 20 Jahrhunderts*, ed. P.-A. Schilpp and M. S. Friedman (Stuttgart: Kohlhammer, 1963), 130/"Martin Buber et la théorie de la connaissance," in E. Levinas, *Noms Propres* (Montpellier: Fata Morgana, 1976), 46/"Martin Buber and the Theory of Knowledge," in *The Philosophy of Martin Buber*, ed. P.-A. Schilpp and M. S. Friedman (La Salle, Illinois: Open Court, 1967), 147.

57. TeI 23, 147/TI 52, 172.

58. TeI 49, 187/TI 76, 212.

59. TeI 89, 120/TI 117, 146.

60. TeI 122–131, 145/TI 148–158, 170.

61. TeI 242, 244/TI 265, 266.

62. TeI 54, 97, 145/TI 82, 124, 170.

63. TeI 55, 178/TI 83, 203; DEHH 175.

64. TeI 192, 231/TI 217, 253; E. Levinas, *L'Au-dela du verset* (Paris: Minuit, 1982), 216.

65. E. Levinas, "La pensée de Martin Buber et le Judaisme contemporain," in *Martin Buber: l'homme et le philosophe* (Bruxelles: l'Université Libre de Bruxelles, 1968), 54; TeI 175/TI 201; DL 205; QLT 107; AEAE 5, 51/OBBE 4f., 38.

66. T. S. Eliot, *Collected Poems 1909·1962* (London: Farber, 1963), 189, 193, 210, "And the way up is the way down."

67. AEAE 24, 58f., 80–89, 101, 178, 188, 191, 195–207/OBBE 19f., 45f., 64–71, 80, 139f., 147f., 150, 153–162.

68. Levinas, *Noms Propres*, 181; TeI 218f/TI 241f.

69. TeI 184, 192/TI 208, 217.

70. TeI xvii/TI 29; DL 219.

71. TeI 35/TI 64; DL 38f.

72. DVI 143.

73. QLT 24.

74. DEHH 140, 143, 156; TeI xv/TI 27.

75. See the new version of Levinas, "Signature," in DL(2d), 374/"Signature," trans. M. E. Petrisko, ed. A. Peperzak, *Research in Phenomenology* 8 (1978), 178.

76. TeI xiii/TI 24f.

77. TeI xvii/TI 28.

78. DVI 139f.

79. Edmund Husserl, "Philosophie als strenge Wissenschaft," *Logos* (1910), 340/"Philosophy as Rigorous Science" in E. Husserl, *Phenomenology and the Crisis of Philosophy*, ed. and trans. Q. Lauer (New York: Harper & Row, 1965), 146.

80. de Boer, *The Development of Husserl's Thought*, 403.

81. TeI 54, 57f., 60/TI 83, 84ff., 88.

82. DEHH 178.

83. DEHH 188f.

84. DEHH 189; DEE "Avant-propos"/EE "Preface"; see on Heidegger: DEHH 170, 188f.; HAH 89; TeI 274/TI 298.

85. TeI xvii/TI 28f.; See also DEHH 122, 139. Sometimes the confrontation with the other is called "experience preminently," TeI 81, 170/TI 109, 196; DEHH 165.

86. DVI 143.

87. DEE 164/EE 96; "TA" 196: TA 89; TeI 40, 51, 75, 129, 147, 153, 187/TI 68, 78, 101, 155, 172, 178, 212; AEAE 15/OBBE 12f.; see also notes 56 and 65 above.

88. M. Theunissen, *Der Andere*, 266, 273.

89. TeI 31, 91/TI 60, 117f.

90. TeI 31f., 50, 62, 193, 195, 217/TI 60f., 77f., 90, 218, 220, 240.

91. TeI 61, 78/TI 88, 104f.

92. TeI xiv, 122f., 153, 222f./TI 26, 148f., 178, 244.

93. TeI 171, 175, 279/TI 197, 200, 302.

7. Levinas' Logic

The following lines of thought are part of a study that is in progress, aiming to establish that prescriptive statements are not commensurable with denotative ones — or in other words, with descriptive ones. We begin by examining the situation of Levinas' thought in the face of Hegelian persecution. This brings into the center of reflection the question of commentary and, as will be seen, the confrontation with the second Kantian *Critique*. The reader will see by the end of this essay that the implications and conclusions to which these lines of thought should lead are here treated in a very abridged or precipitate manner.

I. Commentary and Persecution

To begin with, this is a discourse that sets a trap for commentary, attracting it and deceiving it. In this course lies a major stake, which is not merely speculative but political. Let us run through the stages of the seduction.

Levinas asks that the absolutely other be made welcome. The rule applies to any commentary on Levinas as well. So, we will take care not to flatten the alterity of his work. We will struggle against assimilations and accommodations. This is the least justice we can do him. Such is the first figure of commentary: the hermeneutic — discourse of good faith.

But good faith is never good enough, or the request for alterity is never satisfied. We will say to ourselves that the best way of answering it is to reinforce the difference between work and commentary. The more, as aliens to Levinas, we speak of Levinas, the

117

more we conform to his precept — and also, the more Levinas will be bound to welcome the commentary. For example, what could be more alien to a Talmudist than a pagan? Second figure: the paradoxical — discourse of ambivalence.

The merest trifle separates it from the third figure (and this trifle means that Levinas dislikes pagans). In the third figure the commentator superadds to the alterity: since you ask for it, he says to Levinas, I will not treat you as my similar, but as my dissimilar; I can do you justice only by mistreating you. Indeed, if in your view to be just is to court alterity, then the only way to be just towards your discourse of justice is to be unjust about it. And what is more, you will have to do me justice, in accordance with your law. So if I say, like Hegel in his *Spirit of Christianity*, that the infinity of your God is the bestiality of your people, that the letter of your writing is your people's stupidity, you and your people will have to say to me: that is just.[1]

Discourse of persecution. It is not even above parodying the persecuted. It will say, for example, *"Do before understanding"*[2]; is this not what the commentator is bound to do with this work, if he understands it? This doing, which in this case is a saying (the saying of the commentary), would not deserve its name, according to the very terms of the work under commentary, and would merely be something *said* if it did not *interrupt* what is said in the work, if it were not a word that stands in sharp contrast to it.[3]

What seems to authorize the parody and the persecution is the principle that justice consists in alterity. So the persecutor reasons thus: only alterity is just, the unjust is always the other of the just, and so all that is unjust is just. If the one who suffers the injustice should protest against this sophism, I will declare that he has only its major term to blame, which is none other than his own law. For if the premise states that the rule is alterity, then it necessarily authorizes retortion, enabling the same to be drawn from the other and the other from the same. If this amounts to persecution, it is the fault of the persecuted alone; he suffers only from his own law and refutes himself. Such is the mechanism of the Hegelian description; this phenomenology is ironic by means of its "I understand you."

Levinas sometimes tries a riposte against the persecuting commentary by keeping on its own ground. For instance, he attacks Hegelian alterity so as to show that it is only a caprice of identity (and that it consequently cannot be just): "The *otherwise than being* is couched in a saying which must also unsay itself so as thus to tear away the *otherwise than being* from the said, wherein the *otherwise than being* already begins to signify nothing more than a *being otherwise*."[4] The absolutely other is not the *other of* a same, *its* other, in the heart of that supreme sameness that is being; it is *other than* being. The just does not relate dialectically to the unjust, because there is no neutral middle ground (except in insomnia) where they might be twisted around, where their mutual opposition might be synchronized.[5] The discourse of the would-be middle ground is presumptuous.

Now this riposte is not irrefutable. And if there is a trap in Levinas' discourse, it consists first of all in tempting its reader to refute this riposte. It seems appropriate to follow the path of this seduction.

II. The Enunciative Clause

In order to escape my argumentation, says the persecutor, it is not enough to plead the exclusive disjunction, in a statement such as, for instance, *The entirely other is other than all that is*. All things considered, the mechanism of the refutation is simple enough. Whatever the operator used in the statement, however strongly negative it may be, to use it always "implies" an assertion in the enunciation. So we could always "infer" an affirmative expression from a negative expression; we only have to bring into play the enunciative clause. In this way, for example, we can maintain that *nonbeing is*, because we can state that *nonbeing is nonbeing*.[6] The enunciative clause that permits this "inference" constitutes the unexpressed premise of this argumentation: *All that is said to be, or not to be, something, is*.

The "implication" in question can be declared a sophism only if it is agreed that it is forbidden to formulate the enunciative assertion in the form of an attributive statement; or in other words, only if the above-mentioned premise is rejected.

But if we are trying to escape from the aporias of positivism and mere propositional logic, it seems inevitable and even desirable to use this premise, and therefore the "sophism" seems necessary. The enunciative clause is indeed the king-pin, which seems to allow us to derive the "substance" of statements from the "subject" of the enunciation, as in the Cartesian meditation on the *Cogito*, or to include the subject in the substance, as in Hegel's phenomenological description. It can be shown that all philosophical discourses, no matter how diverse, make use of this clause, if only in a hidden manner. For the philosopher, to be forbidden this clause as formulated by logicians — by Russell, for example, in the theory of types of statements[7] — would make it impossible to philosophize.

Now Levinas' books abound in such statements. This is obviously true of those texts that thematize the subject of pleasure, in which Levinas describes the constitution of this subject and in which it is methodologically necessary for statements relating to this subject to be proffered, or profferable, by him as well, since in the absence of this authority the theme could not be validated. Such is the "phenomenology" of the early books.[8]

We are tempted to object that this validation procedure applies only to the ego's discourse about itself; that the resulting validity of the statements merely attests simultaneously to the closure of this discourse in the identity of experience; but that, as soon as we come to the other great Levinasian theme — the transcendence of the other — we must not be able to detect the use of the enunciative clause in it. Or else, if we can manage it, if we can show that the absolutely other is so only (or is so in any case) in relation to the assertion that maintains the statement of its exteriority, then we can boast that we have ruined the essential project of the work. Such is the temptation.

On this point, let us take, somewhat at random, the following passage from *Totality and Infinity*: "The interiority assuring separation *must*," writes Levinas, ". . . produce a being that is absolutely closed on itself, not drawing its isolation dialectically from its opposition to the Other. And this closure *must not* forbid the exit out of interiority, in order that exteriority may speak to it, reveal itself to it, in an unpredictable movement . . . ."[9] In this text we find two essential statements: *The self (soi) does not proceed from the other; the other befalls the self.* Let us call them respectively $\sim p$, q. Levinas tells us first that if the self proceeded from the other ($= p$), the other would have no marvels to reveal to it, and no transcendent occurrence would touch it:

1. If p, then $\sim q$.

This relation can also be expressed by the exclusive disjunction $p \vee q$.

After the second *must*, we are told two things. First (and this is in fact implied in the context of the book rather than in our passage), confirming the preceding relation and verifying the disjunction —

that the miraculous transcendence of the other is conditional upon
the closure of the self:

    2. If $\sim p$, then q.

The second is more surprising, although more "natural"; it is
that the other can befall the self only *in spite of* the latter's self-
sufficiency — which would be expressed as:

    3. If $\sim p$, then $\sim q$,

or: if the self does not proceed from the other, then the other does
not befall the self.

We see how Levinas struggles to escape the Hegelian persecution. Far from the exterior's inverting itself into the interior and the
interior into the exterior, as is said of language in the *Phenomenology
of Mind*, a group of statements and relations between statements is
proposed here that could hold the exteriority of the other and the
interiority of the self separate. And yet this group is not greatly different from the group of expressions and relations that could be
drawn from Hegel's discourse. In particular, the "lapsus" constituted
by relation (3) juxtaposed with the first two relational expressions
puts the Levinasian group very close to what, in Hegel, is called
"contradiction" and *Aufhebung*.

The comparison may seem superficial, but it is less so than it
appears. Do we think we have exhausted the connotations of the two
musts that punctuate this passage by translating them into the form
of propositional implication? They express not only the necessity
that, in different ways, links those parts of statements, which p and
q are: they indicate not only an alethic propositional modality (*It
is necessary that* . . .), but also an epistemic propositional modality
(*It is certain that* . . .), and above all a modality that is not propositional but "illocutionary" (directed towards the addressee of the
message) and almost "conversational," all of which makes these *musts*
into an appeal from the author to his reader with a view to obtaining
his agreement to statements (1), (2), and (3) — *failing which*, this
"conversation," which his reading is, will have to be interrupted.[10]
Hence, the "necessity" expressed by this *must* bears upon the
pragmatic nature of Levinas' discourse: if you, the addressee of that
discourse, accept p (i.e., that the self proceeds from the other), then
you must refuse q (i.e., that the other befalls the self), and you will
not be on my side — you will be a Hegelian.

In "propositional" readings of the *must*, its scope is kept at the
level of statements (*énoncés*). But to make a pragmatic, or "perlocu-

tionary," interpretation of it (i.e., one that relates to the locutory situation that defines the message's relations of addresser/addressee), we are obliged to take into account the act of enunciation (*énonciation*). Thus the enunciative clause comes back into the statements.

And it comes back with its customary effect, which is to make the properties of the statements (in the case of our text, the disjunctive exclusion) almost negligible, in favor of the enunciative assertion. This is something one could observe in comparing the *must* of Levinas with equivalent expressions from the pen of Hegel, such as the famous "*es kommt nach meiner Einsicht . . . alles darauf an, das Wahre nicht als 'Substanz,' sondern ebenso sehr als 'Subjekt' aufzufassen und auszudruecken,*"[11] or the equally celebrated "*es ist von dem Absoluten su sagen, dass es wesentlich 'Resultat', dass es erst am 'Ende' das ist, was es in Wahrheit ist*"[12] ("According to my way of seeing . . ., everything depends on this, that one apprehends and expresses the true not only as *substance*, but just as much as *subject*," and, "It must be said of the absolute that it is essentially *result*, that only *in the end* is it what is in truth"). The *musts* contained in these statements seem to have exactly the same connotations as those we have just identified — in particular the connotation that if you, the reader, refuse to say that the absolute is result or that substance is also subject, then our interlocution, or perlocution, ceases. Besides, Hegel does not hesitate to indicate the enunciative clause very strongly with a "*Nach meiner Einsicht,*" an "I assert that . . ," a "constative" that is also, it seems, a "representative," an *I wish that . . .* or an *I insist that . . . .*[13]

Strictly speaking, then, we are not here dealing with mere assertion, regarded by propositional logics as the zero degree of the enunciative modality, but with more subtle enunciative modalities having perlocutionary application. The pragmatic force of statement-elements, such as these *musts*, places Levinas' discourse in the same field as Hegel's. Levinas says, "The interior and the exterior must be exterior"; Hegel says, "The interior and the exterior must be interior." Propositionally, the two statements are contraries. But they have the same perlocutionary form: for the discourse of ethics to hold together, the claim for the exteriority of the interior relation is just as necessary as the claim for its interiority is for the discourse of phenomenology. In this respect the two discursive positions are not different.

They have another feature in common: both these enunciative demands, but in fact Levinas' infinitely more than Hegel's, are not formulated as such but are slipped into the statements as modalities that govern their parts (p and q), and not as enunciative acts that govern the attitudes of the protagonists of philosophical discourse. In both cases they are 'speculative' statements in which the form of the statement (in our example, the *must*) implies the instance of the enunciation while hiding it.[14]

Now if this is so, Levinas' statements can be placed on a par with Hegel's only to the detriment of Levinas, because this would imply finally that the exteriority of the other, expressed by the statements p and q and their relations (1), (2), and (3), even when the author of *Otherwise than Being* declares it to be absolute, can obviously be so only according to the enunciative modality of the "constative-representative" *must*, that is, only relative to the enunciative clause. And consequently it is in the Hegelian discourse, which explicitly needs this clause to be inserted in order to form statements (since substance must also be subject), that the Levinasian discourse must take its place, as a moment of it.

We will thus have shown that Levinas' riposte against ontology is refutable and that the project of emancipating ethical discourse in relation to the same fails in view of the enunciative clause. And we will have thus completely succumbed to the temptation into which the Levinasian discourse leads those who have not broken with the speculative project.

Levinas himself felt this temptation and succumbed to it, as we know incidentally from the last lines of "Signature," which concludes *Difficile liberté*:

> It has been possible, since *Totality and Infinity*, to present this relation with the Infinite as irreducible to "thematisation" . . . . Henceforth the ontological language still used in *Totality and Infinity* so as to exclude the purely psychological significance of the analyses put forward, is avoided. And the analyses, themselves, refer not to *experience*, where a subject always thematises what he is equal to, but to *transcendence*, where he answers for what his intentions have not measured.[15]

III. Prescriptives Against Denotatives

These last lines indicate to the commentator how he has been trapped: by treating Levinas' discourse as if it were speculative when it is not. The word *speculative* designates not only, as previously understood, a discourse whose statements (badly formed ones, from the logician's point of view) "imply" its enunciation by whatever aspect you like. Speculative discourse in this sense is opposed to positive *discourse*, that is, one whose conditions of validity are determined by propositional logic, in its own metalanguage. But in a more "elementary" way, the term *speculative* must be set in opposition to other terms designating other kinds of discourse, such as those of the poet, the politician, the moralist, the pedagogue, and others. This second test leads us to place the speculative on the same side as the positive and opposed to these other genres, as discourses with a denotative function must be placed opposite those with a deontic or aesthetic function. The speculative and the positive alike are in effect kinds of discourse placed under the law of truth: we judge them both as true or false. The problem peculiar to the speculative is to determine in what subgenre of discourse one may describe the criteria of truth or falsity valid for all discourses of the denotative genre; and that is where, as we have said, the enunciative clause intervenes.

The nondenotative genres of discourse, for their part, seem reducible to two, according to Levinas: those placed under the rule of the just/unjust, such as the moral and the political, and those of the writer and the orator, which draw on an "aesthetic" value. Levinas evinces the greatest suspicion concerning the *discursive arts*, which he regularly characterizes as techniques of seduction.[16] We know that his wager is on the contrary to succeed in placing the deontic genre at the heart of philosophical discourse. This implies in principle that the latter consists in describing not the rules that determine the truth or falsity of statements but those that determine their justice or injustice. Hence it seems that the "well-formed" expressions that concern Levinas do not need to be well-formed in the terms required by propositional logic. They belong to that group of statements that Aristotle, in a text often commented upon, declares he leaves to one side of the reflections of the logician.[17] In their deep structure, and regardless of their surface forms, properly Levinasian statements are "imperatives." If justice becomes the unique concern of philosophical discourse, it is then in the position of having to comment not on descriptions (denotative statements) but on prescriptions.

Now to comment on a prescription poses a difficult problem. Take for example an order like *Close the door.* The commentary on this order is not an order but a description. The prescriptive statement gives place to a denotative one.

In the terms of the pragmatics of communication, the commentator is the addressee of a first-order message (here the order) and comes to place himself in the position of addresser of a second-order message having the first message as its reference, while a new addressee (the reader of the commentary, for example) comes to carry out the role previously held by the commentator in relation to the first message. When the initial message is denotative, the commentary, being denotative as well, keeps its own discourse in the same genre as the one on which it comments. But when the initial message is prescriptive, it seems inevitable that the commentary, being denotative, displaces the message's own genre. By taking the order *Close the door* as the object of his discourse, the commentator (whether he is a linguist, a logician, or a philosopher) substitutes for this order an autonym[18] of the sentence or of part of the sentence or, in other words, the name of the proposition.[19]

This substitution, which is the rule of the metalanguage of commentary, may have but little consequence when the object-statement is denotative, since its validity in the matter of truth is not *necessarily* disturbed (even if it should happen to be) by the fact that it becomes an "image" of itself in the metalanguage. But one could not be so confident when a prescriptive expression is involved; for an order does not ask to be commented on — that is, understood — but to be executed. Or perhaps: not only understood but also executed. Now the commentator, whatever turn of phrase he uses, does not go and close the door but asks, for example, how it is possible for the statement to produce an act instead of (or as well as) its intellection.[20] And in so doing he necessarily transforms the natural-language expression *Close the door*, which is "immediately" prescriptive, into a metalinguistic "image" of the expression.

The difference, and it is an immense one, is disturbing because the two expressions can be strictly identical. But the one, which belongs to the natural language (except when the latter makes use of autonyms) "expects" to be executed, whereas in the other, which is merely the reference level of the commentary, the executive is a sense that it connotes. The second expression may be the object of various transcriptions. It is either reported: *He said to close the door.* Or quoted: *He said, "Close the door,"* Or symbolized: $O(p)$, which reads, "It is obligatory that p" where p is, according to some, a well-formed expression of propositional logic[21] (in this case a statement like *the door is closed*), or, according to others, a proposition root[22], which here means roughly "the closing of the door by you". Or else it is symbolized in a perhaps more refined way: $Nx'Oy \propto '$, which would read, "x has ruled: y must do $\propto$," where x is the order-giver, y the receiver, and $\propto$ the action of closing the door.[23]

But no matter how diverse the possible "images" of the order in the commentator's discourse may be (and there are many others), all these transcriptions have in common that they neutralize the executive force of the order. This neutralization is the index of a modification in the constraints that weigh on the addressee. In making himself a commentator, the addressee becomes an addresser: he has understood/heard a discourse, and he utters a second discourse having the first as its reference. The addressee of an order, on the contrary, does not have to come and occupy the position of an addresser. He has only to "cause to exist" the *reference* of the order that he received: to close the door.

Two observations. That it is a question of reference and not of signification in statements of this type is indicated by the use of the deictic: *the door* is understood as *the door of which I am speaking and which you know*; *this door here* (with the force of *ille*). To avoid the problems raised by the deictic and the reference, we will here be content to note that what gives the definite article its deictic force in this statement is the perlocutionary situation: the current relationship between the addresser and the addressee of the order is what permits both parties alike to dismiss another interpretation of the article *the*, for example, its force of generality.

Is it the same for all prescriptive statements? That is a question to be discussed. It seems certain, in any case, that at least a subset of the set of these statements obeys this rule of perlocutionary force. Statements of a code applicable to a definite circumstance generally appear to escape the rule: the "legislator" is not a current addresser. But precisely the current addresser (policeman, magistrate, etc.), who we say is "applying" the statement of the code to the case being considered, is in fact bound to show, by the reasons adduced for his judgment (and if possible in contradiction to the addressee of that decision, who by definition has "his own word" to say about it), that the perlocutionary situation in which they are placed is truly one of those to which the statement of the code makes reference. His order is thus not executive, so long as the statement of his order does not receive its unambiguous force from the situation in which it is uttered, that is, so long as it is not indicated as executable. This is a property we can verify for all pragmatic situations where the message is imperative, for example, in agonistic situations (military, athletic, dialectic): the order is executive only to the extent that it makes reference to the current situation.

This first observation is trivially obvious. Yet it has an important counterpart. *Close the door* does not only make reference to *this door here*, but to a state of this door that does *not yet* exist. It is in this way that the addressee of the order "makes the reference exist": he produces a state of affairs. But it is also in this way that, once it is executed, the order loses all executive force, supposing that we repeat it as it is: we can *no longer* close a closed door. If we were to judge the value of an order according to its *conformity* to its reference, we would find ourselves faced with a difficulty that is peculiar to this genre of statement: such statements are never true in the sense of conforming to that of which they speak, for they either anticipate it when the reference is not correct, or they must not be correct when the reference is.[24]

Let us be content with this vague formulation and draw from it an important consequence: that the time put into play in the pragmatic of commands is not only "punctual" in that it takes its ephemeral origin from the perlocutionary situation, but also that this time occasions paradoxes, at least according to the truth functions used in propositional logic, notably that of noncontradiction ($p \lor \sim p$), in that from this point of view to assert p (*the door is closed*) is always false at the moment when the order ($O(p)$: "it is obligatory that p") is given.

This temporal property is not the least of the reasons that would incline us to think that the operators of "Aristotelian" propositional logic do not enable us to judge the value of prescriptive statements. More than any others, these seem to require a "Diodorean" or suchlike logic, which introduces into the calculation of predicates and of propositions a time variable t that allows us to specify whether the proposition or reference being considered is true (or false) at the instant (now, n) of its enunciation, or before or after that instant. This relativization has significant effects on the logical calculation of propositions, and it is shown elsewhere that many classical "paradoxes" arise from it.[25] But here there is more at stake: if we want to situate commentaries on the scale (or on the lack of scale) demanded by Levinas, it is into the logic of prescriptive statements, not descriptive ones, that we must introduce the temporal variable. You may well imagine that the results will be all the more surprising.

For the present, let us merely show for one text of Levinas' that the two observations we have just made about the singular validity of prescriptive statements, according to the perlocutionary situation and the moment of their enunciation, are not alien to his work. It is a simple, and at the same time scandalous, text: for it declares that God himself, the number one enunciator by all accounts (though it is doubtful whether Levinas would agree with this title), is not concerned to, nor has no power to, calculate his orders as a function of situations anterior or posterior to, or independent of, the instant of giving them; and that accordingly there does not exist a tribunal (or stock exchange) of history where all acts (or shares) would be offset against one another with a view to liquidating debts. "Driven out of Abraham's house, Hagar and Ishmael wander in the desert. Their supply of water is finished; God opens the eyes of Hagar, who notices a well where she can give her dying son drink."[26] So far, nothing abnormal — we would expect no less from a god who is also goodness itself.[27]

Yet this generosity arouses the concern and reproof of the heavenly counselors, the angels, who practice a rather unexpected Hegelianism, looking farther than the ends of their noses, calculating, thinking of world history: "The angels protest to God: 'wilt Thou give water to him who will later make Israel suffer?'" and God in his defense invokes the time of ethics and singular situations: "'What matters the end of history,' says the Eternal One. 'I judge each for what he is and not for what he will become.'" What each one *is* is what he alone is at the moment I am speaking to you.

It is not suggested that God judges without a criterion, nor that he has no criterion — although thought that ignores inference is perforce closely related to skepticism.[28] Some things must be refused, at least; so there must be a sign by which to recognize them, and it should be injustice.[29] But blood is not always a sign of injustice; injustice is not always and only the shedding of blood.[30] Ishmael will shed innocent blood: then he is unjust. But at the moment when God is speaking, he is dying of thirst; then he is suffering injustice. Injustice cannot be detected by any constant signs; on the contrary, to have recourse to the constancy of would-be clear signs, to the articles of the code, to established institutions, recourse to the *letter* as that which allows the just to be separated from the unjust — that is unjust. The criterion "exists" but cannot be the object of omnitemporal descriptive statements. If it is grasped, it is not understood; it is grasped in the command received "before" it is understood, before it can be repeated by the addressee of the order, before it can give rise to commentary. It is grasped as beyond the appearance, as trace.[31]

We can see what is at stake in this question of commentary: the status to be given to the relations between prescriptive and descriptive statements, and hence between ethics and propositional logic; this is also the tension proper to Levinas' work, which aims at nothing less than raising above tautology the expressions of obligation, or forbidding, of permission — that is, that entire region of the language where demands, pleas, orders, wishes, prohibitions, and so on are formulated. It aims at freeing the criterion of validity of "orders," that is, the criterion of their justice, from any justification by truth functions.

An expression like *Welcome the alien*[32], for example, must be able to be valid, not because it can be inferred from statements previously admitted, not because it conforms to older statements, but by the sole fact that it is *an order having in itself its own authority*. Hence it is in some sense an *order of an order*.[33] In this refusal to infer normative statements lies, in particular, the considerable importance attached by Levinas to the idea of *an-archy*.[34] Likewise, it is from such a refusal that his attacks on ontology — not only Heidegger's but also Spinoza's, for example,[35] draw their vigor: ontology is, after all, merely another word for the metalanguage that is applied to descriptive statements.

It is interesting to translate this repudiation of the *archè* and of being into pragmatic terms. In the order of the perlocutionary situation, it corresponds to the decision not to conduct a discourse having as its reference and model a prior discourse, even an enigmatic one, given by no matter whom. The hatred of the *neutral* constantly evinced by Levinas[36] is not directed at the unnameable in general, nor even at an unnameable that is presumed to speak, but at an unnameable that is assumed to be both speaking and spoken: that unnameable *of which* I speak or, to use the autonym familiar to philosophers, *of which* the *I* speaks and of which it (or I) speak(s) in order to say that it (this unnameable) speaks in its (or my) place, that is, in the place of the *I*, or of me. This aims at that constraint proper to the discourse of truth functions, which lets the enunciator attest the authenticity of his statement only if he assumes that what he is talking about is also what speaks through his mouth:[37] only if he assumes that the subject, which he is, is also (and is no less) the substance of which he speaks. The neutral that Levinas hates is precisely this substance assumed to be subject in the discourse of ontology. Whether this substance be called 'being' and the discourse resting on it 'ontology' rather than 'metaphysics' is of scant importance when it is a matter of thinking exteriority as "marvel."[38]

The pragmatic reason for hating the neutral is that its assumption implies that the philosopher, the addressee of the message from the unnameable, comes and places himself in the position of addresser, in order to proffer his commentary from the same place as the assumed first addresser, the unnameable itself. In this replacement, ethics necessarily dissolves. Prescriptions drawn from ontology will be inferred from statements relative to the unnameable and assumed to have issued from it. It matters little whether they are true or false; what matters is that the imperatives of ethics will be judged good or bad only by their conformity with these statements, according to the rules of propositional logic. Now, that is enough in Levinas' eyes to make ethics pass under the jurisdiction of the true — a Western obsession — and succumb.

In this subordination of prescriptives to denotatives, the executive force of the former is lost, and so is the type of validity peculiar to them. To put it another way, this subordination has the effect of transforming all orders into metalinguistic "images" of themselves and each of the terms composing them into an autonym of itself. In ontological ethics we can no longer understand *Welcome the alien* but *the /Welcome the alien/of Levinas,*[39] that is, a proposition transcribed into the metalanguage that speaks of the same proposition placed in the natural language. By this fact alone it passes under the legislation of truth functions and loses the remarkable properties that it had in the natural language, notably those we observed pertaining to perlocutionary situation, time, and execution.

IV. Levinas and Kant: the Kantian '*Widersinnige*'

Levinas' concern to safeguard the specificity of prescriptive discourse seems closely akin to the care with which Kant, in the second *Critique*, makes the principles of practical reason independent of those of theoretical reason.

After recounting the episode of Ishmael's great thirst, Levinas adds: "For human consciousness has the right to judge a world ripe at every moment for judgment, before the end of history and independently of that end."[40] This world, he says, is "peopled with persons." If it can be judged at every instant with no consideration of teleology or strategy or even of empirical context, it is because the power to judge not only inhabits it but constitutes it. This power is intact on principle and is not subject to any alteration deriving from situational factors; no alienation could be invoked to excuse or pardon bad judgments.[41]

This faculty of commanding and obeying in complete freedom, regardless of the circumstances, cannot fail to remind us of the autonomy of the will that is for Kant "the unique principle of all moral laws and the duties which conform to them."[42] The author of *Otherwise than Being* seems to agree with the author of the *Critique of Practical Reason* that in order for the principle of the will to be moral, it cannot be inferred from statements describing the empirical context, whether psychological, social, or historical, and that it cannot be justified by the various "interests" of which it is made up. Such statements, which would be denotative, would inevitably explain the act as the effect of causes and would thereby take away its specificity: that it is an uncaused cause. It is owing to this specificity that the act is not a phenomenon, not the object of a science of what is, but the expression of a noumenal freedom — and not apprehensible by any sensory intuition.

Yet this assimilation, however tempting, must be rejected. Practical reason is not an-archy. In Levinas' eyes, the specificity of prescriptive statements is not, and cannot be, sufficiently assured by the Kantian procedure. The reason for his mistrust is contained in a sentence that will serve as our guide: "There is no point in formally distinguishing will from understanding, will from reason, when you decide at once to consider as good will only the will which adheres to clear ideas, or which makes decisions only out of respect for the universal."[43] Although Descartes is a target here no less than Kant, we will restrict our cross-examination of the logic of the prescriptive to the latter.

The obstacle to logical justification posed by the prescriptive is the object "Of the Deduction of the Principles of Pure Practical Reason" in the first chapter of the "Analytic of Pure Practical Reason."[44] How can we deduce the moral law (the prescriptive statement) without making it lose its specificity? Although in the case of statements of theoretical reason, which are denotative, we cannot deduce the principles that govern their formation speculatively on the basis of "a priori sources of knowledge," we can at least have recourse to that *Surrogat*[45], that expedient, which is experience/experiment — which on the whole, other things being equal, proceeds in the same way as does the logician of the sciences who extracts, from the denotative statements given in the corpus that serves as his reference, the axioms (in the modern sense) that these statements presuppose. We know that for Kant, as a reader of Hume, the chief among these axioms is causality.

The relation between the statement of these axioms in the metalanguage of the Deduction and the object language, which is the discourse of the sciences, is isomorphic to the relation linking the language of science to the "givens" of experiment/experience. The isomorphism of the two relations in no way contradicts the fact that the first derives from the transcendental level and the second from the empirical level. On the contrary, it is this isomorphism that allows Kant to declare that the deduction of principles, which cannot be done directly "from the sources," uses experience/experiment as a *Surrogat*. It follows that this metalanguage — the discourse of the deduction of scientific principles and especially of causality — remains isomorphic, on its own level, to the object language that is its reference. This isomorphism is what makes the metalanguage possible. Without it, and without the above-mentioned "sources," how could the principles of theoretical reason, notably causality, be determined?

For the language of prescriptions, this isomorphism between the metalanguage of deduction and the object language, whose principles it must extract, fails. Prescriptive statements, far from being governed like denotatives by axioms such as causality, are themselves the causes of acts that they engender. This pure causality, or spontaneity of the moral law (i.e., the prescriptive statement par excellence), is not a fact of experience, since everything given in experience is governed by the infinite sequences of causes and effects, and since the cause of such-and-such is necessarily also thought of as the effect of so-and-so. Hence, there is an insurmountable allomorphism between the metalanguage of deduction, even considered as the establishment of axioms governing an object language, and the object language that is the prescriptive statement. This is why Kant asserts, concerning the deduction of the practical principle, that "one cannot hope to succeed as well as with the principles of pure theoretical understanding."[46] He even exposes the failure of the practical deduction with a sort of satisfaction when he writes: "No deduction, no effort of reason whether theoretical, speculative, or aided by experience can prove the objective reality of moral law; even if one were willing to renounce apodictic certainty, this reality could not be confirmed by experience and thus proved *a posteriori.*" But he adds at once (and this seems to be the source of his satisfaction): "And nevertheless it sustains itself by itself."[47]

Must we then abandon any attempt to deduce prescriptive statements? Here the Kantian analysis takes a strange turn (which is what Levinas' thought breaks with), for while Kant is pleased to recognize the impossibility of deducing the practical principle, that is, of deducing a metalanguage bearing upon prescriptives, he still maintains its functioning but inverts its direction (*sens*): "Instead of this deduction, sought in vain, of the moral principle, one finds something other and entirely paradoxical" ("*etwas anderes aber und ganz widersinnisches*").[48] One finds something *widersinnig*, a deduction that proceeds in the reverse direction to the one that was sought. The metalanguage that is Kant's transcendental discourse had to try to draw the principle of prescriptive statements (i.e., the moral law) from an object language (having as its model some experience or other). As we have just seen, if it had succeeded in doing so it would have been at the cost of abolishing the principle. It is therefore by failing that it succeeds.

This failure, however, does not do away with the possibility of the metalanguage; it inverts its direction, at the cost of modifying its object. What can still be deduced, in the absence of the law, is freedom. This deduction is made on the basis of the law. Thus, in the new deduction the law is placed not as a conclusion, as a statement extracted by the metalanguage from the object language, but as a premise, as a statement in the object language, about which the metalanguage infers that it presupposes a statement bearing on freedom. This is the reversal of direction: "This moral principle itself serves inversely as a principle for deducing an inscrutable [*unerforschlichen*] power . . . , I mean the power of freedom . . . ."[49]

It follows that freedom is not expressed in any statement in the natural language, but can only be the object of a metastatement in the commentary. In contrast, the law or prescriptive statement is an expression in the natural language that cannot have a place in the metalanguage. The *Thou shalt* is "felt" by the empirical subject, the *Thou canst* is constructed by the philosopher in the transcendental language: empirically it remains unfathomable.

Apparently Levinas has no objection to this distribution — on the contrary, it corresponds to one of the most important themes of his work, the priority of the seizing (or dispossession) by the *Do* of the content of the order (*Do this*, or *that*) from any understanding, that is, from any commentary, which is necessarily denotative.[50]

We may even be tempted to assimilate the place he assigns to freedom to the one that Kant reserves for it: does not the author of the *Critique*, by giving the expression about freedom the status of an inferred proposition in the metalanguage of practical reason, encourage the suspicion that moves Levinas to relegate freedom to the status of a second-order, inferior infatuation of the ego?[51]

Yet it is with respect to this hinge between law and freedom that the difference bursts out: a difference that is all the more profound because the two thoughts are related. Both, in effect, place the law in the domain constituted by the object language of their own commentary, and both recognize that this object domain is not that of experience. Kant proposes to "call consciousness of the fundamental law a fact [*Faktum*] of reason."[52] In this *Faktum*, "pure reason manifests itself as really practical in us"; but for that very reason this "absolutely inexplicable" fact ("*ein schlechterdings . . . unerklaerliches Faktum*")[53] is rather a sort of fact, a quasi-fact. Kant explains that the reality of pure will is "given *a priori* in the moral law as if by a fact" ("*gleichsam durch ein Faktum gegeben*").[54] "As if by a fact," not "by a fact." This fact is only a quasi-fact, since the determination of will by the prescription of law is not empirical and may never be established as a simple fact by means of a commentary, whose denotative model would be the deduction of the principles of theoretical reason.

This fact of prescription is so far removed from what a fact in the empirical sense is, so little capable of being subsumed under a concept that, once deduced, would permit us to fix its place in a moral experience, that Kant, in comparing it to sensory experience, calls it an idea: "The moral law transports us, in an ideal manner [*der Idee nach*] into a nature where pure reason, if it were accompanied by a physical power in proportion to itself, would produce the sovereign good."[55] The reference domain circumscribed by the quasi-experience of the *Thou shalt* is not nature, but "a supra-sensible nature," whose "idea serves as a model for the determinations of our will."[56] Moral experience is not an experience; the *Thou shalt* is not received in the realm of the sensible like something given in that realm. Yet it is received — that is why it can be called a fact; but it is received in the ideal.

Here again, Levinas would apparently not need to change anything, Levinas who tirelessly devotes himself to dissociating what belongs to the experience of the ego (material to be enjoyed or given a denotative commentary, within the limits we have stated) from what arises out of an untestable making-present of the other, by which is opened up a world of responsibilities transcending the world of enjoyment, although its effects are determined there.[57] Kant for his part, pursuing the theme of the *Faktum-Idee* right to its ultimate implications, concludes with that "marvel"[58] provided by moral law, which is, as in Levinas, the presence of transcendence: if the "fact" of the *Thou shalt* circumscribes an ideal nature (it is nevertheless efficient since it gives rise to those effects that are the acts that correspond to it — Levinas' 'responsibilities'), it follows "that reason is itself through ideas an efficient cause in the field of experience," and that "its transcendent use" is thus, thanks to the *Faktum* of moral law, "changed into an immanent use."[59] Reason remains transcendent when it aims to circumscribe in its commentary the essence of empirical nature; but this transcendence is what assures its immanence when, in the form of the prescriptive, it constitutes ideal nature.

Now it is precisely there, on the question of efficiency, that Levinas must turn his back on the Kant of the second *Critique*.

V. Logical Analysis of the Kantian Statement of Moral Law

Causality is indeed the axis upon which Kant makes the deduction of the practical principle operate in reverse. Let us try to demonstrate this briefly. The prescriptive statement *Thou shalt* cannot be deduced: it is a sort of fact (as the scientific statement is for the critique of theoretical reason). The question asked of this "fact" by the *Critique* is not "How does this kind of statement find objects to which it may be applied?" (the critical question bearing on the theoretical use of reason).[60] It is rather: "Strictly speaking, how can this statement prescribe?" Now, to prescribe (and here is the axis) is "to be a cause without objects."[61] The question that the *Critique* asks of the denotative statement is the question of the causality of objects upon representations: the classical question of truth or reference, in short. But when the object of commentary is the prescriptive statement, the *Critique must* invert the direction of the causality.[62] This is the inversion of direction.

All the rest — the deduction, properly speaking — comes in consequence of this reversal, which is stated in the exposition of the principle of practical reason. For if prescription *must* be the cause of objects, it cannot receive its power of efficiency from any object given in experience. In this way all hypothetical imperatives are eliminated. And the only answer left to the question, How does the law prescribe? is "by an 'immediate,' 'transcendent,' 'unintelligible,' 'inscrutable,' power." This transcendent power is freedom, which is none other than pure reason itself, acting as a practical cause.

It seems that the properties able to qualify its power can be applied, just as they are, to the "other side of the face," which in the other, according to Levinas, commands us to act. Yet no one should be more hostile than the author of *Otherwise than Being* to this deduction of freedom, even when it is an inverted deduction: he would not fail to see therein the return of the denotative, and this in the very procedure by which the *Critique of Practical Reason* seeks to exclude it. This return is indeed effected in the form of the reversal of the Deduction, and first of all in the reversal of causality. In inverting the direction of causality, Kant believes he is emancipating will from experience. But the inversion leaves the concept itself, that of causality, intact, and nothing of this is inverted except the relation of order among the elements that it puts together (synthesizes). Kant justifies himself for this throughout the section that follows the Deduction, entitled "Of the Right of Pure Reason, in its Practical Usage, to an Extension which is not Possible for it in Speculative Usage."[63] What is more, he there calls openly for the inverted (i.e., noumenal) use that is made of causality in the second *Critique*.

Kant writes: "We are not satisfied with applying this concept [causality] to the objects of experience," and further, "We want to make use of it for things in themselves."[64] Now we are authorized to do so by the *Critique* of speculative reason itself which, in making this concept a principle of understanding and not as Hume claimed a *habitus*, a general appearance, born of experience, endowed it with a transcendental status. That this a priori cannot be valid outside its application to the givens of experience is the rule of knowledge. However, "it maintains a different relationship with the faculty of desiring,"[65] an inverse relationship whereby the effect is not received from a phenomenal cause but produced by an unconditioned cause. What authorizes the *Widersinnige* of causality (and of Deduction) is, in short, that the same concept of cause is put to two contrary uses, the one in knowing, the other in desiring.

What follows from this as regards statements? That the form of a denotative statement must not be fundamentally different from that of a prescriptive statement. The former effects the synthesis of two phenomena under the category of cause, while the latter effects the synthesis of an agent and an act under the same category (i.e., of cause). Admittedly the agent is noumenal, and the act is not given; these features are registered in the imperative aspect taken by the moral law. But it is simple to show that the main function of the statement of the law is to maintain the imperative within the limits of the indicative, that is, to subordinate the "inverted" mode of causality in desire to its direct mode in knowledge, or in other words to identify the predication that denotes a given "nature" with the predication that prescribes an ideal "nature." Let us try to expose the denotative form concealed by the categorical imperative.

The fundamental law of practical reason is enunciated thus: "Act in such a way that the maxim of your will can always be valid as the principle of a universal legislation also" ("*Handle so, dass die Maxime deines Willens jederzeit zugleich als Prinzip einer allgemeinen Gesetzgebung gelten koenne*").[66] This statement can be analyzed intitially into two parts: *Act*, and *In such a way that . . . . Act* can be rewritten as *Do something*, which in turn may be understood as (i) *Thou shalt*, the pure prescriptive, *It is obligatory that . . .*; (ii) *To do something*, which as we have seen may be taken either as a well-formed expression in propositional logic, *A thing of some kind is done*, or else as a proposition root, *The doing of something* (by you). In Von Wright's notation,[67] this part would be expressed $O(p)$, where O is the operator of obligation and p the proposition being considered.

But it will not be forgotten that the moral law must not determine the will except by its "form," and that the "matter" to be found in it (e.g., a motive ([*Triebfeder*])[68] could not operate in it as a cause, except by falling back into the phenomenal and the infinite chain of causalities. It follows that the expression p must present some remarkable properties.

These appear easily if we rewrite the expression in the notation of Alchourrón and Kalinowski:[69] $O(p)$ is written $Oy\propto$, which reads, "y must accomplish $\propto$." Let it be agreed that y here designates the particular (or singular?) addressee of the order, named "*Thou*." The order would have the developed expression $\exists y(Oy\propto)$ and the signification "There is at least one y and this y must accomplish $\propto$."

But especially since the aim is to write a prescription that does not determine the "matter" of the action to be accomplished, it is appropriate in the expression $Oy\propto$ to substitute for $\propto$, which designates a determined action, a symbol ζ, which will designate the action not determined by itself, the unspecified action, which is the target of the Kantian law — or a variable of an unknown action. The first part of the statement of the law is thus written $Oy\zeta$ and read, "Accomplish an undetermined action."

To move on to the second part of the statement of the law: "That the maxim of your will can always be valid as the principle of a universal legislation also." It indicates that the maxim of the will that motivates the action (by itself the action is a matter of indifference) is equally formulable as a universal norm. The maxim of the action is none other than $Oy\zeta$. According to the chosen convention, the fact that a prescription should be valid as a norm (or as the principle of a law) is written $Nx'-'$, which is read, "x has ruled: –," where x designates an agent and N a norm function that presents as a norm the expression placed in inverted commas on its right.

This operator is not to be confused with the one designated by the symbol O. "It is obligatory that . . . ." The latter belongs to deontic logic, or the logic of prescriptions, while the operator marked N derives from the logic of norms. An expression such as $Nx'Oy\propto'$ reads, "There is a norm decreed by x which declares: y must accomplish $\propto$." This reading brings out that the function N is descriptive; it denotes the fact that the expression placed on its right is a norm, whereas the function O is prescriptive, indicating that the action $\propto$ must be accomplished by y.

It can be seen that the expression $Nx'-'$ is to the expression $Oy\propto$ as a metastatement is to a statement in the object language. The inverted commas around $Oy\propto$ in the statement of the norm attest that the statement of the prescription is here a quotation made by x, and that the reader, the addressee of the complete message, is dealing with the "image" of the deontic statement in the metalanguage of norms. These observations refer back to those made above[70] on the subject of the neutralization of the prescriptive in the metalanguage that comments on it: the commentary that concerns us consists in declaring that the prescription is a norm.

It is in this metalanguage of norms that, according to Kant, the maxim of a particular action can be declared the principle of a universal legislation. The obligation $Oy\zeta$, obligation for a particular subject y to accomplish the indifferent action ζ, is taken as the object of a meta-assertion, which declares it a universal norm. The one who can declare it such is any subject whatever. Thus, x in $Nx'-'$ symbolizes here an agent which has the universal quantifier, and this is developed as $\forall x(Nx'-')$.

We can now write the second part of the statement of the law, still agreeing, however, to ignore for a moment the operation that links it to the first part, which Kant enunciates as *in such a way that*. Isolated then, this part is expressed, *The maxim of your will can always also be valid as the principle of a universal legislation*. The "maxim of your will" is the norm enunciating that the act is obligatory for the agent. Let us recall that the act in question was posited in the first part of the statement as an indeterminate act. Finally, if this norm is only subjective, the subject who enunciates it as such is the same as the one who makes for himself an obligation to act as he does. The "maxim of will," which commands the particular obligation to act, is thus written $Ny'Oy\zeta,'$ which reads, "At least one subject has ruled: At least one subject must accomplish the said indeterminate action."

As regards the end of the second part of the statement of the law, *can always also be valid as the principle of a universal legislation*: It names the predicate that is always attributed to the "maxim of your will," at least if the action that the will commands in accordance with this maxim is just (or moral). This predicate is *the principle of a universal legislation*. The principle of a legislation is a norm. If the legislation is universal, this norm is decreed by any subject declaring norms. Moreover, the obligation thus elevated to the status of a universal norm is evidently the same one that commands the agent designated at the beginning (*Thou*) to accomplish the (indeterminate) action in question in the first part of the statement. Ultimately Kant does not intend only for that agent at least to be made to submit to the said universal legislation, but any agent whatever. Hence we will write the predicate in question $\mathbf{V}x(Nx'Ox\varsigma')$.

The expression *can always be valid as*, which links the predicate to the subject of this second part of the statement of the moral law, is to be understood: "Each time that $NyOy\varsigma$, then it is necessary that $NxOx\varsigma$." We must not let ourselves be deceived by Kant's use of the modal verb *can* (German *können*). It cannot here have the force of probability, or even of very great probability, which it can elsewhere denote in French, as in German;[71] such meaning would ruin the scope of the law that Kant would have "fundamental" and that would then merely be very likely. The fact that the particular maxim *can always be valid as* a universal principle signifies that every time there is the maxim, then it is valid every time, as that principle. What commands the meaning of the necessity that we attribute to the modal verb is the adverb *always* (*jederzeit*, every time), which is the temporal index of the universality of a proposition, as *necessary that* is its modal index. So we will express this meaning by the sign of implication (or logical conditional): *If p, then q*, or $p \supset q$. This provides the following expression for the second part of the statement of the moral law: $(Ny'Oy\varsigma') \supset (\mathbf{V}xNx'Ox\varsigma')$, that is, "If at least one subject has ruled: The said subject at least must accomplish the said indeterminate action, then any subject whatever has ruled: Any subject whatever must accomplish the said indeterminate action."

Let us finally come to the operation by which the preceding statement, which expresses the second part of the statement of the fundamental law, finds itself modified into the complete statement. The question is to know how this second part is articulated with the first. The articulation of the Kantian statement is *in such a way that* (*so, dass*). This is of the greatest importance for Kant, since it is what comes to determine the action, otherwise indeterminate, that the subject makes for himself the obligation of accomplishing, and since the determination takes place (as Kant repeats) only through the "form" of the maxim and not through its "matter." Now, what Kant calls the "form" of the maxim is none other than the second part of the statement of the law that we have just described. It is only if the norm bearing on the obligation to accomplish an action can be decreed as a universal norm that the accomplishment of the said action can be obligatory. It follows that the subjective obligation is legitimate, that is, constituting the object of a norm, only if it can also constitute the object of a universal norm.

The operator that unites the two parts of the Kantian statement is thus that of equivalence (or of biconditionality): *p if, and only if, q*, or $p \equiv q$.

Do whatever it is if, and only if, the norm of what you must do is also a universal norm. Or to put it more rigorously: "At least one subject must accomplish such-and-such an action if, and only if, one subject at least having ruled: At least one subject must perform the said action, then any subject has ruled: Any subject must perform the said action."

To write this, we will replace the sign of the indeterminate action with the sign of the determinate action, since the complete statement of the law henceforth allows us to determine (formally) the action to be accomplished. We get the following expression:

$$Cy\alpha \equiv [(Ny'Oy\alpha') \supset (\forall xNx'Ox\alpha')].$$

We find in many of Kant's explanations confirmation of the proposed reading of the expression *in such a way that* as an operator of equivalence. This operator is not a simple conditional (or inference). For the moral law does not only say, "If the norm of such-and-such an action is a universally obligatory norm, then you must perform this action." It also says, "If you must accomplish such-and-such an action, then the maxim of your will (= your particular norm) is a universally obligatory norm." Not only *if p, then q*, but also *if q, then p*. That the universality of the norm is a condition of validity of the action is something that no one can fail to understand in the second *Critique*. But we cannot restrict ourselves to this simple condition; the morality of the act must also be a condition of the universality of the norm.

The first condition is to be understood as the determination of the will by the pure law, that is, by pure reason in its practical usage. The second condition is to be understood as the determination of the law by pure will, that is, again by pure reason in its practical usage. In effect, practical reason is both legislation, (that is, pure synthesizing power and, so to speak, power to enunciate a nature) *and* at the same time efficient causality, that is, power to produce and power, so to speak, to institute a nature. As legislation, it requires universality as the condition of any obligation to act. As causality, it requires pure will, that is, freedom, which emancipates its effects from nature as explained by theoretical reason, which places them in a suprasensible nature.

Thus the equivalence indicated by our operator appears to be merely the transcription into the conventions of logical notation, of the identity admitted by Kant between reason that rules and reason that wills. The reciprocal implication, or biconditionality, between these two powers appears clearly in a phrase like the following: "Pure practical laws are . . . necessary, if freedom is assumed, or inversely freedom is necessary, because these laws are necessary, as practical postulates."[72]

The same applies for Kant's insistent emphasizing that will is pure only if it is "absolutely" and "immediately" determined. Then "it is all one (*einerlei*) with pure practical reason."[73] This immediate identity is only possible if the will is guided solely by the legislation of reason, which has universal value. If will, then reason, that is, universality; and if reason, then will.

VI. Levinas Against Kant

What have we shown by this? That a prescriptive statement, the obligatory symbolized by O, is equated with the description of this statement, which makes of it a norm N — on one condition only, it is true. This is that the norm of particular obligation can be rewritten as a universal norm: but this condition can itself be entirely expressed in the logic of norms and does not make any new obligation appear, only an implication of propositional logic attributing a change of quantifier to the subject who enunciates the norm.

This equivalence of the prescriptive and the descriptive in the statement of the law was prepared, so to speak, by the inversion of the practical Deduction, and above all by the reversal of usage of causality. The latter is valid as a model for any synthesis of elements in the descriptive statements of science. When Kant detects its new usage in the prescriptive statements of morality, he declares it to be inverted as to its effects: in theoretical reason, causality synthesizes the givens; in practical reason it produces them. But this reversal now seems to be something other than an inversion of direction on one and the same axis.

A simple inversion of that sort would result from a reciprocal transformation. A reciprocal transformation manifests in particular the property of transforming an implication p⊃q in such a way that where R symbolizes the transformation in question, we have $R(p \supset q)$ = $q \supset p$. This transformation is situated in the realm of propositional logic and affects only the form of the statements.

But that is not true of the Kantian *Widersinnige*. The transformation noted by Kant escapes from propositional logic: in displacing the cause from the "noumenon" side on the basis of the "phenomenal" position accorded to it by theoretical reason, it does not operate, or does not only operate, as a reciprocal transformation, inverting the order of the premise and the conclusion in the statements; nor for that matter does it operate as any one of the other three transformations admitted by propositional logic. What it introduces as the premise of that conclusion (i.e., the prescriptive statement of the moral law) is the "subject" of the enunciation of this statement itself.

The practical Deduction does indeed start out from the moral law, as from an ideally tested premise, but only in order to deduce it and substitute for it a premise that is untested even ideally and that is even inconceivable — namely, will. If will remains "unintelligible," it is because it cannot be placed in a propositional statement, that is, in a discourse with a denotative function, arising from theoretical reason and having nothing to do with this genre of unintelligibility. When Kant says that will, if it is pure, prescribes the law, he keeps it in principle outside the statement of that law — which is marked by the imperative form of that statement. Hence the will does indeed occupy the place of the subject of the prescriptive enunciation, which escapes *ex hypothesi* from any descriptive statement (i.e., from all intelligibility).

This 'absolute exteriority' of that which commands, so precious to Levinas but also to Kant, is precisely what Kant causes to vanish, by identifying the power of the subject of the practical enunciation with causality and by conceiving causality as the same category that permits theoretical reason to form its denotative expressions well. Or in other words, by identifying reason as prescriptive will with reason as descriptive causality.

In the language we are using here, we will say, then, that what is at stake in the discourse of Levinas is the power to speak of obligation without ever transforming it into a norm.

VII. Pragmatic Analysis of the Kantian Statement of Moral Law

To clarify the scope of what is at stake, let us go back to the pragmatic point of view, in which we have noted,[74] that the addressee of an order is in a quite different situation from the addressee of a discourse of knowledge. The discourse of knowledge is a genre of discourse that authorizes, and even encourages, the addressee to begin to speak, either to proffer in his turn some statement on the same "subject" (i.e., the same reference) as the first enunciator, or to comment on what the latter has said about this same reference, or to mix the two in a composite discourse. But the recipient of an order has hardly any latitude, at least not if he means to restrict himself to the world of prescriptions: he can only carry it out or not carry it out. If he argues about it, comments on it, negotiates over it, he inevitably substitutes for the order received the "image" of this order that the negotiation, commentary, or argument take as their reference, and he escapes *ipso facto* from the universe of prescriptions into that of denotations.

Now we have just seen that the insertion of an order into a statement declaring that order to be a norm is a particular case of the above situation. The one, whoever he is, who promotes an obligation to the dignity of a norm is an addressee of that order who takes it as the reference of his discourse and, in so doing, moves into the position of addresser of a new statement, the commentary that makes the order into a norm. It is of course conceivable that he did not gain knowledge of that order directly but was told of it; it could be objected that the order thus did not reach him equipped with its executive power, but was already neutralized and repeated as a quotation in a descriptive discourse. This is possible; but the situation is then merely displaced: someone, whoever he is, necessarily, rightly or wrongly, must not have "taken upon himself" the order he heard, so that this order could be made the object of a commentary, even if this commentary consisted of a declaration that the order were valid as a norm.

Such, in particular, is the situation of the enunciator named Kant in respect of the moral law. We have just described the statement of the moral law in the conventions of Alchourrón and Kalinowski. If we now had to write the Kantian statement that declares this law to be the "fundamental law" of practical reason, that is, a norm par excellence, it is clear that we would have to place before our expression of the law a supplementary prefix such as $Nk'-'$. This prefix belongs to the logic of norms and reads "*Kant has ruled: '-'*," where the symbol ' - ' designates the statement of the law, properly speaking.

The complete Kantian statement would then be expressed:
$$Nk'Oy\propto \equiv (Ny'Oyx') = (\forall xNx'Ox\propto ')'.$$
This reads (omitting the outer quotation marks so as to simplify the notation):

> A subject named Kant has ruled: "One subject at least must perform the action $\propto$ if, and only if, one subject at least having ruled: One subject at least must perform the action $\propto$, then any subject has ruled: Any subject must perform the action $\propto$."

A reading like this brings out that Kant — one at least of the addressees of the obligation y — comes to occupy the position of an addresser, inasmuch as he sets up the first obligation as a norm.

The same goes for the reader of the *Critique of Practical Reason*. By reading Kant's commentary, he makes himself the addressee not of the obligation enunciated by the moral law encased in this commentary (as an "image" of itself) but of the discourse by which Kant raises this obligation to the dignity of a norm. As the addressee of denotative propositions, he is required to understand but not to do. He can comment on the commentary in his turn and thus pass into the position of enunciator by the same right as Kant.

This substitution appears legitimate in the case of the reader of the *Critique of Practical Reason*: what he reads is not an order but the declaration that the order *Act in such a way that* . . . is a norm. Now, the statement of an obligation is not an obligation. In this respect, it seems that the reader of Levinas is in a position no different from that of the reader of Kant. If he reads the order *Do before understanding* in this or that book by Levinas[75] it is, so to speak, understood (*entendu*) that he will not stop understanding (or reading) in order to do and that he "must" understand this statement, not as a command but as the quotation or image of that command reported in Levinas' metalanguage.

There is no difference between the two readers in this regard: the one, like the other, is authorized by his position as reader of a book of philosophy to neutralize the executive force of the order that he reads there and to place himself in the position of possible commentator; but the same does not hold true of the two "authors."

Kant can denote the moral obligation as a norm because universality is already implied in its formula. When "Kant has ruled: 'One subject at least must accomplish such-and-such an action, etc.,'" he is doing nothing other than applying to the order *Act in such a way that . . .* the argument *from the moment that the obligation to which you are submitted can be universalized as a norm.* Kant's commentary can denote the order as a norm since this order is executive only on condition that it has been denoted as a norm by the one who is to execute it. Kant can comment on it as a norm since that is what the agent must already have done in order for his action to be moral. To speak in formal terms, the k that we have made appear in the Nk is a case of the Nx that the Ny must imply for the obligation to be valid.

For the moment we will not follow this clue any further, despite its importance. Let us be content to observe that the moral imperative, which on the one hand is set up as a universal norm by Kant and on the other hand equates the obligation with the universal norm in its statement, appears to rest on a *petitio principii*, belonging to the first type recognized by Aristotle, when "one postulates the very thing one has to demonstrate." Kant has to demonstrate that the statement of the moral law is universally valid. Now, by introducing into this statement the biconditional *if and only if . . .* what else is he doing but postulating that the maxim, if it is valid, becomes the moral law?

Yet, if we reestablish the different levels of language the *petitio principii* is not certain:

Object language: *Do that.*

Metalanguage 1: *Do that iff/Do that/is universalizable.*[76]

Metalanguage 2: *Do that iff/Do that/is universalizable/is universalizable.*

The first level of language here is prescriptive; the second, that of the metalanguage or commentary, establishes the equivalence of prescriptive and denotative; the third, which cites the second, is purely denotative. For there to be a *petitio principii*, the metalanguages (1) and (2) would in reality have to be of the same species and at the same level. This would be the case, for example, if the last statement, that is, the Kantian commentary, were prescriptive and if one could substitute /*that*/ for the expression /*Do that iff /Do that/ is universalizable/*. In that case the statement would be: *Do* (= *Say*) /*Do that iff /Do that/ is universalizable iff/ Do* (= *Say*) //*that*// *is universaliz-*

able, where the last /*that*/ is substituted for the first complete expression between bars. Intuitively transcribed, and with simplified quotation marks, we have: *Say [Statement of the moral law] iff [Say (Statement of the moral law)] is universalizable.*

Obviously, this is not the Kantian statement: Kant does not order his reader to declare the statement of the law obligatory on condition that it is universalizable. Kant does not order his reader to do anything practical. That the reader *may* or *must* say something about the statement of the moral law is not on account of a permission or an obligation; it is a modalized inference. The reader of the book is placed before a universe of denotative statements, to which the third-order statement fully belongs. The prescriptive statements that he encounters in the Kantian commentary are always only "images" of themselves. Hence it is legitimate to assert that what saves the Kantian statement from the *petitio principii* is the recourse to denotative metalanguage.

VIII. "Obey!"

But this recourse is at the same time a kind of scandal, since it rests on the equivalence, in the second-order statement, of a prescriptive and a descriptive statement: this is the scandal that Levinas denounces in a sentence we have already quoted.[77] For this equivalence is nothing other than the ego's infatuation with knowledge. By promoting the order he receives to the dignity of a norm, the addressee of the prescription subordinates the obligation that is linked to the prescription to the comprehension that what he understands (the maxim of the action) can be understood, and hence executed, by everyone. The order he receives is really an order only if it is mediated by a denotative metastatement. In consequence, the addressee of the moral law ceases to be in the place of the *Thou* to whom the prescription is addressed and who is expressed in the statement of this law by the second-person imperative, and he comes to occupy the place of the *I* who delivers the opinion that this prescription is or is not universalizable. By the fact of this displacement, the other from whom he receives the order — that other whom Kant, however, admits is "inscrutable" and whom Levinas strives to maintain in his transcendence — finds himself "placed in symmetry" with the ego. The irreducibility of the prescriptive is ruined, if it is true that it assumes an ineffaceable dissymmetry between the addresser and the addressee of the order.

This supposition, which governs the whole discourse of Levinas like a kind of metaprescription of alterity, can be expressed by the following statement: *That /Thou/ shalt never be /I/!*[78] Among the numerous occurrences of it that can be found in his books, the following is a philosophically-inspired one:

> The differences between the others and me . . . depend on the I-Other orientation conjuncture, on the inevitable *orientation* of being 'on the basis of oneself' towards 'the Other' . . . . Multiplicity in being, which refuses totalisation, but takes form as fraternity and discourse, is situated in an essentially asymmetrical 'space'.[79]

But it is Levinas the commentator on the Talmud[80] who seems to grasp most closely the metaprinciple of asymmetry:

> The incomparable character of an event like the giving of the Torah [is that] it is accepted before it is known . . . . The deed in question . . . is not simply the opposite practice to theory, but a way of *actualising without beginning with the possible* . . . . They execute before having understood: . . . To understand a voice that speaks to you [is] *ipso facto* to accept the obligation in respect of the one who is speaking . . . . In this impossibility of hiding from the imperious call of the creature, the assumption does not in any way go beyond passivity.[81]

The question, then, is to know how to formulate a first-level prescriptive statement, expressed in the natural language of orders, that would satisfy the metaprinciple *That /Thou/ shalt never be /I/!*

Let us start again, according to the rapid description we made at the outset,[82] from the situation of the commentator who finds himself faced with the works of Levinas: if he understands it, he must not understand it, and if he does not understand it, then he understands it.

In the batch of "paradoxes" that have come down to us from the principle adversaries of Plato and Aristotle, the Megarians and the Cynics, there exists a prescriptive statement that appears to produce a similarly contradictory effect. This is the order *Disobey!*

Aristotle notes it in the following context. Among the procedures of refutation used by the sophists, he gives the name *paralogisms* to those that, operating *exo tès lexeôs,* do not (or do not only) play on the *lexis* (or *dictio*) of the statement but make bad usage of the categories of thought.[83] In this way, a subset of these paralogisms rests, according to Aristotle, on a confusion of the absolute and the relative in attribution: *to aplôs versus kata ti,* or *to aplôs versus pè.* An example of a statement that plays upon such a confusion is . . . : *If the nonbeing is opinable* (= the possible object of an opinion), *then the nonbeing is.*[84] In order to refute this sophism. it is sufficient to reintroduce the obfuscated category *relation.* For, says Aristotle, "it is impossible for contraries and contradictories, affirmation and negation, to belong absolutely [*aplôs*] to the same object, but there is nothing against each of the two (properties) belonging to it in some way or in a certain regard or in a certain manner.[85] There then follows a further example of the same paralogism: "Is it possible for the same [subject] to obey and disobey the same [order or subject]?" Aristotle rejects such a possibility by a lapidary argument: "He who disobeys does not simply obey, but he obeys in something."[86]

One can thus reconstitute the statement aimed at by the Stagirite as *Disobey!* However, this order is a paradox only on one condition, namely that it be understood as a complete statement. What does this mean?

Let us examine the case of its affirmative correlate: *Obey!* Customarily this statement is understood by its addressee as an abbreviation of a complete statement: *Obey the order that you have received in another connection!* One can thus distinguish two orders here: a first order, which carries the instruction about the act to be performed (*Close the door!*), and a second order (*Obey!*), which recalls that the first order is executive. Note that the sequence *first order, second order* must be conceived as a logical rather than a chronological succession: the expression *Obey!* can, in "real" time, precede the order that gives the instruction, without this reciprocal transformation of the sequence's affecting the logical properties of its terms. In particular, the reminder of the order has in both cases an exclusively perlocutionary function: it orders its addressee not to perform an action but to receive the anterior or ulterior prescriptive statement in an attitude of carrying it out or, in other words, of being obliged by this statement.

One can always reject the expression *Obey!*, taken in isolation, because it is an incomplete statement, lacking an instruction. That is how Jean-Michel Salanskis[87] compares its inconsistency to that of an axiom such as *If a, then b. And a.* It is known that in order to make this axiom executable, Lewis Carroll's tortoise[88] demands a new instruction *c*, expressed as *If a, then b. And a. Then b.* But this instruction *c* must in turn be introduced into the inference that allows us to conclude *b. If a, then b. And a. And c. Then b.* This constitutes a new instruction *d.* And so on.

It is the same, observes Salanskis, for *Obey!* if we claim that it is a complete statement. Let *O* be the order *Obey!* and *e* its execution. This gives: *If O, then e. And O.* The instruction needed in order for the order to be executed is *If O, then e. And O. Then e.* But this instruction (which is here an order *O': Obey the "Obey"!*) introduces itself into the previous inference as a supplementary condition for the execution of *O: If O, then e. And O. And O'. Then e.* And soon the execution of the order will always be postponed, or — there will always be one instruction lacking.

One can use this argumentation (leaving aside for the moment the temporal properties of the expression *Obey!* which we will discuss elsewhere) the better to distinguish an interesting property of the statement *Obey!* This is the same property that Salanskis notes, we believe, in classifying this statement among the protodoxes. It is not one of the well-formed expressions, which satisfy a set of lexical and syntactical rules fixed in the metalanguage of deontic logic. It is one of the expressions that, in the natural language, allow us to gloss the metalinguistic symbol *O*, which also reads "It is obligatory that . . . ." This symbol is an operator whose property is to change the proposition or proposition root placed on its right into an obligation. By itself it could not constitute one of the well-formed expressions of deontic logic: those are (in monadic logic) of the form "$O(p)$," where *p* is a well-formed expression of propositional logic.[89] The logician makes clear, as well, that among the other expressions that are not well-formed deontic expressions are "those which repeat (iterate) a deontic operator."[90] He thus excludes as inconsistent not only an expression like "*O*" but also an expression like "*O(O)*." Thanks to this exclusion, the logician declares himself secured against some "paradoxes," which he does not name, but which we can guess.

There is thus a temptation simply to place the symbol *O* in the lexicon of the metalanguage that allows us to speak about the language of commands. But this solution is unsatisfactory because of the confused usage in it of the word *metalanguage.* According to the acceptation of Russell and Tarski, it is defined as a second-order language in which it is possible to decide the truth value of expressions belonging to the first-order language. The operator O in no way fulfills this function, not even for the sake of the interest that might accrue to it as a result. That is because, once again, the propositions it permits us to put into form are not descriptive or attributive but prescriptive. If there exists some metalanguage relating to prescriptive propositions, it must no doubt be denotative as we have said; but then the operator of obligation, if it is part of it, does not there fulfill the same function as the truth functions imported from propositional logic. These alone enable us to declare that a relation between two prescriptive statements is true because, for example, one can infer the one from the other or false because, on the contrary, the one and the other are contradictory (operator of exclusion). But the operator of obligation, taken in itself, neither derives from the claim to speak truly when we encounter it in the prescriptive expressions of the natural language nor allows us to decide the validity of those expressions when we consider it as a deontic operator. It is indispensable, on the other hand, in whatever form of words it may occur, to the formation of prescriptive expressions. On the hither side of all alethic validity, it is the prescription that accompanies any instruction so as to make it obligatory.

Is this *hither-side* (*en-deçà*) what Levinas means to signify by his *beyond* (*au-delà*)? Perhaps; but even then we must not forget what such a statement has as its pragmatic correlate, which Levinas calls "passivity."[91] Kant said of the *Ich denke* that it accompanies all our representations. This remark merely circumscribes what we previously called the enunciative clause.[92] But the *Thou shalt* or the *Obey!* could not in the same way accompany all our prescriptions. The form of the statement of obligation is not only different from that of a statement in propositional logic but it also does not derive from the philosophy of enunciation alone. Because of the use that it necessarily makes of the second person, the prescriptive necessarily connotes a pragmatic — which is not the case for reflexives.

It follows that the enunciative clause cannot figure in the universe of prescriptive statements, for lack of an enunciative instance capable of making its very assertion an expression or a part of an expression. The exclusion of this clause has not at all the same function as the exclusion to which propositional logic proceeds in order to sanitize its field. Here this exclusion signifies that an expression can be considered prescriptive only from the point of view of its addressee. Whether or not one executes the order contained in it is another question; in any case, it is received as obligation and seizes the one who receives it (or dis-seizes him, as we would prefer to say) as its "obligee." Such is the condition that Levinas calls, among other names, "hostage."[93]

The expression *Obey!* seems then to cover several of the properties that Levinas attributes to the ethical situation. It is an absolutely "empty" proposition, since it is not provided with an instruction to make it executable, not even the meta-instruction of universality conceded by the Kantian statement of the moral law. It is not executable, but it is that which renders executory.

So it is not understood (*entendue*) in the sense of being comprehended (*comprise*), but only in the sense of being received. However, it is never in fact received in its own right but merely hidden in the form of complete or "full" prescriptive statements, that is, instructives. So it is indeed a "simple form" as in Kant, but this form is not that of universality, which is denotative; it is that of obligation, which is pragmatic. According to Levinas, "it" is not obligatory because "it" is universal; "it" is simply obligatory. Thus, "it" is to be done *before* "it" is understood. In this way, the Lord requires of Israel not obedience but rather obligation towards Him, before he instructs the people as to what they will be obliged to do.[94]. In this way the domination of knowledge, that is, the infatuation with the enunciation, is interrupted.

In saying this, we place the accent on a pragmatic property of prescriptives that seems indeed to correspond to the metaprinciple of alterity *That / Thou/ shalt never be /I/*! which we took as our guide. For to find oneself placed in the pragmatic position of being obliged is incommensurable with the position of enunciation, even of enunciating prescriptives. This incommensurability is the same as that of freedom with the condition of being a hostage. If there is freedom, it always and necessarily plays itself out on the enunciative instance. But the ethical and political question does not begin with that of the freedom enjoyed by the "*I*"; it begins with the obligation by which the *Thou* is seized. Not with the power to *announce* . . . , but with the other power, which in the West is regarded as a powerlessness[95] — that of being *bound to* . . . .

This is so much so that, in the end, there is not even any need to have recourse to the negative form *Disobey* in order to restore faithfully the discomfort in which any addressee of an order finds himself. That would give too much credit to the power of the enunciative clause by itself. It alone can allow us, in the universe of denotative propositions, to transform any negative statement into an assertion; it is thus the safeguard of the profundity of paradoxes, if not of their validity, in this universe. But in the universe of prescriptions, it is not necessary to resort to the negative form of the statement (as in *Disobey,* or *Do not understand,* or *Do nothing but command*) in order to reveal the power that is attached to them and that preoccupies Levinas. For this power is not polarized on enunciative spontaneity but on receptivity to the order, on prescriptivity. The Megarians and the Cynics seek by means of paradoxes to shake the system of knowledge from the inside; for the Jews, the point is to escape from it. The simplest prescription, instructively empty but pragmatically affirmative, at one stroke situates the one to whom it is addressed outside the universe of knowledge.

At least two questions are left hanging: How does Levinas' commentary on this situation, a situation incommensurable with denotations, escape the trap of denotative metalanguage? How does his reader receive the commentary? Must we not revise the assimilation we made of Levinas' reader and the reader of the second Kantian *Critique?*

Notes

1. See DL 2d ed. 304–308, "Hegel et les Juifs."

2. See QLT.

3. DL 2d ed. 268, 234; AEAE 6-9, 58-75, 195–205/OBBE 5-7, 45–59, 153-161.

4. AEAE 8/OBBE 7.

5. On the "there is" and on insomnia, see DEE 93ff./EE 57ff.; TeI 114ff./TI 140ff.

6. Aristotle, *Refutation of the Sophists* 167a1, 180a32; *Rhetoric* 1402a5.

7. B. Russell, *My Philosphical Development* (New York: Simon & Schuster, 1959), chap. 7.

8. See TeI 81-160, *Interiorité et economie*/TI 109-186, "Interiority and Economy"; DEE passim/EE passim.

9. TeI 122/TI 148; emphasis added.

10. Cf. J.L. Austin, *How to Do Things with Words* (New York: Oxford University, 1968); P. Grice, *Logic and Conversation* (unpublished, 1968); H. Parret, *La Pragmatique des modalités* (Urbino: Università di Urbino, 1975).

11. G.W.F. Hegel, *Phaenomenolgie des Geistes* (Hamburg: Meiner, 1952), 19/*Phenomenology of Spirit*, trans. A.V. Miller (New York: Oxford University Press, 1979), 9-10.

12. Hegel, *Phaenomenologie*, 21/*Phenomenology*, 11.

13. Terms borrowed from J. Habermas, "*Vorbereitende Bemerkungen zu einer Theorie der kommunikativen Kompetenz*," in Habermas and Luhman, *Theorie der Gesellschaft oder Sozialtechnologie — Was leistet die Systemforschung?* (Frankfurt: Suhrkamp, 1971). See J. Poulain, *Vers une pragmatique nucléaire de la communication.*

14. On the properties of philosophical or 'speculative' statements, see V. Descombes, *L'inconscient malgré lui* (Paris: Minuit, 1977), 142-178.

15. DL (2d) 379/ "Signature," trans. M.E. Petrisko, ed. A Peperzak, *Research in Phenomenology* 8 (1978), 188-189.

16. Hence the necessity to remove the writing of a Blanchot or a Roger Laporte (who are for Levinas the expression of *proffering*) from aesthetics and to class them on the side of ethics. This can be confirmed by reference to E. Levinas, *Sur Maurice Blanchot* (Montpellier: Fata Morgana, 1975), 78 n. 3; and E. Levinas, *Noms propres* (Montpellier: Fata Morgana, 1976), 133-137.

17. Aristotle, *On Interpretation* 17a3; cf. *Nicomachean Ethics* 1138b15-1140a24.

18. See J. Rey-Debove, *Le Métalangage* (Paris: Thèse de Doctorat d'Etat, Université de Paris VIII, 1977).

19. G. Kalinowski, *Du Métalangage en logique* (Urbino: Università di Urbino, 1975), 24.

20. "We say 'the order orders this' and we do it; but also 'the order orders this: I must . . . '. We transfer it now into a proposition, now into a demonstration, now into an act" (L. Wittgenstein, *Philosophical Investigations*, § 459).

21. See Von Wright, "Deontic Logics," *American Philosophical Quarterly* 4 (1969) no. 2.

22. Wittgenstein, *Philosophical Investigations*, § 22; R. M. Hare, "Imperative Sentences," *Mind* 58 (1949), 21-39; H. Keuth, "Deontische Logik . . . ," in *Normenlogik*, ed. Lenk (München: K. G. Sar, 1974), 68.

23. The symbolization preferred by G. Kalinowski, *Du Métalangage en logique*, 18-19, and taken up by C.E. Alchourrón, "Logic of norms and logic of normative propositions," *Logique et Analyse* 12 (1969), 245.

24. Cf. Wittgenstein: "Here we mean: an order would be the image of the action which was executed in accordance with this order; but also an image of the action which must be executed in accordance with it" (*Philosophical Investigations* § 519).

25. See J. L. Gardies, *La Logique du temps* (Paris, PUF, 1975), 29.

26. DL (2d) 260; [*Genesis* 21:14-19 — Ed.]

27. Cf. HAH, "Humanisme et an-archie," 72-82.

28. See AEAE 57, 210-218/OBBE 44, 165-171; cf. the critique by Sextus Empiricus of categorical syllogisms.

29. "Where would the Jew get the strength of his refusal . . . ? the *No* requires a criterion. Rabbi Yossi will give the required sign: 'Let the waters of the cave of Pamais be changed into blood! and they were changed into blood' (Sanhedrin 98a) . . . . The men who see cannot turn their eyes away from the innocent blood which they are diluting" (DL (2d) 278).

30. "In the just war waged upon war, tremble — yea, shudder — at each instant, because of this very injustice" (AEAE 233/OBBE 185).

31. TeI 161ff./TI 187ff.; HAH 57-63; AEAE 125-130/OBBE 99-102. [The next paragraph begins the portion of Lyotard's article that appears in *Textes pour Emmanuel Levinas*, ed. F. Larvelle, 127-150 — Ed.]

32. TeI Section I (1-78), 187ff./TI Section I (31-105), 212 ff.

33. "[The Other] commands me like a Master. A command which can concern me only insofar as I am a master myself; consequently a command which commands me to command" (TeI 188/TI 213).

34. AEAE Chapitre IV (125-166)/OBBE Chapter IV (99-129).

35. E.g., TeI 193/TI 217. Unless we read Spinoza transparently, as that which shelters the word of the law from demonstrative discourse, as Levinas means to do via S. Zac's *Spinoza et l'interprétation de l'écriture* (Paris: PUF, 1965). Cf. DL (2d), "Avez-vous relu Baruch?" 148-159.

36. E.g., TeI 274-275/TI 298-299. And the following: "None of the generosity which is supposed apparently to be in the German term '*es gibt*' was shown between 1933 and 1945. This has to be said!" (DL (2d) 375).

37. Except, of course, if he chooses the alternative hypothesis, which is to begin by defining the conventions thanks to which the metalangage

will be defined in which we can say whether the statements of the object language are true or false.

38. "Exteriority is not a negation, it is a marvel" (TeI 269/TI 292).

39. One can see the importance of the conventions of notation in these matters. The methodological remarks of J. Rey-Debove, *Le Métalangage*, 15-18, are particularly illuminating for the philosopher, as is her analysis of the Metalexicon, chap. 3.

40. DL (2d) 260.

41. Concerning pardon, see, e.g., TeI 259-260/TI 282-283.

42. Immanuel Kant, *Kritik der praktischen Vernuft* in *Werke in Sechs Bände*, Bd. VI (Insel Ed., 1956), I §8 /*Critique of Practical Reason*, trans. L.W. Beck (Chicago: University of Chicago Press, 1949) Part I, Bk. I, chap. I, §8 (144).

43. TeI 192/TI 217.

44. Kant, *Kritik* 155-165/*Critique* 152-160.

45. Kant, *Kritik* 161/*Critique* 157.

46. Kant, *Kritik* 160/*Critique* 156.

47. Kant, *Kritik* 160/*Critique* 157. This is why Kant attributes to it a sort of credit, "*Diese Art von Keditiv*" (Kritik 162/*Critique* 158).

48. Kant, *Kritik* 161/*Critique* 157.

49. Kant, *Kritik* 161/*Critique* 157.

50. See QLT, second lesson, "*La tentation de la tentation*" ("The Temptation of Temptation").

51. "Imperialism of the Same," "effrontedly before the non-Ego," TeI 59/TI 87.

52. Kant, *Kritik* 141/*Critique* 142.

53. Kant, *Kritik* 156/*Critique* 153.

54. Kant, *Kritik* 170/*Critique* 164.

55. Kant, *Kritik* 157/*Critique* 154.

56. Kant, *Kritik* 157/*Critique* 154; and again: "This moral law must be the idea of a nature which is not given empirically, but which nevertheless is possible via freedom: the idea of a supra-sensory nature" (*Kritik* 158/*Critique* 154).

57. See, e.g., TeI "Moi et dependance," 116–125/TI "I and Dependence," 143–151; AEAE "La proximité," 102–124, "La Signification et la relation objective," 167–195/OBBE "Proximity," 81–97, "Signification and the Objective Relation," 131–152.

58. *"Ein merkwuerdiger Kontrast"* (Kant, *Kritik* 155)/ "A marvelous contrast" (*Critique* 153).

59. Kant, *Kritik* 162/*Critique* 158.

60. Kant, *Kritik* 158–159/*Critique* 155.

61. Kant, *Kritik* 158/*Critique* 155.

62. "In the former [nature to which will is submitted], the objects *must* be (*sein muessen*) the causes of the representations . . . while in the latter [nature submitted to a will], the will *must* be (*sein soll*) cause of the objects" (Kant, *Kritik* 158/*Critique* 155).

63. Kant, *Kritik* 165–173/*Critique* 160–166.

64. Kant, *Kritik* 170/*Critique* 164.

65. Kant, *Kritik* 171/*Critique* 164.

66. Kant, *Kritik* 140/*Critique* 142.

67. Von Wright, "Deontic Logics," 136.

68. Kant, *Kritik* 146/*Critique* 146.

69. See Alchourrón, "Logic of Norms and Logic of Normative Propositions" and Kalinowski, *Du métalangage en logique*.

70. See Section III above.

71. On the linguistic value of modals, see: Culioli, "Modality," in *Encyclopédie Alpha* (1970), 168; and his "Ébauche d'une theorie des modalities," paper given to the Societé de Psychanlyse, May 6, 1969; and his Seminar at the Ecole Normale, 1972–1973.

72. Kant, *Kritik* 160/*Critique* 156.

73. Kant, *Kritik* 141, 171/*Critique* 142, 164.

74. In section II above.

75. Particularly QLT.

76. Using "iff" to indicate the biconditional. The statements have been simplified on purpose here, at the risk of being inexact.

77. TeI 192/TI 217 (see note 43 above).

78. / *Thou* / and / *I* / being autonyms in this statement, we will write them in italics and between oblique strokes, in keeping with the conventions adopted. Cf. Rey-Debove, *Le Métalangage*, 17–18.

79. TeI 190, 191/TI 215, 216.

80. To be more exact, on the tractate *Chabat* 88a–88b. The passage in the *Chabat* that Levinas comments on is given in French in QLT 67–69.

81. QLT 91, 95, 98, 104–105, 108.

82. See Section I above.

83. Aristotle, *Refutation of the Sophists* 165b24.

84. Aristotle, *Refutation of the Sophists* 167a1.

85. "*Pè méntoi ékatéron è pros ti è pôs* . . . " (Aristotle, *Refutation of the Sophists* 180a26ff).

86. "*Oud'ho apeithôn peithétai alla ti peithétai*" (Aristotle, *Refutation of the Sophists* 180b1.

87. Jean-Michel Salanskis, *Autochronie et effets*, unpublished; "Genèses 'actuelles' et genèses 'serielles' de l'inconsistant et de l'hétérogène" (*Critique* 379 (December 1978), 1155–1173).

88. Lewis Carroll, "What the Tortoise Said to Achilles," *The Complete Works of Lewis Carroll* (New York: Modern Library, 1960), 1225–1230.

89. At least this is the position taken by Von Wright, "Deontic Logics." Cf. N. Rescher, *The Logic of Commands* (London: Routledge & Kegan Paul, 1966), chapters 2 and 3.

90. Von Wright, "Deontic Logics," 136.

91. See, among others, AEAE 141–143/OBBE 111–112.

92. See Section II above.

93. See, e.g., AEAE 150–151/OBBE 117–118.

94. See *Exodus*, chap 19.

95. Cf. the expression "X has no lesson to learn from anyone." We find the exact opposite view of this infatuation in the Levinasian theme of reading, study, of the *to learn*, and finally, in that cardinal idea that the other is by virtue of its position the master of the *I*, *no matter where the prescription comes from, because it transcends the freedom of the I.*

8. *Skepticism and Reason*

They acknowledged what they had accepted.

Treatise "Chabat"

In his article "De la signifiance du sens," Levinas says that he would like "briefly to consider *further* the contradiction of principle which *would arise* in affirming the independence of ethical intelligibility both from theoretical thought and being, within a discourse that is itself theoretical."[1] The "further" not only leads us into the second, and last, part of this very short article; more than anything else, the three pages thus introduced make allusion to the section of *Otherwise Than Being or Beyond Essence* called "Skepticism and Reason."[2] The latter constitutes one of the original parts of *Otherwise than Being*, since it is not a revision or repetition of any text that had appeared previously. But there is surely no reason to return with a sequel that merely gives a summary of the original argument.

We believe that if Levinas feels the need to recall the argument put forward in "Skepticism and Reason" it is because it provides him with an answer to the objections formulated by Derrida and others, which can be put, most briefly, as follows: The rupture between ethics and ontology cannot be stated except by returning once more to the repudiated language of ontology. One can only say in Greek that one cannot (or can no longer) speak Greek. At least, if one wants to continue to do philosophy.[3]

Levinas is certainly aware of this objection, since he asks,

Are we not *at this very moment* in the process of barring the issue that our whole essay attempts, and of encircling our position from all sides . . . [4]

. . . since the very discussion which we are pursuing at this moment counts by its *Said*, since in thematising we are synchronizing the terms, forming a system among them, using the verb to be, placing in *being* all signification that allegedly signifies beyond being?[5]

We have posed the same question of method in borrowing from J. Ladriere the distinction between discourse and word. Discourse would correspond to the totalizing movement of reason, or more generally, to the Western philosophical tradition, while the word would be the rupture of this totality, resistance to totalization, itself irreducible to exhaustive thematization through discourse.[6]

Insofar as it wishes to remain philosophical, Levinas' enterprise is open to an objection that from *Totality and Infinity* to *Otherwise than Being* remains unchanged, namely *the contradiction that arises in saying that which is supposed to escape discourse.* An "Essay on Exteriority" (subtitle of *Totality and Infinity*) can only be a thematization — and hence for Levinas an interiorization — of the nonthematizable character of this exteriority. *Otherwise than Being* can only conceive of itself, or express itself, as a "being otherwise than being," or as an "otherwise than other," which is to say, always still in the guise of being or identity — at least, according to the principles of what Levinas refers to as "formal logic." Yet it is precisely this formal logic that he invokes with the words "the contradiction of principle *which would arise,*" in speaking of *that which is "said" to be unsayable.* The use of the conditional suggests that the contradiction is only apparent and, hence, nonexistent.

We propose to consider how far the argument elaborated in "Skepticism and Reason" provides a satisfactory response to objections and whether one could not reply differently, without having to resort to some kind of philosophical extraterritoriality. Let us just examine the thrust of Levinas' argument and what is to be understood by the "classical refutation of skepticism."

It is necessary to begin by denouncing an interpretation that immediately presents itself as plausible but that renders the text incomprehensible. According to this interpretation, skepticism would consist in calling into question the very discourse of Levinas himself: if it is true, as Levinas affirms, that discourse synchronizes, even when its subject is unsayable diachrony, then a doubt is raised as to the very possibility of *enunciating* the priority of saying over said, of bad conscience over the self-consciousness that is "whole" and "good."

Since the refutation of skepticism consists in proving the possibility of progressive development, Levinas' work would prove that there is merely a contradiction of principle, showing *by its exposition alone* that this contradiction is only apparent since, in actual fact, it is contradicted *actu exercito.* Such an interpretation is untenable, although it correctly links the refutation of skepticism, with good reason, to a saying that is irreducible to a said — that is to say, to the impossibility of saying's reducing itself to that which it enunciates or expressing its own irreducibility. It is untenable, because a more diligent reading of the text shows that the case is precisely the opposite.

Skepticism consists in being able to call into question, or in rendering uncertain, truths that are expressed, not by Levinas, but by the Western philosophical tradition. To be sure, this second interpretation is only apparently possible if we accept that whenever Levinas talks about "philosophy," what is at issue is not what he himself is doing, but the work of totalization. And the refutation would simply be to point out that in thematizing the rupture of the totality, Levinas is working towards totalization, through the very act of producing a work of philosophy.

Thus it is Levinas who now adopts the position of skeptic in regard to that which appears as evidence for reason, namely the objections put forward against his own philosophical work, which he considered to be of no more value than the refutation of skepticism. We must therefore consider the feebleness of this refutation, which reveals a contradiction in Levinas' work that is *only apparent.*

Strangely enough, in "De la signifiance du sens," Levinas writes about the power of refutation:

> The intellectual vigour of this mode stems from the fact that the negation of truth isn't capable of preventing the reflexive return of thought upon this negation, a reflexive return which grasps within itself the statement of a truth that sets itself in the place of the negation of the truth.[7]

What does this mean?

Since the skeptic's position comes down to *saying* that it is false that it is true that . . . , the refutation of skepticism will accordingly come down to affirming that it is true to say that it is false that it is true that . . . , and so on. In other words, and to avoid all ambiguity or infinite regress, we must introduce quotation marks and recognize that what we have in front of us is an illustration of the distinction between language and metalanguage, useful for the "resolution" or solution of various paradoxes created when a statement refers to a totality of which it itself is a part.

We will try to justify this by starting with Levinas's own text, and we will seek to propose some suggestions for putting his thesis in relation to other philosophical concepts of language.

"Skepticism is a refusal to synchronize the implicit affirmation contained in saying and the *negation* which this affirmation states in the said."[8] But what exactly is this implicit affirmation? Is it *the act of saying* or the proposition that is asserted? The proposition-act or the proposition-content? The enunciation or the enunciated? It is not likely to be the proposition asserted, for that can only be explicit. Thus the implicit affirmation is not "I affirm that" or "It is true that," or even "I affirm that it is true that," and so on, but the fact of *declaring* oneself — that is, the act of saying.

The negation that this implicit affirmation expresses in the said is by contrast itself explicit, since it is asserted in the statement and through the enunciation of saying. But now it is a matter of the affirmation of a proposition of negative form, as when one affirms that nothing is true, or that my evidence is not certain, or simply: "That's not true."[9] The problem of skepticism as inseparable from its own refutation, rejection, or denial derives from the difference between *the act of saying* or asserting and *the negation that is said* (and in this sense asserted).

"The contradiction is visible to the reflection which refutes it, but skepticism is insensitive to the refutation, as though the affirmation and negation did not resound in the same time."[10] We are rather tempted to say that "on reflection," there is only an apparent contradiction in affirming a negation. More important is to see why the affirmation resounds in a different time from that of the negation.[11] Skepticism, as the refusal to *synchronize* the implicit affirmation and the expressed negation in the said, belongs to what Levinas calls the movement of "diachrony." Thus, following Derrida, the difference that skepticism perceives in the separation of saying from said could be written as "differance," a *diachronizing* or *deferring* difference.

"Between *my exposure* — without reserve — to the other, which is Saying, and the exposition or statement of the Said."[12] The exposure without reserve "differs" from the exposure as statement, as the act of affirmation and the content affirmed are different, even in negative form. Sometimes what is revealed is the subject's own exposure, despite himself; sometimes what is revealed is that which is exposed as a theme by the subject, or by the philosopher. But we may progress in our reading, for since the first exposure is *without reserve*, it allows the introduction of an ethical dimension. In effect, it is clear that the one who is without reserve(s)[13] runs "a great risk"; he is laid open and is no longer able to protect himself. Thus he is not only accused, but even guilty, a *self* without presumptive evidence. He is disarmed, not because he is poor but because he is without arms or display — he is exposed "point blank";[14] he is no longer able to ignore the rectitude of what "faces" him, that is, of what is a face.

Without reserve(s) means that the subject, more exposed than he could ever expose himself, can no longer retreat and take a distance — to reflect; that is, *he can no longer defer in order to make good later.* Exigency of immediacy and rectitude. *One must act before understanding.*[15]

Once again, there is only an apparent contradiction between the impossibility of deferring by postponing and the fact of diachrony — that is, between *différant* and different time. For the immediacy of the *exposure* of self to other will always be prior to the *exposition* that could be given of it. The unreflectiveness of the extra-ordinary and the extra-vagant will always be anterior, *already past*, in relation to the reflection that would reduce it to the order of representation again. Discourse thematizing the extra-ordinary — the servant recounting the extra-vagances of his master — is *always already behind* the unreflective rectitude of "acting before understanding."[16]

But that is also why the last word does belong, perhaps, to philosophy, to the servant who has not finished babbling, because the "interval" that skepticism places between saying and said is *directly* (but then paradoxically not immediately) reclaimed, described, recounted, and made good by the discourse that refutes skepticism. Thus the diachrony refractory to synchronization enters into the present *after all*; its unrepresentable past or passage (which thus passes away . . .) appears, displays itself, and *proclaims itself anterior.* Hence, "the posteriority of the anterior . . . ."

But the discourse that refutes skepticism is equally the discourse that skepticism refutes; for skepticism will argue against reason that this anteriority is not properly chronological. The past, the passage that makes or leaves its trace, is not a completed past but a *passivity* as *patience* — we let it pass, as suffering, or *as a way of enduring the intolerability of the present.* It is a passivity prior to every assumption of the claim of conscience, "an actualizing which does not commence with the possible."[17] Reason, refuting skepticism, will object *in its turn* — and thus not immediately — that skeptical discourse is still obliged to make use of expressions like "before" and "beginning." And it will also be able to interpret this nontemporal usage by arguing that the *arché* is not only the beginning but also the principle, making possible the very expression of "the posteriority of the anterior."

Therefore, "in a certain sense," philosophy *does not have* the last word, for the servant speaks and slanders in vain; *from the outset* the master will never cease to behave any less thoughtlessly and extravagantly. And in a certain — but different — sense, or paradoxically, it does have the last word, for "the logos *said* has the last word dominating all meaning, the word of the end. . . . In relating the interruption of discourse or my being ravished into discourse I connect its thread."[18] For even if the said disavows saying, it is still as something said that this disavowal can be denounced or denied.

But is there a final word? Can one say that reason does not have the last word and that "at the same time" it does have it, albeit only "in a certain sense"? No, for skepticism and its refutation *are not contemporaneous*: there is no "at the same time" here, but at best only reprises, disputes that are *directly* made good or done away with. Directly, but each in its turn.

Thus it is the *alternation*[19] that is the enigma, the "time" or the "equivocation" of philosophy,[20] its way of proceeding — or limping — in the bad company of skepticism which, as a "ghost," never ceases to trouble or haunt it, like a shadow or phantom.

And yet, "in a certain sense," there is a final word. For if there is alternation or enigma, it is *finally* because *straightaway* there is the Other (*autrui*) who can reclaim me (but whom I can reclaim also).

> And I still interrupt the ultimate discourse in which *all* the discourses are stated, *in saying it* to one who listens to it, and who is situated outside the Said that the Discourse says, *outside all it includes.*[21] *That is true of the discussion I am elaborating at this very moment.* This reference to an interlocutor permanently breaks through[22] the text that the discourse claims to weave in thematizing and enveloping all things.[23]

> . . . the fact of speaking about it and thinking upon it *at this very
> moment*, the fact of enveloping it in our dialectic, doesn't this signify
> that thought, language and dialectic are sovereign with regard to
> this Relation?
>
> But the language of thematization *which we are using at this very
> moment* has perhaps only been made possible by this Relation and
> is only ancillary.[24]

Even Derrida's hardly ancillary commentary moves in the same
direction:

> As I see it, his response [that of Levinas to the question, "How can
> one take account of the Other?"] and this *actual response*, if one may
> say, this *response in act* . . . does not respond to any problem or ques-
> tion,[25] it responds to the other — for the other — and enters upon
> writing in directing itself toward, this for-the-other . . . . [26]

which is, in fact, a "to God" (*à-Dieu*).

Thus, while the discourse that says the excess may recover the
excessive, it cannot close itself and have the last word; for in addressing itself to someone, it once again breaks open its own totality. The
allocutive dimension of language prevents its closure. *The final word
therefore is that there is no final word.* On the other hand, there always
was a word before every beginning, in an archic speech; for if all
discourse *responds* to the other, it is because the question already
existed as a calling into question.

> Isn't the very opening of dialogue a way for the I to disclose itself
> and to expose itself, a way for the *I* to put itself at the displsal of
> the *Thou*? Why would one have to speak there? Could it be because
> in thinking about it one has *something* to say? But why should one
> *have to say* it? Why wouldn't it be *enough* for one to think whatever
> one is thinking? Doesn't one say what one is thinking, precisely
> because one goes beyond what is *sufficient* and because *language* fun-
> damentally supports this movement? Beyond sufficiency, in the
> indiscretion of thou-saying and the vocative, signifying at the same
> time a claiming of responsibility and allegiance.[27]

Speaking doesn't give me any rights; I only have the right to speech
because with each vocative the subject is already in the accusative —
that is to say, subjected and called upon to answer its summons, to
justify itself. Speaking obliges.[28]

But is it true that the most global discourse remains ruptured because it still addresses itself to the Other? Shouldn't we say, on the contrary, that for Levinas the movement does not go from me to the other but from the other to me, who, in the accusative, declines my identity? *Here I am* (*me voici*) — the uncondition of the hostage — can only be said in response to an "appeal" or a "preliminary citation." Convocation precedes invocation; and thus publication can be exhibition and exposure.

The question can certainly be a demand put to the Other. But the first question, evoking the "Here I am," is produced as *my* being put into question *by* the other and not my putting *of* the other into question. In no way is it a putting into question by the ego, even if I have already eaten of the tree of knowledge. The "Here I am" is already the response to the initial question "Where are you?" that calls man to the responsibility of justification.

Our question is to know if it is because all language addresses itself to the Other that there could never be a closure of language or if it is because language responds to the Other in taking responsibility for him. The other is "outside the theme" (even, and above all, in Levinas' discourse, which is only accomplished in speaking), not because language, addressing itself to someone, can never comprehend its addressee but because the essence of language is ethical: language is responsibility and not initiative. Such seems to us to be Levinas' "thesis," which inevitably lends itself to refutation by reason.

To go further, it is important to find another outcome than that, proposed by Levinas, of a "periodic rebirth" or an "equivocation" stemming from the "unavoidable alternation" of skepticism and its refutation — an alternation that Derrida, sensitive to the traces of writing and rending, calls "*sériature*."[29] It is necessary to see if there might not be some other possible outcome that would avoid the alternation and periodic return of interruption, which is always temporary because it is directly resumed or, to take up sewing terms again, because it is directly and ceaselessly *mended*.

Levinas' discourse is open to refutation not so much because it speaks about the one to whom it is addressed as because this discourse speaks about itself. Apparently, the difficulties we have encountered stem from the fact that the rupture of discourse cannot be achieved *because it is said* and, being said, it therefore reenters the order of discourse. (On one page of *Otherwise than Being* Levinas stresses three times: "The signification known *and said*; . . . discourse absorbed in the *said* . . . the logos *said* . . . .")[30]

But is to say the unincludable unincluded, to thematize the unthematizable, or to thematize the fact that it is thematized anything else than to speak of a totality, of which the discourse that "at this very moment we are speaking" is part? This sort of problem has received a classical answer in the distinction between language and metalanguage. Let us then examine whether this distinction can be of use to break up the skepticism-reason couple.

It offers a double advantage. On the one hand, it allows us to distinguish different orders of language — or better, languages of different orders. In this sense, it seems to reply to the difficulty Levinas acknowledges when he writes:

> The truth of skepticism is put *on the same level* as the truths whose interruption and failure its discourse states, as though the negation of the possibility of the true were ranked *in the same order* restored by this negation, as though every difference were incontestably reabsorbed *into the same order.* But to contest the possibility of truth is precisely to contest this *uniqueness of order and level.*[31]

The distinction equally allows one language to take another language as its explicit object. Clearly it thus allows — if not resolving, at least formulating otherwise than in an aporetic way — Levinas' project of *saying* that saying can only be unsaid once it is said. But precisely by prohibiting saying to bear upon itself, it appears as the negation, or exclusion, of this project. The end, or consequence, of the language-metalanguage distinction is to exclude the possibility of self-reference.

To be sure, one could point out that Levinas sometimes writes "Saying" with a capital letter and sometimes as a simple verb (just as he writes "Said" and "said"). But granting that this is neither poetic license nor a typographical error, any final distinction between Saying and saying is not likely to be derived from the distinction between language and metalanguage since, for Levinas, Saying cannot in any way become the object of saying — that is, something said, commented on, or simply cited, written between quotation marks, as "Saying."[32]

Diachrony, as more than perfect and forever (nonre-) presentable, cannot itself be captured within the language-metalanguage distinction. It is not because it speaks of saying that the said is already posterior to its object, for saying itself has always denied itself presence and contemporaneity. *It is something of which there can only be a trace.*

Lyotard has allowed us to proceed further in the foregoing essay, "Levinas' Logic,"[33] by his linking of the language-metalanguage distinction to the distinction that can be made between descriptive and prescriptive language. The two distinctions are indeed linked, since his thesis consists in affirming that descriptive language cannot adequately render an account of the prescriptive: or better, that descriptive language cannot adequately *render* the prescriptive. The prescriptive can only become an object of description on pain of being "cited" — and what is more metalinguistic than citation? — and of no longer being able to function as order or prescription.

And as a matter of fact, to hold to a descriptive discourse dealing with prescriptive discourse is straightaway to expose the latter to an "infelicity" or "failure": it cannot succeed. (Here it is sufficient to think of Austin and to ask why, at the level of language, a journalist's reporting of the sentence pronounced by a judge is a different situation from the actual act of "sentencing.")

Now, what is Levinas doing when he writes that *one must act before understanding*? Surely he isn't issuing an order or prescription, even if "he has obliged"?[34] In a text whose very title makes an allusion to metalanguage, he comments on a quotation of a quotation that is itself a commentary.[35]

To be sure, the commentator can *in his turn* say that by this Levinas intends the idea that the ethical resists or precedes the ontological and that this latter is not ultimate, in the sense of being fundamental. But the situation does not become any less paradoxical. The subject — on this occasion, the reader — reads and comprehends, thus understanding that "one must act before understanding." He might interpret this as the expression of an extreme urgency refractory to a thematization of the situation. But "if he understands this then he ought not to understand it, and if he does not understand this, well, then he understands it."[36] A situation that Lyotard compares to the prescriptive "Disobey!" This statement, like that prescribing the urgency of immediate action, can be read here only in inverted commas, as the object of a discourse that is itself descriptive and of another order. Now "he has obliged." For it is really this that attests to the relation between skepticism and its refutation. A descriptive metalanguage lays claim to the possibility or to the power of saying the exigency of the other "outside the discourse."

We have seen that Levinas justifies this exorbitant possibility by the fact that all discourse admits of an allocutive dimension. One does not speak to say nothing, but *before all*, one would not have spoken if *from the origin* there had not been the Other.[37] Here, the anteriority is not that of parents; it is not the fact of having to learn a language, be it our mother tongue. One must not understand the différance between the order of narration and that of interpellation in terms of chronological anteriority, for the anteriority here is principial and, paradoxically, an-archic.

Thus we can move from a descriptive metalanguage towards a nondescriptive language of orders, prescriptions, questions, and prayers — the language of *obligation*. And thus,

> Although, for example, as an indirect question, the indicative proposition in its categorical form can support and comprehend the *question* as a modality derived from assertion, *apophansis*, belief, understood as the originary modality. The philosopher, in thematizing the problematic of the *question*, as if it were that of being, can seek out its own original meaningfulness, even if this has to take us back, as we have suggested, to the bad conscience of being.[38]

Bad conscience is a consciousness of responsibility in the face of the Other, un-easiness. Originary language is ethical, and even discourse on ethics must still take account of the other to justify itself, For,

> that rationality can call itself *justification* and not always demonstration, that intelligibility refers itself to justice, is not simply a play of metaphors.[39]

One could object that metalanguage appears only because there is writing and that wherever discourse is oral, we are in the presence of a "language of the first order." And in fact, in *Totality and Infinity* Levinas many times recalls the preeminence of the oral over the written, over discourse in which the one who speaks or writes is already absent and therefore no longer able to justify himself, discourse that addresses itself to possible readers, to become the object of commen-

tary and interpretation, or simply a dead letter. One might thus
think that if the essence of language is ethical, if the true language
is in fact the responsibility of a subject given over to the Other, this
language is that of the face to face. Written language would already
have withdrawn from this originary situation and could *thus* take the
latter for the object of its discourse, without having to justify its
directly metalinguistic and descriptive character.

But it is a fact that oral discourse can quote even more easily
than can the artifice of inverted commas or italics, since it is enough
to say "I quote" or "end of quotation." Moreover, the prescriptive is
very often written, and even a normative statement of indicative
grammatical form is directly comprehended as a prescriptive and not
as the metalinguistic description of a norm.

If, finally, Levinas has obliged, it is precisely because with him
it is never a matter of a neutral and impersonal discourse, such as
might constitute a treatise of morals. His "work" is not metalinguistic
relative to the language he presents as a texture of disinterestedness;
it is neither commentary nor exposition but, on the contrary, *self-
exposure.*[40] What is characteristic of Levinas' work is that the "here I
am at this very moment in this work" exposes itself, but not as a
theme. It is a self-exposure, bearing on the self and this very
exposure,

> insofar as it has already surrendered itself, in the propositions
> where it exposes itself to a regime whose legitimacy it is only in
> the process of establishing.[41]

> It negotiates the non-negotiable and not with one or another part-
> ner or adversary, but with negotiation itself, with the negotiating
> power that believes itself capable of negotiating everything.[42]

A metalanguage can never hold a discourse upon that which *at
that very moment it is in the process of expressing.* It explicitly excludes the
possibility of this. On the other hand, the force of what Levinas calls
"skepticism," against the discourse claiming to refute it, consists in
the possibility of skepticism being practiced, exercised — that is, *in
the possibility of its proving itself by showing* and saying, oblivious to the
paradoxes, "what is true of the discussion I am elaborating at this
very moment."[43] Derrida, commenting on the same passage of
"Skepticism and Reason," has interpreted the following *series* of
expressions, which recur, after an *interval*, every few lines and which

are all characterized by a fixed form of self-referentiality: "at this very moment," "in the discussion we are conducting," "in the present work," "this book," and finally, what appears throughout the book as the condition of the subject-hostage, *"Here I am" ("Me voici"*).[44]

To prove itself, or "better," *to justify itself by showing* — we have chosen this formula by design, because it evokes the distinction proposed by Austin between illocutionary and perlocutionary acts (*in saying, by saying*). A comparison with *speech act* theory is twice suggested by Derrida[45] and would merit being exploited.

We would like to be able to interpret the "Here I am" as a performative that takes account of the asymmetry of my relation with the Other, and this at the level of language. For, in this *act of presenting oneself* — this self-presentation, which is already a response to a convocation, or "call," and which then is already an "election" — the ego speaks directly, starting from a place where it must justify itself but which it never has to justify: *He presents himself*, not *he represents himself*, as would be the case with a consciousness totally in control of itself and its situation. The subject, exhibited, is not master of bringing about its being put in place, since this being put in place is rather that which establishes its *Self*-identity, before the tautology of ego = self can be made.[46] In the "Here I am," the *I* is directly in the accusative.

And yet it is he who *ordains*, for the "Here I am," in French at least, is originally an imperative: "See me here"; "Look at me." It is an order given by the subject. To be sure, this imperative can have the illocutionary force of a demand in the insistent mode of a petition, or a request, that does not expect anything. Then again it could have the force of a threat, but one that warns the Other that he must take notice of me — that is, that he should not count on me, but take account of me.

But doesn't this threat equally express my fear for the Other? Not my fear in the face of the Other, but the fear that I have for the death of the Other, as if I still had to answer for his death? As if *for me* his death could only be like murder?

What an odd way for the ego to impose itself on the other and unsettle him — "Here I am." This contrasts particularly with the embarassment of "being seen" in Sartre, and also with the demand for reciprocal recognition in Hegel. The asymmetry resides in what the *Here I am* uttered by the Other brings "from above," as the prohibition of murder in the defenseless expression of the face, and in what, as response to this ethical putting into question of the ego by the Other, the *I* can only utter: a *Here I am* that comes "from below," as the exigency of self-justifying and of expiating in the place of the other. For, strangely, *"Here I am"* uttered by the Other is not a threat, while at any moment my own can turn into violence.

We can perhaps rediscover the marks of this asymmetry in the theory of performatives. We know that in seeking grammatical criteria for the recognition of performatives, Austin at one time selected the first person singular pronoun with the present indicative tense ("I promise . . ." is a promise, while "you promise . . ." or "I would promise . . ." are constatives). It matters little that he had to give up this criterion along with every other grammatically relevant criterion; we will maintain that most explicit performatives function like this and that the use of the privileged pronoun *I* in the present tense suggests a fundamental *asymmetry when, by saying, it is a matter of doing before understanding.* The *I* is not substitutable; no one can pledge or promise himself in my place. (The comparison is, however, quite superficial and deceptive, for if there is any asymmetry in Levinas, it is at the expense of the subject. The latter is irreplaceable, to be sure, but precisely because it substitutes itself for others!)

We will retain as well the self-referential status proper to performatives, for it allows us to avoid paradoxes without having to fall back on the language-metalanguage distinction. This autoreferentiality exists insofar as the statement expresses the proposition that what the statement claims to produce is the statement itself,[47] without this being merely a turn of phrase "for the pleasure of speaking," for if in the performative to say is to do, then one is doing something other than simply speaking.[48] It can be realized, for example, by the use of locutions like "hereby," "presently," "here is," and, in Levinas, by a "here I am." These expressions can take various forms, and the use of the pronoun *I* in the explicit performative may be considered as filling this function of autodesignation.

Let us keep in mind that the performative does not *represent* what it accomplishes but that it *presents* it, and this *presentation* is the effectuation of what it sets up. For Levinas, ethical language is not an exposition but an exposure and a setting up of an asymmetrical structure between the subject and the other. In the performative there is an identification between the expression, what is expressed, and the act accomplished by these; the subject who promises is exactly the same as the one who says "I promise." Consequently, the use of the explicit performative is the first person singular is only paradoxical if one keeps to the level of syntax and semantics. Pragmatically, it is not, and this is what allowed Descartes to stop at the *cogito* without having to say *cogito me cogitare*.

In fact, the *cogito* is ultimate and reflexive because it is pragmatically self-referential and not because it would be a speculatively indubitable truth. Moreover, the doubt is not theoretical; it can only be something practical-practiced.[49] But this is exactly what we said about skepticism! Now what could be a better prize for skepticism than the self-assurance of the cogito: "*I think, (therefore) I am.*" — "*That's what you think!*" It is precisely in order to avoid the paradoxes involved in a language that refers to itself (but also to avoid having recourse to a metalanguage) that we have proposed a conception of skepticism that we now call pragmatic, as the "refusal to synchronize the implicit affirmation contained in saying with the *negation* that this affirmation expresses in the said." We have said that the value of skepticism consists in what it proves *actu exercito*. And isn't this to justify itself in showing itself?

Along with Plato, Descartes is one of the few philosophers Levinas calls upon without judging severely. For Levinas, however, it is not the *cogito* that saves Descartes but rather his idea of infinity. Thus we can say that Descartes appears to him equally as one of the greatest refuters of skepticism and as one of the moments of Western egological and theoretical thought. But at the same time, we discover in the *cogito* that which makes for the force of skepticism as Levinas understands it, namely, to be pragmatically its own guarantee.

The allocutive dimension — the fact that all discourse addresses itself to someone who remains outside of discourse — has been invoked to show the weakness of the refutation of skepticism. But we must point out that the refutation of skepticism is addressed equally to everyone, including the skeptic. Thus, in the end, we cannot see any reason to privilege skepticism, which always returns in relation to its untiring refutation, for the force of the one is what makes the other return; and both have the same pretension of challenging the other, suspending it, and proving itself by its own activity.

Thus it is entirely as Levinas has described it: in "inevitable alternation, thought comes and goes between two possibilities,"[50] continually resumed and mended. It is the "enigma of philosophy" and the "permanence of its crisis."[51] There is no final word . . . .

The article that we started with, and have just come back to, concludes that "for philosophy, the ontological proposition remains open to a certain reduction, disposed to unsay itself and to intend itself in other words entirely."[52] And the last chapter of *Otherwise than Being* — that is, the pages that immediately follow "Skepticism and Reason" — is entitled "In Other Words" (*Autrement dit*). As a final word, we would like to suggest the possibility of saying the ethical character of language in other words. Obviously, we shall not try to reduce Levinas' thinking to these other ways of speaking philosophically about language; in the alternation, we are proposing some possible convergencies, thus agreeing all the while to refute skepticism and to be refuted by it. We will consider only two approaches, which seem to us capable of expressing the relation between the subject and the Other in other words; both could serve as a prelude to an ethical thought of language, however, or at least, they would not exclude it. The first has, for the most part, already been attended to: it is the performative theory of truth.

According to this theory, to say that a statement is true does not consist in making a metastatement but in performing the act of being-in-accord, of agreeing, accepting, or "endorsing," that is, "taking upon oneself" the truth of the statement. Similarly, to say that a statement is false is not *to negate* the statement but *to deny* it, as unacceptable or unjustifiable — that is, *to oppose* it otherwise than at the level of a declaration of negative truth value.

Thus, when a suspect who has been found guilty is condemned, his response, spontaneous but pragmatically coherent, will not consist in saying "That's false; I'm not condemned" — it will consist in protesting his innocence. It is the same with Levinas (even if it is a matter of admitting one's culpability) insofar as affirmation and negation must be understood not as *declarations* that admit of a truth value but as *proclamations*, that is to say, statements that engage and commit the one who has engaged himself by what he says. Commitment thus acquires a moral dimension that engages the speaker more than the addressee. One could speak here about the proposition, provided that we do not understand it in its logical sense but in the sense of proposing a common world, which is to say as (self) deliverance.

A second orientation can be found (probably without the knowledge of, or to the great astonishment of, its authors) in the texts of Searle and Grice, in that they extend the notion of context to the pragmatic level, to introduce a *rule of sincerity* (which Searle does not limit to the single case of the promise), a *principle of coopera-tion*, and a *maxim of quality*. [53] To be sure, one could object that nothing in all this introduces an ethical dimension into language and that the maxims seem to be conceived in a manner privileged for the exchange of "neutral" or "objective" information. But even the declarative language of true and false propositions is not socially neutral, for one never speaks from nowhere in particular, directed to no matter who. Moreover, one can imagine that in the declarative language of information, there would be, beyond Grice's maxims, maxims that tended more explicitly to "moralize" the discursive or conversational exchange. For examples, one can imagine a *maxim of politeness*,[54] and even a *maxim of morality*,[55] where we take part in the explicit introduction of *ought* and *should* (even if the indicative form of other maxims already has a prescriptive usage). To be sure, we scarcely engage these maxims beyond the exigencies of the good functioning of communication and do not even reach that elemen-tary politeness which is, according to Levinas, the "After you, please" (*"Après vous, je vous prie"*) — a formula remarkably consonant with that of the "Here I am." Even though the conversation governed by these rules and maxims exceeds, for the most part, the neutral exchange of information, it nevertheless includes the play of ques-tions, wishes, demands, and insinuations.

To situate such conversation in an ethical context goes beyond the scope of pragmatic linguistics. But Levinas' "doing before understanding" perhaps calls us to extend the notion of the pragmatic, to situate it in a larger context than that of the conversa-tional. It is then a matter of thinking the exchange in the mode of change — alteration without alienation — otherwise than being before being otherwise (than being). It is perhaps this to which Levinas has not only called us, but also obliged us, for his language assigns and imputes.

Notes

1. E. Levinas, "De la signifiance du sens," in *Heidegger et la question de Dieu*, ed. R. Kearney and J. St. O'Leary (Paris: Grasset, 1980), 243. Reprinted in part, with the title "Façon de parler," in E. Levinas, *De Dieu qui vient à l'idée* (Paris: Vrin, 1982), 266–270. Henceforth "DSS."

2. AEAE 210–218/OBBE 165–171.

3. Cf. J. Derrida, "Violence et metaphysique: Essai sur la pensée d'Emmanuel Lévinas," in *Revue de metaphysique et de morale* 69 (1964) nos. 3 and 4; reprinted in *L'Ecriture et la différance* (Paris: Seuil, 1967), 117–228/ *Writing and Difference*, trans. A. Bass, (Chicago: University of Chicago Press, 1978), 79–153.

4. AEAE 215/OBBE 169; our italics.

5. AEAE 213/OBBE 167; "being" is italicized by Levinas.

6. Cf. J. De Greef, *Discours et parole: Étude sur la pensée du langage chez Levinas* (Louvain: ISP, 1969); and "Philosophy and its Other," *International Philosophical Quarterly*, 10 (1970) no. 2, 252–275.

7. "DSS" 244.

8. AEAE 213/OBBE 167.

9. It is "evident" that nothing would be profoundly modified if one "affirmed" propositions of an affirmative form, like *that is false*. What matters is that the content affirmed (affirmatively or not) runs counter to the truth that saying admits of, "despite itself."

10. AEAE 213/OBBE 167–168.

11. A strange question, but if our interpretation of saying as affirmation-act is correct, it may appear more familiar and closer to Levinas when formulated as follows: Why does saying resound in a different time from the said?

12. AEAE 213/OBBE 168.

13. Cf. our article "The Irreducible Alienation of the Self," in *Analecta Husserliana* VI (1977), 27–30.

14. E. Levinas, "Notes sur le sens," 111, in *Le Nouveau Commerce*, no. 49; reprinted in *De Dieu qui vient à l'idée*, 247.

15. QLT, "La Tentation de la tentation," ("The Temptation of Temptation"). passim.

16. Cf. E. Levinas, "La servante et son maître," in *Sur Maurice Blanchot* (Montpellier: Fata Morgana, 1975), 42; and "Le Nom de Dieu d'après quelques textes talmudiques," in *L'au-delà du verset: Lectures et discours talmudique* (Paris: Minuit, 1982), 157.

17. QLT, "La tentation de la tentation," 95.

18. AEAE 214–215/OBBE 169; our italics.

19. AEAE 213/OBBE 167; "DSS" 246; and Levinas, "De la lecture juive des Écritures, "L'au-dela du verset, 141–142.

20. AEAE 213/OBBE 167.

21. Or outside everything that includes him (and embarrasses?).

22. Albeit in a manner "regularly" interrupted.

23. AEAE 216-217/OBBE 170; our italics and notes.

24. Levinas, "Le Nom de Dieu," *L'au-delà du verset*, 157; our italics.

25. Here we interpret this disjunction not as the "question" that is considered in the following paragraph, but as a synonym of problem.

26. J. Derrida, "En ce moment même dans cet ouvrage nous voici," in *Textes pour Emmanuel Levinas*, ed. F. Laruelle (Paris: J. M. Place, 1980), 27-28; our italics.

27. Levinas, "Le dialogue: Conscience de soi et proximité du prochain," *De Dieu qui vient à l'idée*, 229.

28. Even if, in other respects, dialogue obliges the other to enter into the discourse that is going to unite him with me.

29. Derrida, "En ce moment," 48.

30. AEAE 214/OBBE 168-169.

31. AEAE 213-214/OBBE 168; our italics.

32. This distinction, which is deliberately in the hypothesis rather than the product of a simple liberty of expression, acquires a philosophical significance invariably suggestive of a certain German line of thought. But here we are concerned with something quite different from the refusal to hypostatize Being as being. The ontological difference differs from the diachrony or anarchy that separates — *but within language* — saying from the said. There is something irrecoverable, already committed — the damage has been done — prior to ever happening, more than perfect; yet otherwise than through an engagement with Being, even if this is nothingness.

Besides, in claiming that we are unable to mention "Saying," we are aware of leaving ourselves open to refutation and contradicting certain important texts of Levinas, such as the Talmudic commentaries, where the commentary and citation are essential.

33. Jean-François Lyotard, "Logique du Levinas," in Laruelle, *Textes pour Emmanuel Levinas*, 127-150/"Levinas' Logic," above, (117-) 129-158.

34. Derrida, "En ce moment," 21.

35. "Haven't I yielded to the temptation of putting exponents onto words as if they were numbers?" (QLT, "La tentation de la tentation," 69).

In quoting the tractate *Chabat*, Levinas comments there on a quotation commenting on a passage of the Bible.

36. Lyotard, "Logique de Levinas," 144/"Levinas' Logic," 148 above.

37. See note 27 above.

38. "DSS" 254; our italics.

39. "DSS" 246; our italics. And, "This self-criticism can be understood as a discovery of one's weakness or a discovery of one's unworthiness — either as a consciousness of failure or a consciousness of guilt. In the latter case to justify freedom is not to prove it but to render it just" (TeI 54–55/TI 83).

40. Perhaps it is because of this that the commentaries to which it nonetheless exposes itself should be paraphrases, which are doomed to fail in their purpose. And at this very moment we are commenting . . . .

41. "DSS" 245.

42. J. Derrida, "En ce moment," 32.

43. AEAE 216–217/OBBE 170.

44. J. Derrida, "En ce moment," 32, passim.

45. J. Derrida, "En ce moment," 34, 46–47.

46. F. Flahaut, *La parole intermédiare* (Paris: Seuil, 1978), 52.

47. "To get the thesis of self-reference we just need to add that the utterance also expresses the proposition that the something which by the utterance is asserted to occur, is the utterance itself" (S. Danielson, *Some Conceptions of Performativity* (Uppsala: Filosofiska Studier, 1973), 40). There is undeniably an ambiguity, for *utterance* can signify equally the content of enunciation or the act of enunciation.

48. J.L. Austin's book *How to Do Things with Words* has been translated into French under the title *Quand dire, c'est faire* (Paris: Seuil, 1970).

49. Cf. J.L. Mackie, "Self-Refutation — A Formal Analysis," in *Philosophical Quarterly* 14(1964); J.M. Boyle, Jr., "Self-referential Inconsistency, Inevitable Falsity and Metaphysical Argumentation," in *Metaphilosophy* 25 (1972); C.K. Grant, "Pragmatic Implication," in *Philosophy* 33 (1958); J. Hintikka, "*Cogito, ergo sum*: Inference or Performance?" in *Philosophical Review* 72 (1962); J.M. Finnis, "Scepticism, Self-Refutation, and the Good of Truth," in *Law, Morality and Society: Essays in Honor of H.L.A. Hart*, ed. P.M.S. Hacher and J. Raz (Oxford, Oxford University Press, 1977); F. Recanti, *La transparence et l'énonciation* (Paris: Seuil, 1979).

50. "DSS" 246.

51. "DSS" 246.

52. "DSS" 246.

53. Cf. J.R. Searle, *Speech Acts* (Cambridge: Cambridge University Press, 1969); H.P. Grice, *Logic and Conversation* in *Syntax and Semantics*, vol. 3, ed P. Cole and J.L. Morgan. (Orlando, Florida: Academic Press, 1975).

54. Cf. K. Bach and R.M. Harnish, *Linguistic Communication and Speech Acts* (Cambridge, Mass.: M.I.T., 1979).

55. "Morality (MO): The speaker (in speaking) behaves morally, that is S:

    i) does not reveal information which he ought not reveal,
    ii) does not ask for information he shouldn't have
    iii) does not direct H to do/tell something H should not do/tell
    iv) does not commit himself to do something for H that H does not want done"

(Bach and Harnish, *Linguistic Communication and Speech Acts*, 64).

9. Levinas and Derrida: The Question of the Closure of Metaphysics[1]

I

The notion of the end of philosophy underlies all of Derrida's writings. This is never more explicit than at the beginning of the essay "Violence and Metaphysics : An Essay on the Thought of Emmanuel Levinas," where he announces the questions he brings to his reading of Levinas.[2] First, did philosophy die a sudden death or is it suffering a lingering one? Notice that, although the first thought is that philosophy is dead, the possibility remains that it is still dying and perhaps has always been dying. The mortality of philosophy is not in question; that question is no longer a question. Second, how is the future of thinking related to philosophy? For Derrida, these are the only questions now capable of establishing a fruitful dialogue among thinkers. Or, in his own rather more cautious formulation:

> These should be the only questions capable of founding the community, within the world, of those who are still called philosophers; and called such in remembrance, at very least, of the fact that these questions must be examined unrelentingly, despite the diaspora of institutes and languages, despite the publications and techniques that follow on each other . . . .[3]

The fact that the first question is not philosophical, "is not philosophy's question," already makes the second more pressing. I wrote that Derrida brings these questions to his reading of Levinas, but throughout the essay Derrida is concerned to show that his questions are "questions put to *us* by Levinas."[4] Does Levinas ask such questions? What is Levinas' relation to philosophy, particularly to the thinkers who have announced the end of philosophy? Derrida names four of them at the beginning of "Violence and Metaphysics" — Hegel and Marx, Nietzsche and Heidegger — and the first and last mentioned play an important part in Derrida's study of Levinas, not least because Levinas' debt to them is enormous. First, how do Hegel and Heidegger think the end of philosophy?

"The end of philosophy" does not mean the same for Hegel and Heidegger, but it has the same source for both of them — the experience of the historical nature of philosophy. The insight into philosophy's historical nature is the end of philosophy's naiveté about itself, particularly that naiveté expressed in the presumption of a Descartes or a Husserl that we have within our own resources a procedure for making a fresh start. The connotation of being freed from the tradition, which often now accompanies the phrase "end of philosophy," is quite foreign to the thinking that gave rise to it. Heidegger's own phrases, "the destruction of the history of ontology," "overcoming metaphysics," and "leaving metaphysics to itself," may perhaps be partly responsible for the idea that we can turn our backs on the history of philosophy and ignore it. But closer attention to what he wrote shows a continued insistence that "whatever and however we may try to think, we think within the sphere of the tradition."[5]

Nevertheless, to experience the history of thought means much more than simply to recognize the dominating power of the philosophical tradition. For both Hegel and Heidegger, it means that the true subject matter of philosophy, which has hitherto remained hidden, is now accessible in the history of philosophy. For Hegel this subject matter is the absolute; for Heidegger it is being. The remembrance (*Erinnerung*) of the previously hidden subject matter of philosophy brings about a transformation in the manner of thinking, particularly in respect of the thinker's relation to language and his conception of truth, so that following the old procedures (for example, analysis or argument) no longer seems to the point. And it is because the concealed subject matter of previous thinking has now been brought to remembrance that this transformation of thinking may now be recognized as the end of philosophy. For Hegel, now that thinking has attained its element — "pure self-recognition in absolute otherness" — it becomes possible to apprehend the whole, hence the true, as system. It is only in the completion (*Vollendung*) of truth in the system that the absolute is attained. The end of philosophy means its completion as a fulfilment, a perfection. For Heidegger, by contrast, it is when the thinker finds himself in anxiety, at a loss for words, that he comes to recognize for the first time that his vocation as a thinker within the philosophical tradition was to name being. The lack of a word of being is a disruption of philosophy. And yet, because that disruption belonged to the destiny of philosophy, the disruption — though not a fulfillment in the sense of a perfection — is nevertheless the completion of a destiny, and end.[6]

It has sometimes been suggested that Derrida attempted to divorce himself from Heidegger when, in 1967, preferring the term *closure* (*clôture*) to that of *end*, he insisted that there could be no sudden passage beyond philosophy. And yet Heidegger equally did not maintain that there was such a "royal road" accessible to us. There is even a word in Heidegger's essay "Overcoming Metaphysics," *Verendung*, that seems to correspond to Derrida's *clôture*.[7] More important still, there seems to be agreement between Heidegger and Derrida about the transformation undergone by the language of metaphysics when read from the closure. Metaphysics, where presencing (*Anwesen*) is privileged, comes to resound with the echo of absencing. Or, more strictly, the opposition of presence and absence upheld by philosophy gives way to a play of presence and absence. The reading of texts, as it is practiced by both these thinkers, shows this play at work within metaphysics, particularly in the ambiguity of certain crucial words on which those readings come to hang. Heidegger refers it to the concealment at the heart of truth, the *lethe* in *aletheia*, that reverberates through language at the end of philosophy as a ringing of silence (*Gelaeut der Stille*).[8] Derrida gives it a variety of names, including that of *differance*. A "saying not-saying"[9] — a phrase Heidegger uses to characterize "another possibility of saying," a possibility other than that offered by metaphysics — aptly describes Derrida's own way with language, where books are not (will not have been) books, prefaces are not prefaces, and philosophy is not philosophy.

When at the beginning of "Violence and Metaphysics" Derrida raises his question about the death of philosophy and names Hegel and Marx, Nietzsche and Heidegger, he is placing his thinking within a context. Four years later, in the lecture "Differance," the names have come to be those of Nietzsche, Saussure, Freud, Heidegger, and Levinas himself. The decisive figure for Derrida's thinking of the end of philosophy is Heidegger, because it is Heidegger's history of being that provides the essentialy model governing Derrida's relation to previous thinking exhibited in his deconstructive readings. Derrida never sought to conceal that the history of the determination of being as presence was what inspired his understanding of the history of the text or history of writing and that — after certain lessons had been learned from reading Freud — it was still Heidegger's notion of the forgottenness of being that underlay "the analysis of a historical repression and suppression of writing since Plato."[10] The debasement of writing is effected through the privilege accorded to presence: writing lacks the support of the presence of a speaker. It should be understood that Derrida does not simply repeat the Heideggerian moves, either in general or, still less, as part of a regional investigation of language. Derrida may, in the opening pages of the essay "Structure, Sign, and Play," have given a list of the determinations of being as presence that essentially repeats those given by Heidegger — *eidos, arché, telos, energeia, ouisa* (essence, existence, substance, subject) *aletheia*, transcendentality, consciousness, God, man, and so forth[11] — but he did not mean to suggest thereby that the words in which his readings culminate are to be understood as additions to Heidegger's list. In his readings Derrida forms his own chain of words, which includes, for example, *pharmakon*, supplement, *hymen*, arche-writing, and so on, arising from his readings of Plato, Rousseau, Mallarmé, and Husserl respectively. Thus Derrida's chain consists of more marginal words than those announced by Heidegger, but by virtue of their marginality, they have a claim to being regarded as less implicated in the tradition. The Derridian chain does not function simply as an addition to Heidegger's words of being; they are *supplementary* in Derrida's sense and thereby maintain the parasitic relation of Derrida to Heidegger.[12]

If we turn now to Levinas, we find a tendency — not wholly absent from "Violence and Metaphysics" — to associate him with the early Heidegger, who announced "the destruction of the history of ontology," rather than the later Heidegger, the Heidegger of the history of being, whom we have been considering in relation to Derrida. Certainly, Levinas' description in *Totality and Infinity* of how he sought to accomplish the break with ontology carries echoes of Heidegger's elucidation in *Being and Time* of the destruction as an attempt to break through the barriers of inherited self-evidence, in order to win access to certain original experiences.[13] Levinas wrote that "what counts is the idea of the overflowing of objectifying thought by a forgotten experience from which it lives."[14] Even though, at this point, Levinas is careful to acknowledge only his debt to Husserl, we cannot ignore the Heideggerian heritage that is also operative. Levinas also characterized his efforts as an attempt to make a break with Parmenides. Having announced the task in 1947,[15] he felt able to declare, by 1961, that the break had been made.[16] And again it is clear that language learned from the early Heidegger is being used, in an effort to distance himself from a tradition now understood to include Heidegger. In this context, Parmenides represents for Levinas the philosophy of the unity of being that suppresses the beyond; both Husserl and Heidegger are to be counted among its representatives. Whereas for Heidegger the forgotten experience is that of being, for Levinas — and he invests Plato's formula with an anti-Heideggerian ring — it is that of "the good beyond being," which he also calls "metaphysical exteriority," "transcendence," and "infinity." The good surpasses 'being,' 'objectifying thought,' 'objective experience,' 'totality,' and 'history.'

But although, as we shall see, Derrida draws attention to such debts entered into in the very attempt to pass "beyond Parmenides," "beyond history," he ignores the passage in *Totality and Infinity* where Levinas specifically confronts those thinkers who announce the end of philosophy. Levinas asks whether they do not continue to suppress the good, and he names Hegel and Heidegger, charging them with exalting "an obedience that no face commands."[17] Presumably he has in mind obedience to the concept in Hegel and to the truth of being in Heidegger. Perhaps Derrida ignores the passage because Levinas, in suggesting that the thought of the end of philosophy remains within the neutralization of the infinite and the maintenance of the totality, does not confront the issue of the end of philosophy directly. Indeed, it is not until 1970 and the essay "Beyond Essence," later incorporated into *Otherwise than Being* as its first chapter, that Levinas first does so. He asked, "Should we not think with . . . caution of the possibility of a conclusion or a closure(*fermeture*) of the philosophical discourse? Is not its interruption its only possible end?"[18] Somewhat pointedly, Levinas drew a parallel between this consideration and two others: Hegel's misgivings about philosophical prefaces and Heidegger's reservations about introductions that attempt to lead man to being — as if any movement between them did not always begin with being. Levinas thereby suggested that both Hegel and

Heidegger should have extended to the notion of ends the caution that they exhibited with respect to beginnings. Not that Levinas was thereby simply endorsing that caution: he was rather acknowledging a lesson he claimed to have learned from Husserl, that the inevitability of a certain degree of naiveté, however one might seek to eradicate it, must be left to be exposed by *another* philosopher with his or her own imprudences. The history of philosophy is, one might say, the empirical exhibition of such a *continuing* dialogue, which proceeds by the constant *discontinuity* of interruption.

Is Levinas thereby proposing *interruption* as an alternative model to the totalizing conception of an *end*? On this occasion I shall leave aside the question of the sense in which the Hegelian *end* is totalizing: even though Hegel's conception of *end* frequently conforms to a teleological model, what might be called a speculative reading of Hegel could be developed, not so much in opposition to, but — to acknowledge Derrida's practice — *side by side* with a dialectical reading.[19] As for Heidegger, the idea of interruption plays its part: first, insofar as the fundamental experience of Heidegger's thinking is that of the disruption of the thinker's vocation to name being, and second, to the extent that the naming of being within metaphysics always takes place as an excess inexplicable in terms of what has gone before. The notions of rupture and excess are, if anything, more frequent in Derrida than in Heidegger. To be sure, Derrida does not believe in decisive ruptures: "Every transgressive gesture reencloses [*renferme*] us . . . within the closure."[20] But Derrida's appeal here to the *closure* evokes his attempt to avoid constituting metaphysics as a totality, which would thereby reduce the issue to the simple opposition of inside and outside. At this point the suspicion arises that Levinas' association of the philosophical tradition with the notion of totality makes him more susceptible to his own objection concerning the *fermeture* of philosophy than are either Heidegger or Derrida. Furthermore, both Heidegger and Derrida have, more than Levinas, practiced the continuing dialogue with previous thinking by which Levinas seeks to evade the force of the objection. What then is Levinas' relation to the previous history of thinking?

II

Derrida's strategy in "Violence and Metaphysics" is *in the first instance* to show that Levinas remains under the sway of metaphysics whenever he seeks to transcend it. The fulfillment of this strategy is, Derrida likes to emphasize, made easy by Levinas' acknowledgement in *Totality and Infinity* that language conditions the functioning of rational thought.[21] On these terms, wherever there is metaphysical language there are metaphysical thoughts. Thus, the first step in Derrida's reading of Levinas involves finding instances of traditional language in his writings. Nothing could be easier — such is the sway of the *logos*. When Derrida attempts to clarify the conditions under which it makes sense to talk of transcending metaphysics,[22] his statement is typically cautious:

> The attempt to achieve an opening toward the beyond of philosophical discourse, which can never be shaken off completely, cannot possibly succeed *within language* . . . except by *formally* and *thematically* posing *the problem of the relations between belonging and the opening*, the *problem of the closure*.[23]

Only a thinker who makes the issue of the closure fully explicit writes metaphysical language so that it is transformed into the language of *différance*.

Nevertheless, this careful statement in which Derrida insists on the formal posing of the problem of the closure is itself open to misunderstanding and is, one might eventually want to say, ambiguous. Is Derrida claiming that Levinas fails to raise the problem of the closure "*formally* and *thematically*," or is he merely reflecting on a certain necessity? If Levinas is to be seen as having failed to pose this question, how would we then understand Derrida's claim that the questions of "Violence and Metaphysics" — and particularly the question of language — are engaged by every element of Levinas' thought?[24] Everything depends here on whether one understands Derrida's essay as a *critique* of Levinas, as it is often described, despite Derrida's own denials. Alternatively, one can attempt to read it as a *deconstruction*. Deconstruction — if one may attempt to restore precison to a word that has become overextended through overuse — proceeds by a double reading, which arises through the closure. It is often signalled, as in *Of Grammatology*, by a distinction between the author (to whom explicit declarations are attributed) and the text (which is always hidden).[25] This distinction is already operative as a strategic device in "Violence and Metaphysics," when Levinas is charged with "betraying his own intentions," which is to say that the

text betrays his intentions.[26] One might understand Derrida to be
saying that Levinas' text itself raises the question of the closure that
Levinas, the author, fails to pose — a sense supported by the emphasis on the question being raised "formally and thematically." Levinas'
pronounced intention to break with Parmenides would then be
understood as a way of evading the issue, precisely because it does
not address the difficulties arising from the fact that the traditional
language of ontology is the only one at our disposal. But one could
then no longer understand Derrida to be *criticizing* Levinas. Rather,
Derrida would have isolated one tendency in Levinas' writings
which, as Derrida knows better than anyone, is compensated for
elsewhere in them.

The context of Derrida's comment (that Levinas' text is
betrayed by the intentions announced in that text) is important: "By
making the relation to the infinitely other the origin of language,
meaning, and difference, without relation to the same, Levinas is
resigned to betraying his own intentions in his philosophical
discourse."[27] Derrida seems to charge Levinas with "anhistoricity"
because of his insistence on separating the original possibility of
speech as nonviolence and gift from the violence necessary in
historical actuality.[28] But it is far from clear that, with this reading
of Levinas, Derrida would be doing justice to the account of the
origin of language found in *Totality and Infinity*.

In the section of *Totality and Infinity* called "Ethics and the Face,"
Levinas tells us the first word. The first word is the phrase *you shall
not commit murder*.[29] Or, it would be a phrase if it were not without
words altogether; it is said by the face, the eyes.[30] What comes to
mind here is that the saying *you shall not commit murder* does not seem
like a primordial speech at all. It sounds much more like a *response* to
a threat. But in that case the threat would be the primordial expression. When we turn back to Levinas' account, however, we find that
he neither does nor does not presuppose a prior threat. The prohibition against murder arises from the other, because in meeting him
or her we discover ourselves; we discover our arbitrary, violent, murderous freedom in shame before the gaze of the other. Shame is here
understood as having the structure of an intentionality in reverse
direction, so that I am not the subject of my shame. The subject of
shame, and thus its source and support, is exterior to me.[31] Shame
is governed by the exteriority of an other who exceeds me. *You shall
not commit murder*, says that in the face of the other's transcendence,

his height, his absolute difference; I am disarmed, my powers are paralyzed. "You shall not commit murder," announces the impossibility of murdering the other. This does not mean that I cannot kill him, only that I shall never be able to annihilate him. The memory of the language of his eyes will remain to haunt me. *You shall not commit murder* is the primordial expression, because it is my introduction to the alterity of the other, my introduction to a realm that exceeds my control. It is clearly inappropriate to understand this account in terms of a nonviolence from which every violence has been excluded.

And yet every reader of *Totality and Infinity* will recognize that, taken in isolation, this description of the origin of language gives a misleading impression of Levinas' position as it appears in the book taken as a whole. It is misleading because it leaves out of account the welcome given to the other in his destitution and his hunger. Here Derrida's reference to a discussion of the origin of language as nonviolence and gift seems more fitting. The other appeals to me in such a way as to arouse my goodness.[32] "To recognize the Other is to give."[33] Elsewhere Levinas tells us the verbal equivalent of this welcome: *me voici* (Here I am).[34] Furthermore, he suggests that this admission of a debt "precedes all other forms of saying."[35] In this way we find that Levinas has provided us with two versions of the primordial expression and that the second, like the first, appears to be a response to a call. But again Levinas insists that it is not a response; it is "an obedience that precedes the hearing of any order."[36]

The question of how these two accounts are related now arises. Although Levinas makes no attempt at the level of *description* to reconcile the two versions of the primordial expression, he frequently *declares* their integration, as for example when he says that "to welcome the Other is to put in question my freedom."[37] But the term *integration* would not be adequate to any discussion of the relation between the two accounts, if it suggested that the aim of such declarations was to reconstitute them as a single unitary account. At the level of description we would suppose a separation prior to the encounter with the other but, although the notion of separation belongs also to the order of declaration, the declaration does not follow the description. The face to face encounter cannot be referred to a meeting of two separate individuals; it is a "relation without relation," a relation that cannot be reduced to the conjunction of the related terms. The sense of separation is that the face to face cannot be contained in the gaze of a third party looking on from outside;

that is to say, it is beyond the reach of objectifying thought, because the partners of the face to face are held apart by a distance that cannot be bridged. The notion of separation is in this way referred to the face to face itself and is not to be understood in terms of a temporal sequence that inscribes a system of priorities. That both of the primordial expressions Levinas offers have the appearance of responses is in keeping with this notion of the face to face and shows that the declarations are not simply to correct the descriptions but that the descriptions bear with them their own reflection on the necessities governing description as such. There is no first word in the sense of an arche-point. We speak first only in response, not because we are responding to a more original saying, but because we speak out of responsibility. This responsibility is, he will suggest in a later work, "without a prior commitment, without a present, without an origin, anarchic."[38] Indeed, already in *Totality and Infinity* the term *anarchy* was introduced to call into question the classical conception of origin as "beginning."[39]

So, although the order of declaration serves to reconcile the division between the two descriptions, the order of description plays a crucial part in the discussion of language, by calling into question the traditional language in which the declaration is couched: the language of origins. Levinas has attempted a description in which ethical responsibility conditions the theoretical and is in some sense prior to it, where 'priority' is to be understood neither in terms of a system of ontological dependencies nor a temporal ordering but rather of "the anarchy of what has never been present."[40] It is precisely to convey this sense of priority that the term *trace* was later introduced.[41]

This double origin of language, inscribed in the text of *Totality and Infinity*, not only addresses the question Derrida posed in "Violence and Metaphysics" but raises a further question about the affinity between Levinas and Derrida. In *Of Grammatology* Derrida, employing the distinction between declaration and description, developed a double reading of Rousseau's *Essay on the Origin of Languages*, similar to that just given of Levinas. Rousseau gives two accounts of the origin of language: one for southern languages, another for northern languages. The universal conditions governing the two origins must include reference both to dispersion, constituting a condition of separation, and to pity as an innate, but inactive, principle in the human heart. A further condition, that of need, draws people together and counteracts separation. In the north, people need help from others against the elements, and so they gather around the fire; in the south the need is for water, and they gather around the watering hole. But Rousseau does not maintain the place of need in his account. In the south, it is not need but passion and the striking quality of the other as handsome, as strong, or as fine dancer that draws people together. And whereas in the north, the first words are *aidez-moi* (help me), in the south they are *aimez-moi* (love me). The language of the south, the language of neighbors as a song of desire, is given a certain priority over the language of strangers, the cry of fear and need heard in the north, which is not regarded as language in the full sense. This is not the occasion for exploring either the details of Rousseau's text or the extraordinary rigor and subtlety of Derrida's reading of them. Derrida finds that Rousseau would like the absolute origin to be the language of the south, which represents, in Derrida's reading, the value of presencing and thus of speech as opposed to writing. This forms the basis of Derrida's deconstruction, which shows how no such priority of the south over the north — however much sought by Rousseau, the author, in his declarations — can be maintained by the text and the descriptions in it. Rousseau cannot maintain the south as absolute origin because he cannot efface need from the description of the language of the south. In Derrida's reading, we are ultimately led to question the notion of origin as absolute presence, and in this way the origin is found to rely on that which is supplementary to it. The supplement thus comes to the fore in response to an originary lack, thereby showing that the text may be read as structured, not by an opposition between presence and absence, but by a play between them.

Levinas' account of language, which may at first sight look like a metaphysical search for an *arché* of the kind exposed by Derrida in *Of Grammatology*, is thus found to reflect the very moves Derrida used to expose that search. Many questions are raised by this parallel. What, for example, is the relation between the so-called "logic of supplementarity" exposed by Derrida in his deconstruction of Rousseau and the "logic" of Levinas, a logic he insists does not conform to traditional logic? Derrida, in "Violence and Metaphysics," is particularly drawn to Levinas' refusal to conform to "formal logic," while at the same time emphasizing the difficulties for understanding that follow from this. So, Derrida insists that one can only break with traditional logic while at the same time borrowing one's resources from it. That is what lies behind Derrida's insistence on the term *closure* and his refusal simply to declare the rupture, or interruption, of philosophy. That is clearly only one side in Derrida's approach to a text, but how well did Derrida succeed in doing justice to both sides in his reading of Levinas? When Derrida dwells on Levinas' 'anhistoricity', to what extent is it recognized that the evidence giving rise to such a judgment belongs to an examination of a certain conception of history, one that we shall find Derrida himself also denies? And when Derrida finds in Levinas a separation of the original possibility of speech as gift from the violence of historical actuality, is this reading entirely innocent? Is this blindness possibly governed by the same kind of necessity that led Rousseau to seek in his own work an absolute origin in the south?

Finally, a series of questions about Derrida's own intentions in "Violence and Metaphysics." Does he mean to offer a critique or a deconstruction? To what extent had Derrida, in 1964, already recognized the moves that were later to constitute a deconstructive strategy? Derrida was always clear about the ways in which Levinas' avowed aim to break with the philosophical tradition was inhibited by the fact that the only language available to him was that of the tradition. But was he always as aware of the way in which Levinas transgresses the tradition? This theme is most pronounced in Derrida's discussion of the trace as "impossible-unthinkable-unstatable, not only for philosophy in general but even for a thought of being which would seek to take a step outside philosophy."[42] But the texts in which Levinas discussed the trace only became available to Derrida at a late stage in the writing of his essay, as he acknowledges in a footnote.[43] Was the ambivalence of deconstruction perhaps even forced on Derrida by his attempt to come to terms with these developments in Levinas' thinking? Close analysis of the texts does not support this latter hypothesis. Moreover, these questions are not important, except insofar as they suggest how Derrida's essay might itself be subject to a double reading — once as a critique of Levinas and again as a deconstructive (and thus double) reading of Levinas. In the same way, the question of whether or not Levinas might have *intended* his readers to find a double origin of language in his text would be one-sided. After Derrida, we can no longer ask with innocence how the descriptions that led us to posit a double origin might have appeared to us independently of Derrida, nor does it make sense to try.

III

In *Of Grammatology*, Derrida juxtaposes what Rousseau declares and wishes to say (*vouloir dire*) with another possible interpretation based on what Rousseau describes in the text. In some of Derrida's other studies, a conventional interpretation or a translation sometimes does duty in place of the author's intentions. Derrida tends to operate with two texts: on the one hand, someone's text (the author's, the translator's, an interpreter's text) and on the other hand, the text in some stricter sense. The work thereby becomes ambivalent. Whereas in Derrida's reading of both Levinas and Rousseau the ambivalence is between author and text, in his essay on Plato's *Phaedrus*, the more fundamental ambivalence of the *pharmakon* as both remedy and poison arises, alongside of that between translation and text.[44] The ambivalence is thereby found, not between the metaphysical and the nonmetaphysical, but rather in such a way that metaphysics is transgressed from within. Platonism, and indeed metaphysics itself, can be characterized as the halting of this ambivalence. That is to say, other metaphysical texts and indeed neoplatonic texts like the *Enneads* indicate the closure of metaphysics by transgressing metaphysical thought. A conception of the history of metaphysics that would be "infinite and infinitely surprising" is thus proposed.[45] In this way Derrida clarifies the conditions governing the notion, common also to Heidegger, of an excess within history.

This conception is particularly helpful for clarifying Derrida's concern with the problem of history in Levinas. Derrida's questions concerning Levinas' account of the origin of language were only part of a broader strategy directed to Levinas' notion of a "beyond history": "One wonders whether history does not begin with this relationship to the other which Levinas places beyond history. The framework of this question should govern the entire reading of *Totality and Infinity*."[46] Derrida reads Levinas' "transcendence" as standing outside history and concludes that "the anhistoricity of meaning at its origin is what profoundly separates Levinas from Heidegger."[47] Derrida's point here arises out of the apparent opposition of infinity and history in Levinas. Certainly the notion of a "beyond history" dominates the Preface to *Totality and Infinity*. And yet it should be emphasized that Levinas has in mind here a teleological conception of history, which he refers to Hegel, whereby history is constituted as a totality ordered by a judgment. Levinas' "beyond history" is clarified in two sentences that, better than Derrida's question, might serve as a guide to reading *Totality and Infinity*: "This 'beyond' the totality and objective experience is, however, not to be described in a purely negative fashion. It is reflected *within* the totality and history, *within* experience."[48] These sentences show that the terms of the title *Totality and Infinity* are not related to each other antithetically and that totality in Levinas is not simply the finite totality, for it bears the infinite within it. The opposition of 'inside' and 'outside,' 'within' and 'beyond,' is displaced by Levinas, although we shall have to investigate on some other occasion whether the manner of doing so does not introduce a speculative idea of infinity that rejoins Hegel, albeit another Hegel from that which Levinas seeks to separate himself. What is clear now, however, is that with these sentences Levinas not only departs from the conventional conception of history but takes a step toward the conception that we also find in Heidegger and Derrida themselves. Indeed, having read *Of Grammatology*, one is no longer inclined to suppose that Derrida is simply insisting that Levinas should have made the relation to the other the beginning of history. It becomes more likely that he sought to find in Levinas an oscillation between two interpretations of history as, in his reading of Rousseau, he first found "the perverse substitution" of pity in love described both as the origin of history and as an historical depravity *within* history and then employed the concept of supplementarity so as to think the two interpretations at the same time.[49] We cannot then accuse Derrida of overlooking Levinas' answer to his question about the beginning of history without at the same time recognizing that it is Derrida who has helped us to expose the "logic" of that answer, so that it does not simply appear to repeat the conventional procedures of philosophy — which would, as Derrida himself constantly reminds us, be self-defeating for an attempt to pass beyond philosophy.

Levinas' strategy is to question totality and history so as to show that they themselves refer to the beyond, although *not* as the transcendental conditions of their possibility. Nor when Levinas directs us — to recall the phrase quoted earlier — to "the overflowing of objectifying thought by a forgotten experience from which it lives," does he understand the "forgotten experience" as an historical one. What Levinas has in mind here is what he and Heidegger — and following them, also Derrida — called a "trace" (having explicated it elsewhere I shall not dwell on it here). The procedure whereby

Levinas passes from experiences within the totality back to the rupture that conditions the totality exhibits how and in what sense Levinas supposes that one can pass beyond philosophy. As he already puts it in *Totality and Infinity*, "Without substituting eschatology for philosophy, without philosophically 'demonstrating' eschatological 'truths', we can proceed from the experience of totality back to a situation where totality breaks up, a situation that conditions the totality itself,"[50] The passage beyond philosophy is possible because the "beyond philosophy" already permeates philosophy and is reflected within it. But if this is Levinas' position, it implies — indeed relies upon — an alternative account of history that inscribes this possibility. In this way a Levinasian reading of the history of philosophy imposes itself. It would not be a continuous history any more than Heidegger's history of being and Derrida's history of writing are, although like them it would introduce a dialogue with previous thinking that was constantly to be renewed. I call it a "history of the face"; it must be understood, however, that this phrase does not mean that the face has a history but that the face ruptures history from within just as, in the history of being, being ruptures the history of philosophy as an excess that at the same time conditions that history. The phrase *history of the face* is disruptive.

In a remarkable passage towards the end of *Otherwise than Being*, we find Levinas insisting upon the importance of just such a conception of history for his thinking:

> Philosophy has at its highest, exceptional hours stated the beyond of being and the *one* distinct from being . . . . And we would not here have ventured to recall the *beyond essence* if this history of the West did not bear, in its margins, the trace of events carrying another signification, and if the victims of the triumphs which entitle the eras of history could be separate from its meaning.[51]

Levinas' readers will recognize that Plato's 'beyond being' and Descarte's 'infinite' in the third *Meditation* would belong to such a history for him. One could readily add the names of Plotinus, who is referred to when the notion of the trace is introduced, and Nicholas of Cusa, who is quoted by Derrida in "Violence and Metaphysics" and who gives the notion of face an important place in his thinking. Even Rousseau, although not referred to by Levinas in any of his major philosophical works, can be seen in the *Discourse on the Origin and Foundations of Inequality among Men* to have given an account of the encounter with the other, in his discussion of the festival, that would warrant him a place in such a history of the face.

Derrida himself seems to recognize the possibility of such a history when he asks, "Is not the beyond-history of eschatology the other name of the transition to a more profound history, to history itself?" He emphasizes, in 1967, that it is not a history in any conventional sense when he adds, "but to a history which, unable any longer to be *itself* in any original or final *presence*, would have to change its name?"[52] At the same time, however, he makes another addition, which seems to go against the sense of the original question: "The economy of which we are speaking does not any longer accommodate the concept of history such as it has always functioned, and which it is difficult, if not impossible, to lift from its teleological or eschatological horizon."[53] This second addition seems to equate the teleological and the eschatological conceptions of history, which Derrida did not do in 1964, perhaps because he was then more impressed with the eschatological dimension of Heidegger's thinking in "The Anaximander Fragment." The important point, anyway, is that Derrida, in acknowledging the possibility of "a more profound history," was already making room for a history of the face — albeit without explicitly recognizing its advent in *Totality and Infinity* in Levinas' references to Plato and Descartes.

One might well seek to diminish the differences among Heidegger, Derrida, and Levinas by insisting that the history of being, like the history of writing, exhibits the same play of the beyond and the within that we have now found in Levinas. But there are important differences among the three, and to regard the history of the face merely as a revision of the history of being would be to fail to do justice to ethics as Levinas thinks it. We have already seen that being is for Heidegger the hidden subject matter of philosophy, whereas Derrida is concerned with a more marginal chain. And while Levinas may declare that the 'beyond essence' arises on the margins of the history of the West, he would not wish thereby to diminish its importance and, in a certain sense, its centrality. There is, for example, nothing marginal about Plato's 'idea of the good' or Descartes's 'infinite' in the texts in which they appear. Their marginality arises only for philosophy, which has been unable to sustain such "thoughts." Furthermore, Levinas gives to them an ethical dimension *other* than that with which they might originally have been endowed.

When Levinas adopts the word *infinite* from Descartes, he takes it up as an excess, in the manner of Heidegger's words of being. Levinas finds there a thought that we, as finite beings, cannot think. It is "an idea put in us," an idea thought in us, so that we must say of it that the infinite "is not a thought."[54] The infinite is as unthinkable as the trace. But even though Levinas thereby adopts this word from the history of thinking in a manner that parallels the appropriation practiced by Heidegger and Derrida, the word is transformed in a way different from the transformation of language in these thinkers. Levinas makes this point forcefully when adopting Heidegger's phrase *Geläut der Stille* to describe this transformation. In the 1975 essay "God and Philosophy" Levinas says of the face, "There the resonance of silence — *Geläut der Stille* — certainly resounds." It is not to some play of presence and absence in a face that Levinas refers us, but to a face.

> naked without resources, with the nakedness of someone forsaken, which shows in the cracks in the mask of the personage, or in his wrinkled skin, in his being "without resources," which has to be heard like cries already addressed to God, although without being voiced or thematised.[55]

If the notion of a history of the face is to be sustained, we must ask whether the human face ever reverberates in our dealings with the history of philosophy. Does it not happen whenever — in a "cry of ethical revolt, a testimony of responsibility"[56] — we find ourselves calling into question what we are doing as philosophers? Would we be wrong to suppose that in recent times this questioning has become more widespread? "The moment when, in the spiritual history of the West, philosophy becomes suspect is not just any moment."[57] And Levinas sees in "the insignificant signs of a language in dissemination" — the reference to Derrida is unmistakable — a clear revelation of the poverty of philosophy, and the human sciences generally, with their "impossible indifference with regard to the human."[58]

In "Violence and Metaphysics," Derrida recalled the statement of the ancient Greeks that "if one has to philosophize, one has to philosophize; if one does not have to philosophize, one still has to philosophize." He even found a passage in which Levinas seemed to acknowledge this necessity as it operates in our own times: "One could not . . . arrest philosophical discourse without philosophizing."[59] In "God and Philosophy," Levinas makes his reply: "Not to philosophize would not be 'to philosophize still.'" and

> to recognize with philosophy — or to recognize philosophically — that the Real is rational and that the Rational is alone real, and not to be able to smother or cover the cry of those who, the morrow after this recognition, mean to transform the world, is already to move in a domain of meaning which inclusion cannot comprehend and among reasons that "reason" does not know, and which have not begun in philosophy.[60]

Youth's rebellion against the established order is an example of a reason that has not had its beginning in philosophy, but so too is Plato's testimony in favor of the beyond, and even the thought of the end of philosophy itself.[61]

The notion of a rupture with philosophy has a different, and perhaps an even stronger, force in Levinas than in Heidegger or Derrida, for it represents the overcoming of the priority of ontology to which they, too, remain subject, insofar as they efface the ethical. And yet the contribution of the history of the face would be to invite us to recognize the ethical where we would not otherwise expect it. So Levinas writes in *Otherwise than Being* that "we have the boldness to think that even the Stoic nobility of resignation to the logos already owes its energy to the openness to the *beyond essence*."[62] Might we not find in these lines a reference to Derrida, the very power of whose thinking derives from the "indestructible and unforeseeable resource of the Greek logos?"[63] And if Levinas thereby finds the ethical in the means by which Derrida draws him back "within" philosophy, can we not see it again in Derrida's insistence that the questions about the death of philosophy "*should*" be the only questions for the community of "those who are still called philosophers" — as Derrida himself would seem to acknowledge when he writes in this regard of "an unbreachable responsibility?"[64]

Notes

1. I would like to thank Tina Chanter and John Llewelyn for their helpful comments on an earlier version of this paper. The paper was first drafted during the Spring of 1982 when I was a guest of the Department of Philosophy, SUNY at Stony Brook, and was delivered at a Levinas Sym-

posium held there in April of that year. The discussion of Levinas' treatment of the origin of language and of Derrida's *Of Grammatology* in relation to Rousseau in part II is abstracted from a lecture given at Duquesne University in March 1982 under the title "The Origin of Language." I am grateful to these two universities for their hospitality.

2. J. Derrida, *L'écriture et la différence* (Paris: Seuil, 1967), 117-228/ *Writing and Difference*, trans. A. Bass, (London: Routledge, 1978), 79-153. Henceforth ED and WD respectively. The essay originally appeared in *Revue de métaphysique et de morale*, 1964, nos. 3 and 4 and underwent a number of important revisions before its republication in 1967.

3. Derrida, ED 118/WD 79.

4. Derrida, ED 125/WD 84.

5. M. Heidegger, *Identitaet und Differenz* (Pfullingen: Neske, 1957), 30; trans. J. Stambaugh, *Identity and Difference* (New York: Harper & Row, 1969), 41.

6. I have developed the reading of Heidegger suggested here in *The Question of Language and Heidegger's History of Being* (New York: Humanities, 1984).

7. The essay consists of notes dating from 1936 to 1946. Heidegger says of the *Verendung* that it "lasts longer than the previous history of metaphysics" (*Vortraege und Aufsaetze* (Pfullingen: Neske, 1954), 71; *The End of Philosophy*, trans. J. Stambaugh (New York: Harper & Row, 1973), 85). It would seem therefore that when Derrida pointedly uses the word *closure* rather than *end*, he is addressing only a certain reading of Heidegger popular among some Heideggerians and so it is ironic that it has now been adopted by some readers of Derrida.

8. M. Heidegger, *Unterwegs zur Sprache* (Pfullingen: Neske, 1959), 30; *Poetry, Language, Thought*, trans. A. Hofstadter, (New York: Harper & Row, 1971), 207.

9. Heidegger, *Identitaet und Differenz*, 66/*Identity and Difference*, 73.

10. Derrida, ED 293/WD 196.

11. Derrida, ED 411/WD 279-280.

12. It should be understood that to call Derrida's relation to Heidegger "parasitic" is not simply to subordinate Derrida to Heidegger but, by the so-called logic of the supplement, the former could also be said to enjoy a certain priority over the latter. On Derrida's relation to Heidegger, see my essay "The Transformation of Language at Another Beginning," *Research in Phenomenology* 13 (1983), 5-42.

13. M. Heidegger, *Sien und Zeit* (Teubingen: Niemeyer, 1967), 22/*Being and Time*, trans. J. Macquarrie and E. Robinson, (Oxford: Blackwell, 1967), 44.

14. TeI xvii/TI 28.

15. E. Levinas, *Le temps et l'autre* (Montpellier: Fata Morgana, 1979), 20.

16. TeI 247/TI 269.

17. TeI 275/TI 298.

18. AEAE 24/OBBE 20.

19. For an attempt to introduce a distinction between the speculative and the dialectical in this way, see my "Levinas Face to Face — with Hegel," *The Journal of the British Society for Phenomenology* 13, no. 1 (1982), 267–276.

20. J. Derrida, *Positions* (Paris: Minuit, 1972), 35 and 21/*Positions*, trans. A. Bass, (Chicago: University of Chicago, 1981), 24 and 12.

21. TeI 179/TI 204.

22. The term *metaphysics* is being used here as the later Heidegger and Derrida use it whereby it refers to the previous history of philosophy as seen from the closure. The early Heidegger and Levinas give 'metaphysics' a positive meaning, and they use it to describe their own practices, very different though they are from each other. For Levinas, what Heidegger does is 'ontology'.

23. Derrida, ED 163/WD 110. The translation has been slightly altered. This passage is not found in the original version of the essay published in 1964. See note two above.

24. Derrida, ED 161/WD 109.

25. J. Derrida, *De la grammatologie* (Paris: Minuit, 1967), 326/*Of Grammatology*, trans. G. Spivak, (Baltimore: Johns Hopkins, 1976), 229. Henceforth DG and G respectively.

26. Derrida ED 224/WD 151.

27. Derrida, ED 224/WD 151.

28. Derrida, ED 220/WD 148.

29. TeI 173/TI 199.

30. TeI 37/TI 66.

31. TeI 56/TI 84.

32. . TeI 175/TI 200.

33. TeI/TI 75.

34. E. Levinas, "Dieu et la philosophie," *Le Nouveau Commerce* 30–31 (1975), 124/"God and Philosophy," trans. R. Cohen, *Philosophy Today*, 22, no. 2, (Summer 1978), 141. Henceforth "DP" and "GP" respectively. Also AEAE 145, 180–186/OBBE 114, 142–146.

35. AEAE 183/OBBE 143.

36. "DP" 124/"GP" 141.

37. TeI 58/TI 85.

38. AEAE 195/OBBE 153.

39. TeI 36/TI 65.

40. AEAE 124/OBBE 97.

41. See my paper "The Trace of Levinas in Derrida" delivered to the Warwick Workshop on Derrida, July 1982, and published in *Derrida and Difference*, ed. D. Wood and R. Bernasconi (Coventry, England: Parousia, 1984), 17–44.

42. Derrida, ED 194/WD 132.

43. Derrida, ED 117/WD 311 n.1.

44. J. Derrida, *La Dissémination* (Paris: Seuil, 1972), 145/*Dissemination*, trans. B. Johnson, (Chicago: University of Chicago Press, 1981), 127. Henceforth LD and D respectively.

45. J. Derrida, *Marges de la philosophie* (Paris: Minuit, 1972), 206 n/ *Margins of Philosophy*, trans. A. Bass, (Chicago: University of Chicago Press, 1982), 172n.

46. Derrida, ED 139/WD 94.

47. Derrida, ED 220/WD 148.

48. TeI xi/TI 23.

49. Derrida, DG 253–254/G 178–179.

50. TeI xii/TI 24.

51. AEAE 224–225/OBBE 178.

52. Derrida, ED 222/WD 149.

53. Derrida, ED 220/WD 148.

54. TeI 183/TI 211.

55. "DP" 120/"GP" 139.

56. "DP" 127/"GP" 143.

57. "DP" 127/"GP" 143.

58. AEAE 76/OBBE 59.

59. DL, "Pieces d'identité," ("Identification Papers"), 77.

60. "DP" 127/"GP" 143.

61. E. Levinas, "Ideologie et Idéalisme," *Archivo di Filosofia* (1973): 141–142/"Ideology and Idealism," trans. A. Lesley in *Modern Jewish Ethics*, ed. M. Fox (Columbus, Ohio: Ohio State University Press, 1975), 130–132. A note at the beginning of the English translation explains that it was based on a number of different versions in French and Hebrew. The translation includes the sentences " . . . all metaphysics in Europe is now both laudable and shameful. We are deep into the end of metaphysics, and at the end of metaphysics we are all occupied with it." (122).

62. AEAE 224–225/OBBE 178.

63. Derrida, ED 165/WD 111–112.

64. Derrida, ED 118/WD 80.

Part III

Contexts

ADRIAAN PEPERZAK

10. Some Remarks on Hegel, Kant, and Levinas

Although most pages of *Totality and Infinity* quote Heidegger or allude to his work, it is obvious that Hegel's "system of philosophy" is a paradigmatic case of the "totalitarian" philosophy attacked by Levinas, whereas it is not immediately clear whether his criticism does full justice to Heidegger's long meditation on the difference between being (*Sein*) and the totality of all beings (*das Ganze des Seienden*). Heidegger's name does not occur very often in *Otherwise than Being or Beyond Essence*, but this thought is still more present there than in *Totality and Infinity*, because in the former Levinas' target is no longer the absolutization of totality but the proclamation of being as the ultimate horizon within which all beings, including others and God, must appear. During the thirteen years separating his two main works, Levinas radicalized his nonontological thought about the ways of being and the very different ways of its beyond, but this radicalization has not abolished the validity of the questions formulated in the title of *Totality and Infinity*. The modes of being and appearance, as manifested *in* a philosophy of totality; the possibility of a concept of the infinite within the horizon of such a philosophy; the "otherwise" of a discourse trying to separate and "save" the idea of the infinite from its coincidence with the collectivity of all beings and from being itself — these and similar questions continue to be symptomatic for the struggle that divides not only the scene of contemporary philosophy but also the mind of every philosopher expecting more from philosophy than a passionate game, an aesthetic delight, or a quasi-scientific discovery.

For Hegel, 'being' is the minimal determination of thought and — because thought and reality are one and the same — of all reality. Nothing, either actual or possible, can be conceived of or be what and how it is, if it has not the structure of a being. Being is, thus, the most universal ontological category. It is almost nothing; it is certainly no thing, because a thing presupposes many other determinations as well. Being is as good as nothing: it is not any one of all the predicates that can be attributed to a subject. Concerning all realities and possibilities, however, we must say that they "are," for example, that they "are" a reality or a possibility. The copula affirms this "is" or "are"; it covers all beings — but *a* being is already more than the determination *being* through which it is. Because of its extreme abstractedness, 'being' is empty and therefore open to all possible determinations. It is the quasi-determination of indeterminateness, of pure transparency, of the nothingness of an abstract openness in which all varieties of things and nonthings can manifest what they are. Being can be conceived of neither as a predicate nor as the subject of a sentence. As copula it cannot exist except in something else — a nonbeing — in which it is united to (other) determinations. It includes, therefore, that which it is not: *nonbeing* is its necessary complement. In order to be freed from its (almost) nothingness, being needs a determination that is more of an antidetermination: its opposite. Of course, nonbeing is also not able to be what it is (a "non-is"), unless it relies on its opposite (being), of which it is the inseparable complement. Being and nonbeing cannot be (and not be) what they are unless they pass continuously into one another. The unity of being and nonbeing is their ceaseless changing into their opposite: an endless movement of *becoming*, which — just as Aristotle's *dynamis* — is the onto-logical core and secret of movement and materiality. Nothing can escape from the texture woven by being and nonbeing as they become what they are not and therefore become what they are. There is no other dimension and no other stuff of which a being could be made. If the universe has meaning, it *must* be found somewhere within this texture or in the whole of it. Nothing is, unless it can be developed from this fundamental text.

Hegel's logic is the attempt to show that the universe of thought and being (in which 'thought' and 'being' are two opposite names of one and the same idea) is nothing but the full unfolding of a minimal thought. The movement through which being starts its transformation into its opposite and its adventures following from this first negation could not take place, if being were not animated by a life that is virtually as wide and strong as the universe. Being is the first mark and mask of an inspiration, which Hegel wants to show is the absolute. Being is the first incognito of absolute spirit which, in its full development, reveals itself to be the fully self-conscious insight into the structures and contents of the totality of beings. The texture of being and nonbeing is the neutral light in which the spirit presents and understands all finite beings as moments of its own appearance. This light produces its own shadows by negating its own indeterminate and blinding positivity, in order to reflect and enjoy itself in the darker exterior of a perfect mirror. The first, still very indeterminate, determination of thought produces the horizon within which everything becomes an object of circumscription and definition, whereas every definition and delimitation passes immediately into its opposite, until the horizon of totality is reached by a complete unfolding of all possible determinations, which are . . . and are not . . . and move . . . .

The infinite itself — the breath of inspiration — appears within *and as* the horizon; in fact, it appears twice: once as a being that is not finite but is the ground, the source, the substance, the essence, and the telos of all finite beings, and a second time as the union of all finite beings with that first pseudo-infinite which, if it were isolated from the finite, would itself be a finite being. The light of the ultimate horizon coincides with the appearance of the totality of all beings manifesting the infinite as their ground and subject. The infinite manifests itself as the spirit's throwing light upon its mirror and upon itself and contemplating its own face in this circularly bowing light. The concrete infinite knows that the onto-logical totality is identical with its own inner life. The triumph of knowledge is the full expression of the idea, which is the core and secret of the totality. As thought, in which thought and being are conceptually one, the idea contains all realities and all the lights and shadows of which they are composed. It is the womb in which everything breathes and moves according to the rhythms of its categorical diversifications. There is no elsewhere, nor any margin from which the idea could be looked at, but according to its own universal law of self-negation, the idea must transcend the level of the onto-logic and realize itself concretely as exteriority. The exteriority of the idea is nature. The passage from the onto-logical realm to the level of its most elementary concretization constitutes the first form of concrete phenomen-

ality. What the idea gains by this self-expression, it pays for by a loss
of coherence and light: natural exteriority is the dark and scattered
side of the idea — the side of its not-being what it is, the chaos of
its almost-death. Although the light and the life of the idea are strong
enough to submit and "sublate" its own chaotic night, its nightside
must affirm, strengthen, and organize itself in order to give the idea
its possibility of a mirroring and self-conquering autonomy.

The most primitive level of nature is pure exteriority, without
any interiority. The ongoing drama of the infinite's self-realization
separates the extremes of its pure, ideal light from the restless darkness of a faceless "prime matter," unidentifiable because of its ever-
changing (non-) nature.

When Levinas considers 'being' under the name of *il y a*,[1] he
does not think of an abstract categorical structure, as thematized in
the beginning of Hegel's (onto-)logic, but of the most elementary
form of being real or being there, which resembles the lowest level
of Hegel's 'nature'. The *il y a* precedes the formation and appearance
by which nature organizes and manifests itself. Even space and time,
insofar as they include certain rules of figuration, are still hidden in
this most primitive "stirring" (*grouillement*) and "rumbling" (*bruisse-
ment*). The phrase *there is* points to the dimension of a dangerous
proto-world, the anonymous underworld of faceless monsters, a
chaos that does not give, a neuter without generosity. The *il y a* burdens and bothers us but, at the same time, it seduces us by the magic
of its invitations to self-abandonment and its promises of drunkenness. Magic power and enthusiasm are offered to those who play
with the labyrinthian possibilities of this prehuman, precultural, and
prehistorical "beingness". Its dangers cannot be mastered completely,
but those who have goals can take possession of it by enjoyment,
dwelling, labor, construction, technology, and scientific knowledge.[2]
This presupposes, however, that they have discovered or received an
orientation that comes from something other than being.

The 'being' that Levinas describes — in a retaking of Sartre's *être*
and in contrast with Heidegger's *Es gibt* — is rather similar to Hegel's
pure exteriority, which is exterior even to itself. As first concretization of the interplay of abstract being and nonbeing passing
ceaselessly into each other, it accepts and rejects all the contours of
all beings, having no form of its own. As a sort of prime matter in
movement without end, it is certainly not a totality.

What Levinas rejects most of all in Hegel's theory of being and nature is the thesis that the infinite itself reveals itself within and as the realm of the anonymous in which Leviathans are at home. As the element of magic forces, mythic gods, and delightful enthusiasms,[3] nature cannot reveal the infinite, because it exists and "is" in another way than being, in its oscillation into and out of nonbeing. Levinas' hatred for this conception of the relationship between the finite and the infinite is most clearly expressed in his polemics against Heidegger's attempt at resuscitating the gods of Greece and of Hoelderlin, through a celebration of the divine as it appears in the phenomena of the earth, with its places, woods, and rivers, in works of art, in the heroes of politics or thought, and in the time of destiny.[4] It is, however, easy to adapt Levinas' criticism to Hegel's way of looking at nature and culture as the expressions of the absolute life unfolding itself through the hierarchy of stones and stars, plants, animals, and people, states and history.

However, can we not defend Hegel against this criticism? Doesn't he say that the natural exteriority of the idea should not be isolated from its interior light and that, if it were isolated, nature would indeed be an ungodly, monsterly chaos without any meaning, structure, value, light? And couldn't Hegel ask Levinas how he can avoid a dualistic view, according to which part of the world — being or *il y a* — is essentially unholy and unredeemable? How can being thus be conceived of as created?

Levinas might answer that we are not obliged, nor are we able, to have an answer to every question — or even that we are not permitted to ask every possible question. But such an answer would make him weak in the eyes of a thinker who cannot help reflecting on every answer that seems to imply a contradiction or a gap. A more philosophical answer would be that being, in the sense of "there is," can indeed be redeemed from its chaotic character — and Levinas has shown how; but it is not altogether certain that he thereby fully answers Hegel's question (which does not necessarily mean that the answer is bad, because it is not certain that the question is a perfect one). Approached from the perspective of our hedonic and economic existence, the anonymous stirring of "prime matter" offers the contours of various elements capable of satisfying human needs. The *there is . . .* receives a meaning from our existence. Chaos appears to be a medium in which we enjoy bathing, which we take possession of and transform through labor into a home and

tools.[5] But this existence on the basis of needs and more specific
elements is still ambiguous: it may bow to the gods of nature, but
it can also follow another orientation. Instead of an inspiration from
within, organizing by its breath the living totality of one "great
animal,"[6] another inspiration is possible, coming from "something"
other than the play of being and nonbeing: the breath of the other
— a silent whisper — shakes the foundations of a world based upon
the needs of nature. The meaning of being remains undecided, as
long as the whisper is not heard or orientation of our natural life is
not subordinated to our relationship with another.

Levinas' answer to Hegel's question implies that 'being' and
'nature' do not possess their meaning in themselves, insofar as they
are considered in isolation from human existence and history, and
that the meaning by which they can be saved from absurdity or evil
can be discovered only through morality.

The orientation brought into being by the appearance (which
is not an appearance) of the other, the other's self-presentation
(which does not produce a presence, his being there in front of me),
which is not just "being there" — the otherness of this dimension
cannot be described, defined or known in itself. The other is not a
new sort of phenomenon, which could be located among, and connected with, the other sorts of phenomena, nor is it a new sort of
light within which other phenomena would appear. The 'being there'
of another is not a horizon through which we could synthesize all
other beings; this would still presuppose that the ego takes advantage
of it in order to collect and comprehend all other beings in a universal light. The other would then be the source of transparency within
which everything can be and can manifest what it is. The other
would take the place and the function of Heidegger's being, and the
ego would remain the center of an enlightened universe, the hero of
a theory. But this is not the way in which the other's epiphany produces itself. It is not a source of light, throwing beams and shadows,
but an inexhaustible and incomprehensible claim. The other obliges
me to a straightforwardness without knowledge. I "know" where to
go and how to behave, I have an "idea" of the demands put on me,
but I do not have an insight into the infinite's directing me, as if it
were the object, or noema, of my intentional consciousness. The
answer to the meaning of being and history, and the 'end' of our
desire, can only be discovered through a *nontheoretical* relationship
with (or "idea" of) the infinite.

The structure of our relationship to the other reminds us of the way in which Kant reopened and "saved" the dimension of meta-physics through morality. The spatiotemporal order of phenomena permits us to wrest knowledge of the phenomena, but we do not *know* what and how things and persons in themselves are. We enter, however, into the dimension of 'being-in-itself' through respect for human autonomy as it reveals itself in the existence of others, as well as in our own existence.

Under the title *economy*, Levinas describes not only our theoretical but also our affective and practical familiarity with the phenomenal world:[7] we enjoy its elements, transform and (re)pro-duce and handle parts of it through labor, and know it in science and philosophy. What Kants calls a "fact of reason" corresponds to the epiphany of the other's face and speech. Whereas Kant stresses the universality and fundamental equality of being human manifested in that 'fact', Levinas describes it more truthfully as an asymmetric rela-tionship. Both Kant and Levinas refuse to call the revelation of the other's respectability an "experience" (*Erfahrung, expérience*), because it cannot be understood as a perception ruled by the conditions of empirical schematism or of phenomenological fulfillment, but for both that revelation is an exceptional sort of awareness, or "cogni-tion," from which all philosophy should start, although all attempts at thematizing it necessarily betray it.

In the ethical "experience," the ego of *I think* discovers itself as an *I am obliged*. Kant translated and betrayed the discovery of this submission, or "subjection," by formulating it in terms borrowed from the structure of theoretical reasoning. He described it as a universal law, to which the individual must submit his/her particular inclinations, thus preparing Hegel's synthesis in which morality is only an intermediate moment of the concept of *Sittlichkeit*. But behind this betrayal, the structure of a receptive subject is still legi-ble: I must obey and follow an orientation not chosen by me, but "choosing" me as a reasonable, that is, human being; my being human is the command to respect humanity as an end in itself; my life is being-for-this-end from which I cannot escape — morally rele-vant behavior on the basis of radical passivity.

Levinas opposes the idea that humanity can be defined by autonomy, because the term *autonomy* suggests easily the idea of a *causa sui* — a suggestion made into a thesis by Sartre's exaggeration of an existence choosing its own essence. The other reveals to me that the 'essence' of the self is to be a subject in the accusative: not *I think*, *I see, I will, I want, I can*, but *"me voici"* (*Here I am*). Kant's autonomy was, however, only a metaphor, because he knew very well that, before I become aware of it, *I* am not able to establish the law by which I discover myself to be ruled. Do not the images of a self (*soi*) "more passive than all possible passivity"[8] and of a hostage, a servant, and a victim[9] all hint at the same nonobjectifiable truth? Once again the highest (the lawyer, the ruler of human existence) and the lowest (the hostage, the slave) converge into something that cannot be circumscribed conceptually but that produces itself — albeit awkwardly — in the half-contradiction of opposite metaphors. The exaggeration of a transcendental self-determination together with the emphatic being-for-the-other that no longer belongs to itself seem to point to the same orientation: a 'being-for' that includes a nonphenomenal and unknowable, but practical, awareness of the absolute orienting the subject's life. True, Kant has not made explicit the asymmetry characteristic of duty and respect, but further on, when meditating on the connections associating the other with the third, we will see that this difference between Kant and Levinas is somewhat smaller than it may appear at first sight.

A classical objection against Kant's practical philosophy states that its dialectical part reintroduces the concept of happiness as a fundamental one, on which our belief in God and an afterlife relies. This objection can be reinforced from the perspective of Levinas' sharp distinction between *desire* and *need*.[10] If it is the *good* we desire, and not satisfaction or fulfillment, the separation between *ethics* and *economics*, in the wide sense of the Levinasian word *économie*, seems clear. But in defense of Kant it may be said, *first*, that an absolute separation between desire and needs and between the ends of both seems even more difficult to make than a separation between the chaotic darkness of primitive 'being' and the 'economy' of a human world. No philosopher can be satisfied with the duality of two unconnected levels that thus comes to the fore. *Second*, Kant does not say that he must postulate an afterlife because *he* cannot do without happiness, but because a universe in which goodness and happiness remain forever separated and even partly opposed would not agree with the necessary presuppositions and demands of reason: it would be an unreasonable and absurd, unfair and immoral universe. In it morality and justice would not be accepted as a dominating perspective; it would be ruled by blind fate or a cruel God. Kant's claim can be interpreted in a much less narcissistic and more disinterested and universalistic way than is often done.

From Levinas' perspective, the satisfaction of human needs is necessarily associated with the fulfillment of our obligations, because the ego cannot be for the other concretely, unless the ego offers him/her bread and house and work. 'Being-for' is being a body, is having hands as well as a heart, is building a home in which warmth and meals can be given to the stranger. I cannot be a self claimed by an other if I do not enjoy the world. But also: the other cannot be served by me unless I know his needs and try to procure for him what covers his nakedness and abolishes his poverty. Ethical life is associated with a practical interpretation of messianism in the name of this other of mine and of all the other's others. Contentment cannot be separated totally from morality.

This brings us to a consideration of the relationships between the other and the third(s).[11]

The 'fact' of the other is the revelation of the infinite, because it breaks the totality of my world and urges another orientation upon me — an orientation that coincides with my desire for the absolute. (By the way, if this sentence is true, we may state a certain coincidence of myself-as-desire with myself-as-the-host-of-another, a coincidence that permits us to speak in a certain way of self-realization on the basis of a certain identity between the origin and the end).

Because the other would not be fully other if he/she were my parent, husband or wife, sister or brother or friend, the other is a stranger. But because of her/his infinity, my life does not belong to me any more: the claim of the other is absolute. The love, or proximity, that is thus demanded from me is unjust insofar as it would exclude my being disposed to live also for others than the other, the 'third' and 'thirds', who are present in the other's self-presentation. I am obligated towards *all* others — whom I, however, cannot love with the same exclusive intimacy. From the exceptional perspective of my relationship with the other follows the obligation of universal fraternity, and this implies the organization of a social world through universal laws, social technology, planning, objective knowledge, and so on. Love has to make place for *universality*: I must overcome the perspective of "you and me" by combining it with the perspective of universal rights and equality.

Has not Levinas thus founded and justified, in a new way, the principle of Kant's and Hegel's metaphysics of duties and rights? And isn't this exactly the principle that Hegel opposes to all forms of subjectivism? By adopting the perspective of reason, we adopt the claim of universal justice and condemn every ego's tendency to prefer his own well-being over that of others. Equality and symmetry are the criteria — as Levinas admits — for a society in which the just claims of all others are taken seriously. Levinas agrees with Hegel when he affirms strongly that the existence of others, with whom I do not have an immediate proximity, obliges me to uphold more than moral intentions and behavior. No third can be safe unless (s)he is a member of a well-organized society in which the war of general egoism is suppressed by the concrete universality of collective institutions and customs. A moral life includes, therefore, participation in the good functioning of the economical and political organization of a state and of history, insofar as it is a never-ending attempt to put an end to war by counterviolence.

Levinas accepts the order of inevitable counterviolence-against-violence in the name of universal justice. But doesn't he give more place than Hegel to the dimension of immediate encounter and discourse? Hegel, too, sees a particular place and function for personal relationships. A family is not only a necessary institution of a well-ordered society but also includes the private intimacy of love; it is the best example of a mediation between the perspective of individual morality and the demands of society as a whole. Hegel's system deduces not only the love of husband and wife and parents and children but also friendship, private concern for the poor, and religious fraternity. Private life gets no lesser chance in his picture of human society than in Levinas' social thought. But the real question does not lie here. The meaning of justice, social organization, the state, war and peace, and so on depends on the perspective, the principle (*archè*) or nonprinciple (*an-archy*), from which they are seen as necessary. Whereas Hegel regards the individual, the moral subject, and the perspective of morality as mere moments of a concept that triumphs in the concrete universality of the state, Levinas interprets the state as an essentially violent system of equality and justice, intermediate — and in a sense mediating — between goodness and war. The difference between their perspectives explains why Levinas holds that true peace cannot come from the state and that the dialectics of violence must be oriented by a voice that "comes from the out-side, 'through the door' (*thurathen*),"[12] whereas Hegel — from his "totalitarian" perspective — must defend the state as the highest expression and guarantee of peace, above which no *practical* recon-ciliation is possible. World history, as the history of social, economic, and political life, is unable to put an end to war, because the sovereignty of states hinders their sublation into a wider whole. On the level of practical — moral and political — life, no final reconcil-iation can be found. The bloody madness of history ("a slaughterhouse," as Hegel calls it) distresses us so much that we *must* console ourselves by the artistic, religious, and philosophical con-templation of its tragedies. Through knowledge we know and see and feel and enjoy that the infinite-in-us lives and masters itself in spite of *and on account of* its continuous darkening, corruption, and destruc-tion throughout world history. To the believer and the knower, it is clear that the terrible drama of existence is only a reflection of the eternal *clair-obscur*, which is the way of being of eternal life.

In rejecting the pseudoreligious satisfaction of a final vision, Levinas places the unpredictability of time above eternity. But does he dispose of a place from which he can pronounce his preference for morality over history? When he proclaims the primacy of the moral perspective over the pseudoconcept of a judgment pronounced by history,[13] how can he take enough distance from the life and history in which he is involved? The only distance given to him is the separatedness that the I, in awakening, discovers between the other, coming from elsewhere, and "me." There is, however, no space from which I can have an overview of the duality of my being involved in the moral relationship with this other here and now *and* my being involved as one of the many moments of world history. If both dimensions are dimensions of one and the same subject, we cannot but somehow "think" their unity, yet this thought remains for-mal and abstract; it cannot become a synthetic knowledge, in the style of Hegel's concept or Kant's synthetic judgment a priori. The margin from which Levinas projects a hierarchy between morality and history is minimal; it is no more than a line without any volume, a nonplace (*non-lieu*)[14] in which there is only a little breath: a whisper that can be recognized as an enigmatic voice, or not.

We can neither master nor "know" our own orientation and the meaning of human life, because we cannot have a vision of it. We cannot know what history is doing and where it goes. But we can and must proceed towards the stranger, or let him/her in. The text of our synthetic judgments and nicely coherent papers has to be unwoven, because it converts itself into a fossil as soon as we believe it. No complicated alchemy can extract life from the inscriptions of history; they come to life, however, when touched by the breath of a simple speech interrupting the coherence of a synchronizable time. The "severely calculated strategies" in which other writers have put their hope for a radical transformation of the languages in which we live are new expressions of our old desire to gain mastership by imitating the gestures of a demiurge. Infinity demands more modesty.

My attempt at comparing some elements of the very original text Levinas has written with some texts of Kant and Hegel may have underscored the differences separating them. Certainly the nonphenomenality of the face, the otherness of discourse with relation to the customary methods of philosophy, and the irreducibility of saying (*le Dire*) to a said (*le Dit*) are great discoveries that oblige philosophy to make a new beginning. But within the new discourse of philosophy to be born, classical elements of the modern tradition may be recaptured and transformed into legitimate parts of a text that denies, not only to them but also to itself, the right to function as a highest perspective. The other, our idea of the infinite, the meaning of our desire, the most radical orientation of our behavior can only be formulated in a language by which they are immediately betrayed. This betrayal makes them look like the concepts and oppositions of a Hegelian system. But still it is an approach to the truth, if we do not venerate its text but try to overcome it by an extreme attention to the inconceivable saying, of which all texts, including those of philosophy, are only awkward paraphrases.

Perhaps I am not Jew enough and too much of a Germanic intellectual, full of reverence for the heroes of late Greece and their modern heirs. Perhaps the love for a motherly tradition in which one can feel at home prevents me from a more courageous exodus. It seems, however, worthwhile — and Levinas gives us an example of it — tomeditate on what unites us with the heritage of our Greece-inspired modernity and to plunder it as much as we can before we leave it behind — before we are renewed by the arid sufferings of a desert.

Notes

1. DEE 93–105/ EE 57–64; TeI 116–117, 132–134, 137, 164–165/ TI 142–144, 158–160, 163, 190–191; AEAE 3–4, 207–210/ OBBE 3–4, 162–165.

2. TeI 82–142/ TI 110–168.

3. Cf. E. Levinas, "Levy-Bruhl et la philosophie contemporaine," *Revue Philosophique* 147 (1957), 556–569; "Heidegger, Gagarine et nous," in DL 255–259; TeI 29–30, 49–50, 115–116, 121/ TI 58–59, 77–78, 141–142, 148.

4. Cf. "Heidegger, Gagarine et nous."

5. Cf. TeI 100–125/ TI 127–151.

6. Cf. Plato, *Timaeus* 30b ff., 92c.

7. Cf. TeI 79 ff./ TI 107 ff.

8. Cf. AEAE 65–72, 132–146/ OBBE 51–56, 104–115.

9. Cf. AEAE 114–151/ OBBE 113–118.

10. TeI 3–10/ TI 33–40.

11. TeI 187–191/ TI 212–216; AEAE 19–20, 84 n.2, 103, 116 n.33, 200–205/ OBBE 16, 191 n.2, 81–82, 193 n.33, 157–161; E. Levinas, "Le Moi et la Totalité, *Revue de métaphysique et de morale* 59 (1954), 353–373.

12. Cf. Aristotle, *De generatione animalium*, 736b28, cited by Levinas in "Le Moi et La Totalité," 367.

13. Among many places, one of the finest is the Preface of TeI ix–xviii/ TI 21–30.

14. AEAE 9, 17, 21, 148/ OBBE 8, 14, 17, 116: "null-site."

ALPHONSO LINGIS

11. The Sensuality and the Sensitivity

To sense something is to catch on to the sense of something, its direction, orientation, or meaning. Sensibility is sense perception, apprehension of sense. In addition, to sense something is to be sensitive to something, to be concerned by it, affected by it. It is to be pleased — gratified, contented, exhilarated — or to be pained, afflicted, wounded, by something. A sentient subject does not innocently array object forms about itself; it is not only oriented in free space by their sense, it is subject to them, to their brutality and their sustentation.

Was it ever evident that the sensibility in our nervous circuitry has to be conceived as a passivity of the mind, upon which the physical action of the material world taps out impressions — impressions that a free and spontaneous understanding can then take as signs and for which it can relate and posit referents? Is receptivity passivity? Is there in it a synoptic assembling of the multiplicity of sense data? Is there in it an intentional orientation? But is the sensuous element really a multiplicity of discrete impressions? Is the affective sensitivity but a side effect of sensibility, a factor of confusion and indistinctness in sense perception? Is there opposition between sensibility and responsibility — between the sentiment of respect, which Kant called the receptivity of the spontaneity of the mind, the sensibility of the faculty of understanding, and the sensibility for sensible things? Were the metaphysical correlates of matter and form, activity and passivity really imposed on the classical philosophy of mind by analysis of the phenomenon of sensibility?

There is a movement in sensibility, the moment of ex-isting. Our existence is sensitive. In the receptivity for sense, the capacity to catch on to the orientation and potentialities of things, Heidegger has seen the propulsion that makes our being ex-ist — that is, cast itself out toward entities exterior to itself — and cast itself beyond them to take in the context in which they could move. The given beings make an impression on us, because the active, self-propelling thrust of our being makes contact with them and advances beyond where and how they actually are to their possible positions and employment, to their futures. What we sense when we sense the solidity of the seat is neither a coagulation of chromatic and tactile impressions, nor an idea, an ideal object, associated with them; it is a possibility. Sense perception is, in fact, apprehension of the forces of things, the possibilities things are, anticipation of the future of the world, clairvoyance.

But the propulsive force by which our existence casts itself perceptively into the world is oriented by the layout of things. There is subjection to the world in the sensibility. Our emotions disclose to us, in us, how the things we envisage matter to us; our affective disposition, our moods, reveal how the layout as a whole besets us. The world is not only a layout of contours, whose orientation, whose sense, whose future, we envisage; in our affectivity the facticity of its being is imposed on us. Affectivity, far from being just a subjective factor of confusion and immanence in the mind, is exposure and revelation of the world. Revelation of its being. It is in itself that our being knows the being of the most remote things, of the whole world. The existential elucidation of affectivity is astonishing: Heidegger showed that, while our existence *entfernt*, distances itself from, posits apart, the forms and appearances of things through sensibility, our being is afflicted from the start with the pressure, the gravity, of the being of those exterior things. We find ourselves exposed not merely to the appearances, the phosphorescence, of things that are closed in themselves but to the incontrovertible plenum of their being, all the infinity of the condensation with which their being has replaced and excluded nothingness. Our own being is exposed from the start to the being of the most alien and remote things, exposed to the dimensions of remoteness in which beings can be exterior; the weight of the being of the world presses down on us. In fact, the ecstatic thrust of our existence, by which we cast ourselves beyond their actual forms and positions to their possibilities, is not really a free-floating domination over them; it is rather a continual effort to escape the burden of their being, which oppresses our being from the start.

These two sides to our original contact with the world — projection into it and subjection to it, delineating a line of sense in it and being beset with the fact of its being — Heidegger sought to make intelligible, in their juxtaposition in our sensibility, by understanding them as dimensions of the movement of time, the inner time of our existence. Our presence is realized as an ecstatic transport from the being disposed by the world to the synthetic grasp of its possibilities, a transport conjoining projective comprehension with affective subjection, sensibility with susceptibility, a transport of what has come to pass in us to what is to come to us, ex-istential transport of the being we have been given to our potentiality for being otherwise.

But this transport itself, Heidegger will show, is nothing else than the enactment, the active realization, of a subjection of one's being to nothingness, which is our vulnerability, or our mortality. The propulsion of the sensibility beyond the given to the possible, beyond the present to the imminent, beyond the entity to the world space, is in fact a projection into nothingness. For Heidegger the possible as such, the really possible, is constituted by the eventuality of impossibility. The possibility that the sensibility grasps in things is not simply a representation, an advance presentation, of another format of them drawn by the power of the mind to vary their actual appearances. It is also not simply the arrangement of them, not yet there, that the mind perceives in advance. Neither the calculative skills of the mind nor its recombinatory imagination produces the real possible. The possibilities are the future of things — but a future that is not ineluctable, that is possibly impossible.

Then the universal being that affects us, the being of the world that besets our being, is but a possible being, and possibly impossible. The weight and force of the world's being that presses down on our being is also the imminence and ineluctability of nothingness in which the contingent world is suspended, which we sense in the mortal lucidity of our anxiety. The world that solicits us with its possibilities and its promises, that incites our existence to project itself continually out towards it, draws as it withdraws, draws by withdrawing into its own being and into the imminent nothingness that does not cease to threaten its irremediable contingency.

It is this mortal lucidity of our anxiety that makes our existence perceptive, our sensibility clairvoyant. At the bottom of our concern

for the possible beings, there is a sense of being concerned by the
nothingness that approaches of itself, that closes in, that touches us
already. It is because we are first stricken with the void, haunted by
the death everywhere lurking in the interstices of the world, affected
by its nothingness, that we are touched, affected by, stabilized and
steered by the things, that the things have sense for us. They have
sense and affect us, not as material nor as forms, but as means, as
supporting gear, or obstacles and snares, in the way of our
movements into the world. It is with one and the same movement
that our being projects itself into the open clearing of the world and
into the emptiness of impossibility, the void of the definitive and
irreversible abyss of death. Being-in-the-world and being-unto-death
are one and the same.

For Heidegger, it is thus because we are exposed to the
nothingness that is exterior to all being that we are exposed to exterior beings. For Levinas sensibility is exposure, not to nothingness,
but to alterity. And for him, otherness is not decomposable into
being and nothingness; possibility is not decomposable into actuality
and the impossibility that threatens it.

Levinas' phenomenological exposition shows that, prior to the
anxious taking hold of things that for Heidegger makes our sensibility practical from the first, there is the sensuous contact with
material, there is sensuality. It is not with their "primary properties,"
their contours, but also not with their forces, their instrumental
potentialities, that the things first affect us but, indeed, with their
matter, their substance. In our sensuality we find ourselves immersed
in a sensuous, qualitative medium, supporting and sustaining, a
depth of sustenance. We find things, we find ourselves, in the light,
in air, on terra firma, in color, in tone. Our sensuality makes us find
ourselves steeped in a depth before we confront surfaces and envisage the profiles of objects. Sensibility opens us, not upon empty
space, but upon an extension without determinate frontiers, a
plenum of free-floating qualities without substrates or enclosures,
upon luminosity, elasticity, vibrancy, savor. The sensuous element —
light, chromatic condensation and rarefaction, tonality, solidity,
redolence — is not given as a multiplicity that has to be collected nor
as data that have to be identified but as a medium without profiles,
without surfaces, without contours, as depth, *apeiron*. We find
ourselves in it, in light, in the elemental, buoyed up, sustained by it.

Life lives on sensation; the sensuous element is sustenance, ends, the goodness of being we enjoy before any practical intention arises to locate means for our pursuits.

The sensual sensibility is receptivity for this elemental materiality. Sensuality is not intentionality, is not a movement aiming at something exterior, something transcendent, that objectifies; it is not identification of a diversity with an eidos, an ideal identity term, nor is it imposition of form or attribution of meaning. Steeped in the elemental, contented with the plenum, its movement is that of enjoyment. The enjoyment is the vibrancy and excess of our openness upon the elements, which delineates a movement of involution and ipseity: being sensual, one enjoys the light, the color, the solidity, the spring, the monsoon, and one enjoys one's enjoyment. The most elementary egoism in sensitive flesh is this eddy of enjoyment reiterated; the first ego is this pleasure.

Sensuality is vulnerable and mortal from the start. But this susceptibility, inseverable from sensibility, is not the vertiginous sense of the contingency of all being, the imminence of nothingness threatening one in all beings one touches. The sense of the contingency of the sensible medium, flux or chaos without law or necessity, supported by nothing behind its appearing — for the things will be formed in it, out of it — is not to be identified with an intuition into the nothingness, in which all being would be perilously adrift and which could be foreseen as a real possibility just beyond the thin screen of the actual being. The contingency of the sensuous element is rather in the very fullness and abundance of the present, which plugs up the horizons, the future. Coming from nowhere, going nowhere, it is there by incessant oncoming, not as though grudgingly parceled out by the malevolence of nothingness — but rather as gratuity and grace. Fortuity and goodness of the light, the vibrant colors, the radiance of tones, the liquidity of the swelling forces — yet there is in sensuality a sense of vulnerability, not made of anxiety over the imminence of nothingness but of the liability of being wounded and rent and pained by the force and substantiality of the sensuous element. In pain one is backed up into oneself, mired in oneself, in oneself, materialized; pain announces the end of sensibility, not through a conversion into nothingness, an annihilation, but at the limit of prostration, at the conversion into passivity, at materialization. In savoring the materiality of things, sensibility has the taste of its own mortality. It is in the materiality

of the world and not in its inconsistency, its being already undermined by the imminence of nothingness, that our death already
touches us.

If Heidegger finds, subtending the capacity to be affected by the
impact of beings, an exposure to or a projection into nothingness,
that is because he conceives of sensibility as an outbreak of freedom
from the start, as intentionality or transcendence. There is sensibility for beings and presence to being when our existence finds itself
exposed to nothingness or finds itself in a clearing, or free space. He
conceives of the 'being open' of our existence, as 'being in an openness'. Its first model is the hand that has leeway to move; he conceives
of sensibility as "handling things." But in Levinas, finding oneself in
the light, vibrancy, and plenitude was taken as a primary model for
what happens when life becomes a *lumen naturale*, becomes lucidity.
He saw in the tremor of sensation not an exhilaration and ecstasy
out of being but an enjoyment, an intensity, and an involution.

Levinas' complete analysis of sensibility contains the bold and
strange thesis that the exposure and subjection to beings is itself
subtended by an exposedness and subjection to alterity. He reverses
the Kantian position; for him responsibility, sensitivity to others,
does not conflict with, mortify, sensibility for mundane beings, but
makes it possible.

Heidegger had already located responsibility not in one
suprasensory faculty, the rational faculty, but in the sensible structure of our existence. Responsibility is not a receptivity for an ideal
order, an order of the *ought* over and beyond what *is*. For Heidegger,
being is the law; it is being that is incumbent, being that orders and
ordains, being that destines. His *Introduction to Metaphysics* initiated a
diagnosis of the history of the understanding of being that located,
at the decisive period when metaphysics extended its sway over all
Western culture, a determination of the meaning of being that
separated being from, and opposed it to, becoming, appearing,
thought, and the ought; since that time, being is for us the given, the
actual, the facts, over against what ought to be. Heidegger
repudiates this opposition; for him it is being that binds us, obligates
us, is the law and the destiny. He will show this by showing that in
us being is not just what is coextensive with us as the matter of our
movements or the actuality of our acts; on the contrary, for us to

exist is to relate to our being. Between us and our being there is not coinciding but relationship: in us our own being is a matter of concern. We consider our being, question it, are troubled and afflicted by it, wearied by it, laden with it. We cannot exist without taking up a stand, an attitude, with regard to our being. But our being is not an object we envisage; it affects us, weighs on us, afflicts us. Our affectivity is a sense of our responsibility for our own being. We do not engender our being; it is given to us, laid upon us; we are burdened with it and have to bear it. We do not exist, simply; we have to be. Being is an imperative in us: we are bound to be. Socrates felt that, too, when he castigated suicide as recreancy and desertion. The imperative is first an imperative to exist — in order to answer for existence.

This having to be related to our own being, such that it affects us and afflicts us, is at the origin of the existential option always made between existing inauthentically (i.e., anonymously) or authentically, that is, on our own. For the primary awareness of our own being is an effort to take a distance from it, to evade the burden of having our being as our own, of having to be on our own. Feelings contracted from others, passed on to others, perceptions equivalent to and interchangeable with those of anyone else, thoughts that conceive only the general format of the layout about one, sentences formulated such that they can be passed on to anyone, all make up the rigorous and consistent enterprise of evasiveness in the face of the being that is one's own to be. Evasiveness in the face of one's own being is an evasiveness in the face of one's own time. It makes us live each day as it comes, making it a reinstatement of the day that passed, always expecting another day to take the place of the one that is passing; it makes us live out time as an indefinite succession of nows, of manageable units, of workaday workdays. What makes us so continuously and consistently evasive, with regard to the being that is our own to be, is fear of the anxiety, which has never ceased to be felt, over the nonbeing that is our own to become.

Whereas, responsible being originates at the far end of anxiety. The anxiety that rehearses dying, that anticipates the limits of what is possible for me, casts itself over and takes over the full range of what is possible for me, unto the last limits of impossibility. The anxiety that anticipates the nothingness that is to come for me delivers over to me the full range of all that is mine to become. One becomes responsible in anxiety.

It is one's own being that is imperative; the being that is given to me is a destination to a potentiality for being that my actual being engenders and a destination to the nonbeing that is to come for me. The imperative is not an imperative for the universal and the necessary, but for the singular; it is the imperative that my singular potentiality for being come to be. At the same time, however — and this is the central hinge forged in Heidegger's existential ontology — the being in me that I appropriate is being, being generally. In my own being, universal being, the being of the world, presses upon me. I cannot answer for my own being without undertaking to answer for the being of all that is. That is why I am a pulse of care in the universe, not only anxious for my own exposed, vulnerable, mortal existence but concerned for the world, for all that is. For Heidegger it is this being afflicted with, being concerned for, the contingent being of the world, not merely anxiety over my own subsistence, that makes my existence practical. Responsibility is finding, in the forces of my own existence, the wherewith to come to the assistance of universal being, threatened throughout with nothingness. It is, he will say in a late study, to shelter the most remote things — earth, heavens, harbingers of the immortal — in my own mortal existence.

Responsibility is, then, not measured by authorship; it is not just the will or the project to answer for what has originated in one's own existence. It takes over and answers for a situation one did not initiate; it is answering for what one did bring about and for what came to pass before one was born, for the deeds and failings of others. And it answers already for the sequence of occurrences that will extend beyond one's own power to steer them; it answers already for what will come to pass when one will no longer be there.

Responsibility is coextensive with our sensibility; in our sensibility we are exposed to the outside, to the world's being, in such a way that we are bound to answer for it. The world is not just a spectacle spread before us but a burden with which we are entrusted. What opens us to the exterior, what makes us ex-ist, makes us be a sensibility, is exteriority, which approaches of itself and touches us, affects us, afflicts us. For Heidegger, this exteriority is what is exterior to our being and to all being — nothingness, or death. The approach of this exteriority is also what casts us back upon our own being and upon being and makes existing for us both a response to the nothingness and a responsibility for being.

For Levinas it is not the encounter with nothingness that could make us take on our own being and answer for all being; it is alterity. Alterity is not nothingness, which could only be the nihilation of being. It is not ideality, self-sufficient and absolute in its immobile present. Alterity is what is positive enough to appeal to being and separate enough from it to order it imperatively. This kind of alterity Levinas locates neither in the death that summons all that lives nor in the ideality of law, without executive force, but in the face of another. For the face is not another surface. In his face, by facing, the other takes a stand; otherness itself appeals to us and contests us.

In *Totality and Infinity*, Levinas had worked out the phenomenological analysis of facing in such a way as to show that the perception of the face of another is a responsibility. In turning to face me, the other signals me; his face, his expression, his word is not only indicative, informative but also vocative and imperative. He faces me with his eyes, unmasked, exposed, and turns the primary nakedness of the eyes to me; he faces me with a gesture of his hand, taking nothing, empty-handed; he faces me with a word, which is not an instrument, an arm, which is the way to come disarmed and disarming. To recognize his move in facing is to recognize an appeal addressed to me, which calls upon my resources and first calls upon me, calls upon me to stand forth as I. And he appeals imperatively. To recognize his voice is to recognize his rights over me, his right to make demands on me and to contest me, his right to demand that I answer for my existence.

There would then be two kinds of sensibility: a sensibility for the elements and the things of the world, sensuality, which is appropriation and self-appropriation, and a sensibility for the face of another, which is expropriation and responsibility. But in *Otherwise than Being* Levinas set out to show that the space in which the sensuous material is laid out is already extended by the sense of alterity, which takes form and becomes a phenomenon in the face of another. This thesis involves the idea, already found in Heidegger, that before the beings of the outside world are set forth for me, they are possessed by others; that the material world is "human" even before it is a nourishing medium, and that its elements are "objective" or "intersubjective," elements in themselves or open to others, before they are goods for me.

It is true that in Husserl and in Heidegger, the lateral relationship with others, as other points of view or as other sites where being is exhibited, already entered into the constitution of universal space. But Levinas advances two innovations. First, he thinks that the relationship with the other does not enter only at the point where my perceptual field, already extended by my own intentional perception or by the reach of my utilitarian operations, is fitted into impersonal, universal extension; for him, spatial distance is not extended by a sense of nothingness but by a sense of alterity. Second, the relationship with alterity can have this role because the relationship with the other is not, as in Husserl, perceptual or, as in Heidegger, pragmatic, but ethical. There is then a difference of levels; the argument is not that the other is the first object of perception, or the first instrument with which one could get one's bearings in a field of things. It is that what institutes the first *here*, what constitutes my existence as here, is not the power to keep objects at a distance; it is the pain of being afflicted with the demands of the other.

For Heidegger, what subtends the sense of space is the sense of nothingness; the space of the world is the very abyss of death. This is because Heidegger takes being to be presence, *ens* to be *prae-ens*, and presence to be dis-stancing, distance. It is the *Entfernung* that realizes presence is situating at a distance — and Heidegger took the sense of distance and exposure to contain a sense of nothingness in general and in itself. In boredom and in anxiety nothingness nihilates; in antagonism, rebuke, failure, prohibition, privation, nothingness nihilates; in all distance, including all separateness by which things take their stand about us, nothingness nihilates.

For Levinas, what extends space is not the nothingness that separates and frees the entities of the world to be as they are where they are; it is rather contact, contact with what is other and withdraws in the midst of the contact. He first worked out the notion in the example of the neighbor whose proximity, whose nearness, consists in his touching us, affecting us, while remaining uncomprehended, unassimilable, by us. In this move he is other, shows himself as other. It occurs when the other faces us, that is, appeals to us, contests us.

The contact does not only reveal the proximity of the other; it determines the *here*, determines the one contacted as here. Being here, being a here in being, supposes in our substance not only a capacity to be oriented or disposed by the exterior but a susceptibility to being affected, altered — sustained and wounded. To be here is to be exposed to the other, exposed to pain.

Quite early Levinas studied the immanence of pain. To be pained is to feel one's own substance, as a passive affliction, in the torment of wanting to escape oneself. For to escape pain would be to be able to transcend it towards the world, or to be able to retreat behind it and objectify it. The inability to flee or to retreat, the being-mired in oneself, is the suffering of pain.

Later Levinas was to find this inner diagram of pain in the contact with the other. The approach of the other who faces, afflicting one with his exigencies and exactions, throws one back upon oneself. One is unable to establish distance by rendering present to oneself, by representing to oneself, what afflicts one so pressingly. One is unable to retreat from the demand by apprehending or comprehending it, setting it before oneself by one's own initiative, as though it emanated out of oneself. One finds oneself forced back into the resources of one's own being by the exaction put on oneself. This being backed up into oneself, this having to bear the burden and affliction of the other's wants and failings, without being able to find anyone to take one's place, this being held to one's post, repeats, in the structure of the one approached by alterity, the inner diagram of pain. Thus the *here* is fixed. To find oneself somewhere is to be exposed, not to emptiness and nothingness, but to suffering appeals made on one's substance and contestations made of one's stand.

The recognition of the imperative in the face of another is not an abstract and intellectual respect for the pure form of the law, which the other would instantiate in the diagrams of his moves; it is the recognition of a claim put on my substance and my life, the injunction to answer for the destitution of others with one's own bread and, as a hostage, to give one's life in sacrifice. The other's wants are first of all material; they make claims on my own sustenance and on my own substance, made wholly of the substance of the sensuous element. It is not only some surplus of my possessions that is contested by his imperative need but my appropriative life, by which I appropriate myself. Responsibility is serious when it is not only my surplus that is affected but all that sustains my life and my very occupancy of this post.

To have to answer to the other is to have to answer for what I did not initiate, for his wants and failings, and even for his approach, which puts me in question. It is this position that is constitutive of my being here and of my being vulnerable to being wounded by entities. The exactions put on me by the others make me liable to death — not by taking away the ground under my feet and casting me into the void, but by exposing me to the obduracies and lacks of material things. It is not in being delivered over to nothingness, it is first in being delivered over to beings, having to count only on their sustenance, that I am mortal. To this mortality I am delivered by the exactions of alterity, from the first a claim put on my life, on my life living off the enjoyment of life.

Thus we find Levinas' texts taking on some of the pathos of the Kantian moral philosophy, for which the inclination to obey the moral imperative is always received as a humiliation and a pain by the sensuous nature of man. But in Levinas this pain is not only the intellectual pain of a capacity for feeling negated and frustrated, even when the moral order is carried out by the executive forces of life; it is the pain of the substantial wounding and sacrifice demanded of life. For it is in depriving oneself to answer to others for the hunger of those who have no claim on one but their hunger, and in sacrificing oneself to answer for what one did not do, that responsibility is serious.

12. The Fecundity of the Caress:
A Reading of Levinas,
Totality and Infinity *section IV,*
B, "The Phenomenology of Eros"

On the horizon of a story is found, once again, that which was in the beginning: this naive, or native, sense of a touch, in which the subject does not yet exist. Submerged in *pathos* or *aisthesis*: astonishment, admiration, sometimes terror, before that which surrounds it.

Eros prior to any *eros* defined or measured as such. The voluptuousness of being born into a world where the gaze itself remains tactile — open to the light. Still carnal. Voluptuous without knowing it. Always at the beginning and not based upon the origin of a subject that sees, grows old, and dies, from no longer being in the enthusiasm and innocence of a perpetual beginning anew. A subject already "fixed." Not "free as the wind." A subject that already knows its objects and controls its relations with the world and with others. Already closed to any initiation. Already involved in initiatives that exclude the unknown. Already solipsistic. In charge of a world that it enjoys only through possession. With neither communion nor a childlike acceptance of that which gives of itself. A consumer who consumes what he produces without admiration for what offers itself to him in its unfinished state, before it becomes a finished product.

Voluptuousness can reopen and reverse this conception and construction of the world. It can return to the evanescence of subject and object. To the lifting of all schemas by which the other is defined. Made graspable by this definition. *Eros* can arrive at the innocence

231

that never took place with the other as other. At that nonregressive in-finity of pathetic feeling for the other. At that appetite of all the senses, which is irreducible to any obligatory consumption. At that indefinable attraction to the other, which will never be satiated. Which will always remain on the threshold, even after entering into the house. Which will remain a dwelling, preceding and following the habitation of all dwellings.

This always still-preliminary gesture, which precedes any union and comes first in all nuptials, which weds without consuming, which perfects while abiding by the outlines of the other, this gesture may be called: the touch of the caress.

Prior to and following any positioning of the subject, this touch binds and unbinds two others in flesh that is still, and always, untouched by mastery. Dressing the one and the other without-within, within-without, in a garment that neither evokes, invokes, nor takes pleasure in the perversity of the naked but contemplates and adorns it, always for a first time, with in-finite, un-finished flesh. Covering it, uncovering it, again and again, like an amorous impregnation that seeks out and affirms otherness, while protecting it.

In that place, nothing attests to the subject. The ever prolonged quest for a birth that will never take place, whose due date still, and always, recedes on the horizon. Life always open to what happens. To the fleeting touch of what has not yet found a setting. To the grace of a future that none can control. That will or will not happen. But while one waits for it, any possession of the world or of the other is suspended. A future coming, which is not measured by the transcendence of death but by the call to birth of the self and the other. For which each one arranges and rearranges the environment, the body, and the cradle, without closing the least dimension of a room, a house, an identity.

The fecundity of a love whose most elementary gesture, or deed, remains the caress.

Before orality comes to be, touch is already in existence. No nourishment can compensate for the grace, or the work, of touching. Touch makes it possible to wait, to gather strength, so that the other will return to caress and reshape, from within and from without, flesh that is given back to itself in the gestures of love. The most subtly necessary guardian of my life being the other's flesh. Approaching and speaking to me with his hands. Bringing me back to life more intimately than any regenerative nourishment, the other's hands, these palms with which he approaches without going through me, give me back the borders of my body and call me back to the remembrance of the most profound intimacy. As he caresses me, he bids me neither to disappear nor to forget but rather, to remember the place where, for me, the most intimate life holds itself in reserve. Searching for what has not yet come into being, for himself, he invites me to become what I have not yet become. To realize a birth still in the future. Plunging me back into the maternal womb and, beyond that, conception, awakening me to another — amorous — birth.

A birth that has never taken place, unless one remains at the stage of substitution for the father and the mother, which signifies a gesture that is radically unethical. Without respect for the one who gave me my body and without enthusiasm for the one who gives it back to me in his amorous awakening.

When the lovers substitute for, occupy, or possess the site that conceived them, they founder in the unethical, in profanation. They neither construct nor inhabit their love. Remaining in the no longer or the not yet. Sacrilgious sleepers, murderous dreamers — of the one and of the other in an unconscious state that would be the site of voluptuousness? Sterile, if it were not for the child.

Thus the closure, the sealing up of the society of couples. Barren — if it were not for the child? And the abandonment of the loved one[1] to the anonymity of love. To that touching vulnerability of one who can only be mortal. At least for him and in this place.

The caress does not try to dominate a hostile freedom. However profaning. Transgressing the freedom of God? Voluptuousness nourished by this transgression. Whence its always increasing avidity. Always deferring its possible? The lover sent back to the transcendental, the loved one plunged into the abyss. The caress would not attain that most intimate dwelling place where something gathers itself in from a more secret consummation? In and through a mucous shelter that extends from the depths to the heights? From the most subterranean to the most celestial? A movement from the one to the other that would take place in lovemaking?

Profanation always designates a threshold: the one where the simultaneity of what is hidden and what is revealed is in operation. The movement from mucous to skin? But also, the presentiment of the first dwelling place where, now, there is no one, only the memory and expectation of amorous fecundity. No nudity brings back to light the intimacy of that first house of flesh. Always nocturnal for a certain gaze — which wishes for clothing in order not to see what it cannot see entirely?

The evanescence of the caress opens upon a future different from an approach to the other's skin in the here and now. Stopping at that point would risk relegating the loved one to the realm of animality, once the moment of seduction had passed. Of penetration beyond anything visible. Always alien to the intimacy of the mucous membranes, not crossing the threshold, still staying outside, the lover continues to caress until he founders in some abyss. He does not attain communion with the most inward locus of the feeling and the felt, where body and flesh speak to each other.

In this moment of ultimate sympathy, the feeling and the felt go so far as to get out of their depth, until they are immersed in that which does not yet have an individualized form, until they are returned to the deepest level of elemental flux, where birth is not yet sealed up in identity. There, every subject loses its mastery and its method. The pathway has been neither indicated nor prepared, unless in the call to a future that is offered by, and to, the other in the abandonment of self. Causing the possibles to recede, thanks to an itimacy that keeps on unfolding itself, opening and reopening the pathway to the mystery of the other.

Thus a new birth comes about, a new dawn for the loved one. And for the lover. The blooming of a face whose form was not yet sculpted. Opened up from having flowed to the depths of what nourishes it again and again. Not a mask given or attributed once and for all, but an efflorescence that detaches itself from its immersion and absorption in the night's most secret place. Not without scintillations. The light that shines there is different from the one that makes distinctions and separates too neatly.

Is this to say that the loved one — and the lover — find themselves thus in reversed positions from inside to outside? No. Rather, what is most interior and what is most exterior become mutually fecund. Prior to any procreation.

The son does not resolve the enigma of the most irreducible otherness. Of course, he is not engendered without having had his place in the crypt of the loved one's womb. Where the lover falters, and whence he returns, without any possible recognition or vision of this terrain. Does the son appear to the father as the impossible image of his act of love?

But, before the son appears, the loved one's fulfillment tells him, shows him, the mystery of fecundity. Looking again at the woman he has loved, the lover may contemplate the work of fecundation. And, if the loved one's — and the beloved's — surrender means a childlike trust, an animal exuberance, it illuminates the aesthetics and ethics of the amorous gesture, for those who take the time to reopen their eyes.

The loved one's beauty announces the fulfillment of the flesh. More beautiful, or differently beautiful, after lovemaking than in all her shows and finery. The most intimate fecundity of love, of its caress, of getting beyond all restraints on this side of the other's threshold, is preferred in this parousia — silently. Admiration for what is reborn from the heart's depths through a new conception. Regenerated by having gone back, with him, beyond the fixed, deadly due date of her birth? Returned to the acceptance of her life by the lover and accompanied on this side of, and beyond, a given day of reckoning.

Prior to any procreation, the lovers bestow on each other — life. Love fecundates each of them in turn, through the genesis of their immortality. Reborn, each for the other, in the assumption and absolution of a definitive conception. Each one welcoming the birth of the other, this task of beginning where neither she nor he has met — the original infidelity. Attentive to the weakness that neither the one nor the other could have wished for, they love each other like the bodies that they are. Not irremediably diminished by having been born in different times and places nor by having lived prior to their mutual union and generation.

The mystery of relations between lovers is more terrible, but infinitely less deadly, than the destruction of submission to sameness. Than all relationships of inclusion or penetration that bar the way to that nourishment that is more intimate than all other nourishments, given in the act of love.

Sameness, quantitatively polemical when it comes to its place, occupies my flesh, demarcates and subdivides my space, lays siege to and sets up camp on my horizon — making it uninhabitable for me and inaccessible for the lover.

Porosity, and its utter responsiveness, can only occur within difference. Porosity that moves from the inside to the outside of the
body. The most profound intimacy becoming a protective veil. Turning itself into an aura that preserves the nocturnal quality of the
encounter, without masks. The distance of the impenetrable in the
clarity of daylight. Of that which perceives without ever looking at
itself. Crossing itself like a threshold occasionally, while touching and
being touched by the other, but is forgotten and recollected.

How to remember the flesh? Above all, what is or becomes the
site/source that makes it possible to remember? The place of a possible unfolding of its temporality? Burial ground of the touch that
metabolizes itself in the constitution of time. Secret fold stitched into
the other's time. Eternity of the other?

While there remains the mystery of the touch that goes beyond
touching, the intention of every gesture, how can one recall this permanence? Become it as one recollects it? Make time of this source
of time? Arrive at this nocturnal temporalization of touch?

Without face? The face swallowed up by the nocturnal experience of touching, touching each other, retouching. Veiled by that
which is situated only beyond the project. Invisible because it must
defend itself unceasingly from the visible and the night. Both of
them.

The loved one, the beloved, emerges from all disguises. No
longer rigid within a deadly freedom, but left to a still possible
growth. To a face without habits, which allows itself to be seen in
order to be reborn beyond what has already appeared. And, in the
imperfection, the unfinished state of all who are alive.

In that place, there is no discovery to scrutinize. That which lets
itself go in the most intimate touch remains invisible. Touch
perceives itself but transcends the gaze. And the question of creating
nakedness. Touch never shows itself, not even if its exactness could
thus be made manifest. Reaching the other, or not. But it remains
palpable flesh on this side of, and beyond, the visible.

Analyzed in images and photographs, a face loses the mobility
of its expressions, the perpetual unfolding and becoming of what is
alive. Gazing at the loved one, the lover reduces her to less than
nothing if this gaze is seduced by an image, if her nudity, not
perceived in its ever unceasing palpitation, becomes the site of a

disguise rather than of wonder at that which does not stop its inward movement. The loved one's vulnerability is this unguarded quality of the living, revealed in a form that is never definitive. If he thinks he leaves her like a dead body, could it be that the lover discovers in her what is terrible about the limits of nudity, or dredges up what he needs to move on to a place beyond what is alive?

The face, or at least a certain conception, idea, or representation of it, can be swallowed up in the act of love. A new birth, which deconstitutes and reconstitutes contemplation by returning to the source of all the senses — the sense of touch. There is no longer any image there, except for that of letting go and giving of self. With the hands, among other ways. Sculpting, shaping, as if for the first time, on the first day. The loved one would be engulfed in infancy or animality only in order to be reborn from there as flesh reshaped inside and out. Innocent of absorption in self and of self? Encounter across a threshold that differs from the irreversible one of mortal birth. Approach, communion, and regenerating fecundation of the flesh that touches itself on an ever more distant horizon, repeating, and going beyond, the original conception.

Also surpassing the corruption of what has already been seen. Return to a certain night whence the lovers can arise, differently illuminated and enlightened. They give themselves to each other and abandon what has already been created. By themselves and by reason. Opening to an innocence that runs the risk of folding back on itself in defense of the past. In this gesture, each one runs the risk of annihilation, murder, or resuscitiation.

Lovers' faces live not only in the face but in the whole body. A form that is expressed in and through their entire stature. In its appearance, its touch. A *morphe* in continual gestation. Movements ceaselessly reshaping this incarnation.

The lovers meet in one moment of this incarnation. Like sculptors who are going to introduce themselves, entrust themselves to one another for a new delivery into the world.

And all the senses share in the nature of the caress. The hand serving, in its way, as the most intimate means of approach.

There the beloved is not subjected to alternations of fire and ice. Mirror or frost that the lover would have to pass through to reach the loved one. Given back to her own movements, to the demonstration of her charms, she also revives herself in the warmth and does not simply receive it from the other. Waiting without becoming rigid, she does not close herself in or up in any sepulchre of images or any project that denies her dynamism. She tends towards her own fulfillment, already unfolds herself to gather in more.

Thus, neither the one nor the other will take the initiative of plucking in order to contemplate. Both are contemplative and blossoming. Opening and closing themselves, in order to keep giving each other that which they could never have brought to life. Each one moving along the path to some in-finite, which trembles in the encounter without closing itself up or making decisions according to the limiting dimensions of some transcendental value to be attained.

The beloved falls back into infancy or beyond, while the lover rises up to the greatest heights. Impossible match. Chain of links connecting, from one end to the other, an ascension in which the one and the other do not wed, except in the inversion of their reflections.

When the lover loses himself in a regress through the voluptuousness of the loved one, he remains within her as an abyss, or an unfathomable depth. Both of them lost, each in the other, on the wrong side, or the other side, of transcendence.

The loved one. Not the beloved. Necessarily an object, not a subject in touch, like him, with time. Dragging the lover down into the abyss so that, from these nocturnal depths, he lets himself be carried off into an absolute future.

The loved one sinks into the abyss, founders in a night more primeval than the night, or finds herself dispersed in the shards of a broken mirror. The pearls of ice or frost that are her reflection making a screen for love? From the brilliance of her finery? Desired by the lover, in and through herself. she is removed from the place of greatest tenderness. Bidding her to freeze into the shapes that separate her from herself. Deprived of the suppleness of her amorous mobility, torn away from the source of respiration, which is also cosmic, where she moves in harmony with the fecundity of nature. For her, a living mirror. Tuned differently to the rhythm of the earth and the stars. Intimately tied to universal motions and vibrations that go beyond any enclosure within reproduction. Turning in a cycle that never revolves back to sameness. Continual and patient engendering of an obscure labor. More passive than any voluntary passivity, but not foreign to the act of creating-procreating the world.

Within her something takes place, between earth and sky, in which she participates as in a continual gestation, a mystery yet to be deciphered. Heavy with her destiny.

When the lover relegates her to infancy, animality, or maternity, he leaves unsolved, in part, this mystery of a relation to the cosmos. What is lacking is participation in the construction of a world that does not forget natural generation and the human being's part in the preservation of its efflorescence. A gestation in which the subjective microcosm, does not need to nourish, shelter, and fecundate itself by means of a macrocosm about which it no longer cares. Believing that it is given once and for all, to be exploited endlessly, carelessly irretrievably. Cultivating one's already-enclosed garden. The work of a landlord, without regard for the natural world that makes fecundity possible, without God's concern for this universe of incarnation, for the harmony of its allurements.

Separating her off into the subterranean, the submarine, stone and airborne flight lacking the sparkle of light and fire. Dismissed to a perpetual future. Forgetting that which already persists here, now — already hidden or still buried. Uprooting the beloved from her fundamental habitat.

Annexing the other, in all his/her dimensions and directions, in order to capture him/her, captivate him/her, in a language that posseses as its chief, and internal, resources only the consumption, consummation, and speed of its contradictions. Deployment of a network that extends over everything and deprives it of its most intimate breath and growth. A garment that first and foremost paralyzes the other's movement. Protecting it, like the shield of the hero who defends the loved one from the conquest of some rival.

But how does one stay alive beneath this shield? What future is left for one who is so hemmed in? Even if she plays, within this male territory, at disguising herself in numerous displays, various coquetries, which he will interpret as part of love, she remains without an identity or a passport with which to traverse, to transgress, the lover's language. A more or less domesticated child or animal that clothes itself or takes on a semblance of humanity? Carrying on the subject's involuntary movements, veiling them in softness, in folds, in spaciousness to give him back some room. Wrapping itself up in the remainder of what he has taken in and from love. But what of her call to the divine?

About this he has little to say. And, since she is not to speak when he renders her profane in voluptuousness, is he not also sacrilegious vis-à-vis God? The "God" of lightness, of the "incarnate," the God of life — of the air, . . . blood, and . . . maternity of the son who appears in the "form" of the cloud accompanying the tablets of the law. The lover would take this God into his discourse and beyond, not allowing him the freedom of his future manifestations. He invokes this God but does not perceive him where, in the here and now, he is already held out/withheld: in the beloved's sensibility. In the creation that she perpetuates, while preserving her intimacy, her inviolability, her virginity. God of the universe, God of the fecundity of a future coming, which is also preserved in the beloved.

The lover also summons her to God when he does not reduce, or seduce, her to his needs. Also regressive, she is infintile and animal, for him? Irresponsible in order to give him back freedom.

This lightness of amorous gestures and deeds makes one forget that the beloved loved one's self-abandonment is inspired by the most absolute trust in the transcendence of life. Still in the future, always being reborn. Allowing herself to let go into the nocturnal, she calls forth from there a new morning, a new spring, a new dawn. The creation of a new day? To the source of a light that goes behind and beyond that of reason.

God's first act of creation? Before peopling the sky and the earth. An illumination that precedes any role in the organization, the ordering — of a world. A contemplation prior to any vision. An opening on a less-than-nothing that is not nothing — light. Ultimate incorporation of the newborn man. The first discovery once out of the womb, or in regeneration. Matter without which no creation of form is possible, light is the chance of emergence out of chaos and shapelessness.

Returning to the depth of the night, the beloved waits for light — the light that shines through discourse, that filters through words, that bestows a sense of the cosmos, but also that which is illuminated in the grace of regeneration and transfiguration? Giving herself to nature to be reborn from there, fecund — within herself. A son, perhaps (but why a son and not a daughter, her other self?), but also hers by him. Fecundity of a love that gives itself over, above and beyond reason — at the source of light. There where things have not yet taken their places but remain possible. Future. Still germinating, growing, being revealed. The beloved will have to cultivate the intimacy (the seed?) of this fecundity and the path from the most hidden part of the night to the efflorescence of the day.

When the loved one presents herself and appears to the lover as a paradise to be brought back to infancy and animality, then the act of love signifies a profanation, but also a deposition. Causing her to be dragged down. The loved one would be relegated to the abyss so that the lover might be sent back to the heights. The act of love would amount to contact with the irrationality of discourse, in order to send the loved one back to the position of fallen animal or infant, and to man's ecstasy in God. Two poles that are indefinitely separate. But such is — perhaps — the loved one's secret: she knows, without knowing, that these two extremes are intimately connected.

Beneath her veils, she keeps secret watch over a threshold. A slight opening onto the depths or abysses of all language, of all birth and generation. It is up to the lover to discover, or perceive, there the fall into amorphousness or the astonishment of that which has not yet been given form or revealed from above. To bring about, with her, and not through or in spite of her, the assumption of the flesh. Instead of leaving her to her own profanation, her despoiling, to reconstitute again and again only her virginity. To wrap herself up in a *something beyond* all humanity? While the lover leads her back to the *not yet* of the infant, the *never like that* of the animal — outside of any human becoming. Separating himself from her, once this gesture has been made, to return to his ethical responsibilities.

In this sense, the loved one, she who renounces her obligations as the beloved, succumbs to the temptation of being seduced by the lover. She divests herself of her own will to love, in order to make herself the stake in the lover's exercise of will. Which assigns her to the place of nonwilling in his ethical will. Her fall into the lover's identity cancels out any real giving of self and makes her into a thing, or something other than *the woman* that she needs to be. She lets herself be taken but does not give herself. She quits the locus of all responsibilities, her own ethical site. She is placed under house arrest, lacking the will and movements of love. Except for the expectation and cure for profanation? For the fall into the abyss? Gathering around herself and wrapping herself with what was secretly entrusted to her — without his knowledge. Barely moving at all, but deploying around herself garments for protection and display. Her paralysis, where the dance is concerned, runs the risk of resignation from all amorous creation, except that of remaining desirable. The guardian of the source and secret of her appeal. Without responsibility for bringing to life that something more than the seduction of man in the hidden side of himself? For the unveiling of a difference that would remain coupled with him in the night.

If she comes back to herself, in herself, to himself in her, she may feel that another parousia is necessary. Having to create, give birth to, engender, the mystery that she bears — prior to any conception of a child. No longer staying within the grasp of the one who draws upon the mystery, but taking charge — yes, she herself — of bringing it to light. Engendering love prior to, as something more than, the son. And the daughter.

Generating her space, her site, with the lover. Remaining on the threshold, which is always receding and in the future, of a mystery that she ought to reveal under pain of ethical dereliction? The lover would help her in this parturition, if he does not simply send her back to the abyss. The one for the other, messengers of a future that must still be built and contemplated. The one for the other, already known and still unknown. The one for the other, the mediators of a secret, a force, and an order that touches also on the divine.

Occasionally going their separate ways, meeting again, linking up again, in order not to lose their attentiveness to what transcends their already actual becoming. Listening to what has never taken place, nor found its place but that calls to be born.

This simultaneousness of concupiscence and transcendence is traditionally represented by the angel — the divine messenger. Not foreign to desire and anger, in some dimension that is not one of need.

But here, voluptuousness would hold fast to the fate of an exorbitant ultramateriality fallen away from discourse. Never brought to fruition nor fulfilled in its transcendence. Captive of a destiny, without remission. Of an original sin without possible redemption? Manifesting itself beyond the word, beyond and in spite of reason. Beyond all measures.

For the lover, the transcendence of the other justifies this infidelity of love. Returning to his God in a discontinuity of *eros*. If it were not for pardon.

And what of the beloved? Grace for what has not yet gone sufficiently far into the future nor been sufficiently faithful in the
moment, for what remained unfinished, left over. Remission of
deprivation, of distress, of expectation, which measures out the
chronology of the lovers' unions and separations. Each one fulfilling
the cycles of his/her solitude to come back to the other, wounded
perhaps, but free of a possible return because of the pardon that each
gives. Allowing one to become detached from self and from the
other. Renewal of the attraction that is also nourished in the suspense
of reconciliation. There, sacrifice is neither sacrifice of nor mourning for the one or the other but absolution for what was not perfect.
A marker in time that opens up to infinity, without sending it back
to an origin or a goal deprived of an access, a threshold.

The flesh of the rose petal — sensation of the mucous mem-
brane regenerated. Between blood, sap, the not yet of efflorescence.
Joyous mourning for the winter past. New baptism of springtime.
Return to the possible of intimacy, of its fecundity, fecundation.
But time enters in. Too much involved in numbers and in what
has already been. And how to repair, in a second, an evil that has
lasted for such a long time? Call to the other from a starting point
of virginity, without a trace of scar or mark of pain and self-
enclosure? Love the other above and beyond any labor of healing.
And when others continually interfere with this expectation of
union, how to maintain a candor that neither cries out for remission
nor burdens the lover with the task of healing wounds?
But does the lover not ask the loved one to efface, again and
again, an original wound of which she would be the bearer? The suffering of an open body that cannot clothe itself with and in her,
unless the lover is united with her, in the joy and not the sacrifice,
of the most intimate mucous threshold in the dwelling place. Crossing the threshold, being no longer a profanation of the temple but
an entrance into another, more secret space. Where the beloved
receives and offers the possibility of nuptials. An inebriation unlike
that of the conquerer, who captures and dominates his prey. Inebriation of the return to the garden of innocence, where love does not
yet know or no longer knows, or has forgotten, the profanity of
nakedness. The gaze still innocent of the limits of reason, the division of day and night, the alternation of the seasons, animal cruelty,

the necessity of protecting oneself from the other or from God. Face to face encounter of two naked lovers in a nudity that is older than, and unlike, a sacrilege. Not perceivable as profanation. The threshold of the garden, a welcoming cosmic home, that remains open. No guard other than that of love itself. Innocent of the knowledge of displays and the fall.

Intuition without an end, intuition that does not mark out but inscribes itself in an already insistent field. A prehensive intuition, which inhales from the air something of what is already there to come back to itself?

The loved one would be she who keeps herself available in this way. Offering to the other what he can put to his own use? Opening the path of his return to himself and of his own future? Giving him back time?

When the loved one perceives the lover in this way, does she inscribe herself in a moment of her trajectory as he arrives at a moment of his own? He believes that she is drawing him down into the abyss; she believes that he is cutting himself off from her to constitute his transcendence. Their paths cross but achieve neither an alliance nor a mutual fecundation. Except for the lover, whose double is — the son.

The loved one relegated to an inwardness that is not one because it is absymal, animal, infantile, prenuptial; and the lover, to a solitary call to his God. At both poles distant from the living, they do not wed each other. They occupy the contrapuntal sites of human becoming. The one watches over the substratum of the elementary, of generation, but the act of love would scatter her among the archaic moments of earth, sea, and airborne flight. Caressing her to reach the infinity of her center, the lover undoes her, divests her of her tactility — a porosity that opens up to the universe — and consigns her to the regression of her womanly becoming, always in the future. Forgetful of the fecundity, in the here and now, of lovemaking: the gift to each of the lovers of sexual birth and rebirth.

Taking the other into oneself during lovemaking creates an inordinate separation. There is no opportunity to mourn an impossible identification. Attraction in union, and the chance of its fecundity.

Revealed only in the son, it continues to mask itself as the fecundation of the lovers in difference. As the fruit of the communion between lover and beloved, the son becomes the lover's ornament and display of the same as self, the position of the lover's identity in relation to, and through, paternity.

Conceived in this way, the son does not appear as the fulfillment of love. He bars the way to its mystery? The aspect of fecundity that is only witnessed in the son obliterates the secret of difference. As the lover's means of return to himself outside himself, the son closes the circle. The path of a solitary ethics that will have encountered, for its own need, without nuptial fulfillment, the irresponsible woman, the loved one.

When recognized only in the son, love and voluptuousness bespeak the lover's vulnerability, on the threshold of difference. His retreat and his appeal to his genealogy, his future as a man, his horizon, society, and security. Turning around in a world that remains his own. Contained within and by himself, without a dwelling for the beloved, except for the shelter that she gives to the son — prior to his birth.

If the lover needs to prove himself in voluptuousness, it is in order to sink down into his own otherness/the other of himself. To put down the night side of himself, which he covers up in the reasonable habitat of his life and from which he gains, as he emerges, the form of his highest ascension. The body of the loved one(s) (*l'aimé-aimée*), approached by caresses, is abandoned on the threshold of the nuptials. There is no union. The seduction of the loved one serves as a bridge between the Father and the son. In her, only an aspect of himself, the lover goes beyond love and voluptuousness, towards the ethical.

> In this frailty as in the dawn rises the Loved, who is the Loved one [*l'Aimé qui est Aimée*]. An epiphany of the Loved, the feminine is not added to an object and a Thou antecedently given or encountered in the neuter (the sole gender formal logic knows). The epiphany of the Loved one is but one with her *regime* of tenderness.[2]

The loved one's fragility and weakness are the means for the lover to experience self-love, as a loved one who is powerless. The flesh of which he would remain the very body.

Touching that which is not contained within the limits of his flesh, of his body, the lover risks an infinite outpouring in dead being. He who has no connection to his own death puts the other at a permanent risk of loss of self in the wrong infinity.

Touching can become a limit, also, to the reabsorption of the other into the same. Giving the other its contours, calling it to its contours, means inviting the other to live where she is without becoming other, without appropriating herself.

But he who encounters only self as object in the loved one caresses himself under the disguise of a greater passivity? Adorning and inhabiting it with his own affects? Eventually giving to it the tactile *there is* (*il y a*), caught up in his own subjectivity. Aporia of a tactility that cannot caress itself and needs the other to touch itself.

The threshold is still missing. The access to the most mucous part of the dwelling.

Circumscribing the abyss is the unavoidable alterity of the other. Its absolute singularity. To be protected prior to any positioning or affirmation of another transcendence? The transcendence of "God" can help in the discovery of the other as other, locus where expectation and hope hold themselves in reserve.

Dwelling place, which becomes that of the matrix of the lover's identity. She, having no place of her own? Hiding her dereliction in terror or irony, she calls for complicity with something other than profanation, animality, infancy. She calls — and sometimes in her dispersion — to the feminine that she already is, secretly. Wanting to give herself over without resignation or violation of her intimacy.

Modesty is not found on one side only. Responsibility for it should not go to only one of the lovers. To make the loved one responsible for the secret of desire is to situate her also, and primarily on the side of the lover — in his own modesty and virginity, for which he won't take ethical responsibility.

The beloved's task would be to watch over two virginities, at least? Hers and the son's, to whom the lover delegated the part of himself that is still virginal. A walk in the dark, of course. The lover also seeks himself in this passage where, for him, the threshold cannot be crossed, from the not yet to the still future. Searching, in infancy and animality, for some moment whose obscure attraction remains insistent inside himself. Call to an obscure night that is neither a return to immersion in the mother nor profanation of the loved one's secret, but the weight of his own mystery.

But, if some God obliterates respect for the other as other, this God stands as the guarantee of a deadly infinity. As a resource of life and of love, the divine can only aid and further the fulfillment of the relation with the other. Provide the audacity of love. Encourage the risk of encountering the other with nothing held in reserve.

The fecundity of God would be witnessed in the uncalculating generosity with which I love, up to the point of risking myself with the other. Amorous folly that gives back to the other its last veil, in order to be reborn on another horizon. The lovers becoming cocreators of new worlds.

The lovers. Since to define the amorous couple as lover and *loved one* already assigns them to a polarity that deprives the woman of her love. Object of concupiscence, of the concupiscible, appeal to the alterity of the night or to the regression to need, she is no longer she who also opens partway onto a human landscape. She is part of the lover's world. Keeping herself on the threshold, perhaps. Causing the limits of her world or of her country to founder, to be swallowed up. But remaining passive within the field of activity of a subject who wishes himself to be the sole master of desire. Leaving him, apparently, the whole of voluptuousness, leaving him to a debasement without recourse to herself. What is left for him is dependence upon the son in order to continue on his path.

Thus, the God, like the son, would serve as a prop during the man's ethical journey, neglecting to keep for the beloved the light of her return to self. He looks at her before plunging her into the night of his *jouissance*, his infantile or animal regression. But is it not between God and son that he takes her and annuls her as other? That he profanes her in his transcendence and his relation to the divine?

Voluptuousness would remain that which does not know the other. That which seduces itself, through her, in order to return to the abyss and take up ethical seriousness again. Not maintaining itself in the encounter with an other who is accountable, and for pleasure. But undoing this responsibility in the thoughtlessness of voluptuousness. A shore of indifference that brings repose from ethical fidelity?

Is not the most terrible demand of the ethical played out in that scene? Because it is a confrontation, here and now, with the mystery of the other. Tied to a past and a future of incarnation. Modesty being a sign of an intimacy that calls for, even begs for, a return. A supplication that calls, wordlessly, to reappear, beyond the immersion, in a light that has not yet occurred.

To give, or to give back to the other the possible site of his identity, of his intimacy: a second birth that returns one to innocence. A garment that isn't, but is rather an enveloping which again and again watches over a space for birth — becoming other than the return to self. A becoming in which the other gives of a space-time that is still free. In which he reentrusts me to a genesis that is still foreign to what has already happened.

A gesture that is more modest than the caress. A caress that precedes every caress, opening up to the other the possible space of his respiration, his conception. Greeting him as other, encountering him while respecting what surrounds him — that subtle, palpable horizon in which each person keeps himself within a necessary surrounding, an irradiation of his presence that overflows the limits of his body. Capable of more than the "I can" of the body itself.

This caress would start off from a distant point. A tact that informs the sense of touch, attracts, and comes to rest on the threshold of the approach. Neither paralyzing nor breaking in, the lovers would beckon to each other, at first from far away. A salutation that means the crossing of a threshold. Pointing out the space of a love that has not yet been profaned. The entrance into the dwelling, or the temple, where each one would invite the other, and themselves, to enter in, also into the divine.

Not divided into alliances between highest and lowest, the extremes of day and night, but involving these ultimate sites at the risk of the union and fecundation of each by the other. A passage through the loss of the individual body, through the surrender of the "I can" that opens up a future without the sacrifice of the one to the other. Creation of the love that does not resign from its respect for the ethical.

This union does not forget about voluptuousness but sounds it out in its most vertiginous and most sublime dimensions. Not divided into elements belonging to different domains, the lovers meet as a world that each one reassembles and both resemble. Inhabiting it and dressing it differently. The lover and the beloved's horizons being irreducible.

The loved one — called a child or an animal — is also she who holds the highest note. Whose voice carries the farthest, is the finest, the strongest.

Her fall into the abyss would refer to the loss of her voice. To not listening to her song. To forgetting her vocalism. The loved one would be mute, or reduced to speaking in the spaces between the consonants of the lover's discourse. The loved one relegated to his shadow, his double, that which he does not yet know or recognize in himself, presenting itself to him under the guise of the loved one. Disguising for him the space of the present. An engulfing of his authority in the present, which clings to memory and the song of the beloved. Whom he sends back down to the abyss so that he may rebound into the transcendent. Manifest in and through writing. Absent and awaited in spirit. Whose voice would have been silent for a long time. A seriousness that is hard to maintain, which history would try to rediscover, reuncover through the text.

Neither wishing, nor being able, to see himself in this body that he is no longer, the lover would appear to himself in an other, her, mystery of the site of his disappearance. In order to keep the secret, she must keep quiet, no song or laughter. Her voice would give her away. Reveal that she is not what the lover thinks or searches for. That she is only a cover for what he is seeking, through and despite her.

Before parousia occurs, silence occurs. A silence that rehearses oblivion and that is only filled by music. The voice of she who sings and calls to the lover is still missing there. Stifled by the noise of instruments and of nature running wild. Or abandoned to prostitution.

Unless she, too, disguises herself, under the guise of an angel? Neuter? Perhaps. An interval that speaks between spouse and spirit? Neither the one nor the other expressing themselves. Unless through the mediation of the angelic order.

The expectation of parousia would also mean the death of speech between the sexual partners of the scene. Which foretells the terrible aspect of a new cosmic chaos and the disappearance of the gods. The hope of a new pentecost? Of the spirit's coming to the spouse in the joy of a different union.

The feminine would remain in search of its cause and sought out as a cause, but never thought through as such. Always relegated to another kind of causality. At best, defined qualitatively. Adjectives or ornaments of a verb whose subject they can never be.

The *logos* would maintain itself between the verb and the substantive. Leaving out the adjective? A mediation between the act and its result. The place of attraction? The place of the loved one — masculine/feminine — would be between loving and love. The lovable. Approachable in its realm of tenderness.

The two philosophical gestures would come down to laying the foundation, unfolding, and surrounding that which founds itself: acting and constituting the substantive of the act. Closure of an era. The partly open would be remembered in the qualities. Of the loved one. Already passive appearances or attributes? Over which she keeps watch, however, as they resist being taken up into matter.

Would not the loved one's appeal signify that which is not yet rigidified in the hardness of a name/noun or the seal of a signature? Between the act and the work would be situated what opens up to a future the lover does not understand as the work of love, but as the lightness of voluptuousness. The repository of certain characteristics that the lover does not maintain when he is loved. The loved one's significance derives from this less than nothing, a substitution that does not divulge itself. Brought into a world not his own, so that the lover may enjoy himself and recover his strength for his voyage towards an autistic transcendence. Allowing him, in the quest for a God already inscribed but voiceless, not to constitute the ethical site of lovemaking? A seducer, seduced by the gravity of the other and only approaching the other, feminine, carelessly. Taking away her light to illuminate his path. Without regard for what shines and glistens between them. Whether he wills it or not, knows it or not, turning the divine light to the illumination of reason or to the in-visibility of "God."

Meanwhile, he will have taken away from the loved one this visibility that she offers him, which gives him strength, and he will have sent her back to the nocturnal. He will have stolen her gaze from her. And her song. Her attraction for the divine that becomes incarnate — in the light, in the contemplation of the universe and the other. The divine revealed in its also sensible dimensions. Having already appeared and still to come, and which beauty would call to mind? A half opening. A threshold. Also between past and future. The lover stealing her desire away from her, to adorn his world that preceded love, to spark his voluptuousness and aid his ascension, following the lightness of a fulfillment that did not take place in the encounter between them. A union, or wedding, broken off twice —

at least. In display and in degeneration. No "human" flesh having been celebrated in that *eros*.

Not taking into account his own limits, the lover penetrates a flesh that he consummates and consumes without attention to the sacrificial gesture. He "takes communion" without rites or words. Is absorbed into nothing — unless it is his other? Without detectable transition. Without a trace of this rape. If it were not for the exhaustion and suffering of the loved one. Reduced to infancy, left to herself or to animal savagery.

Confounding the one and the other, bending them to the same logic, the lover does not know the irreducible strangeness of the one and the other. Between the one and the other. Approaching the other to reduce it to that which is not yet human in himself. Voluptuousness that does not take place in the realm of the human. Will not be its work. Neither ethical nor aesthetic.

Placing in the other a trust that goes beyond his possibles, the beloved is relegated to a vertiginous dereliction. Opening herself up to the most intimate point of her being, to the most profound depths of her inwardness, but not retouched and sent back to the most sublime part of herself, she gives way to a night without end. The invitation to inhabit this dwelling being a call to communion in the secret depths of the sensible and not to a defloration of the woman that she is.

The loved one's face radiates the secret that the lover touches upon. Shining with a new light, bathing in a horizon that goes beyond the intention, it says [*dit*] what is hidden without exhausting it in a meaning [*un vouloir dire*]. It fills up with a nothing to say that is not nothing — thanks to the already and the not yet. A taking shape of matter that precedes any articulation in a language. Growth of the plant, animal expectation, sculptor's roughcast. Aesthetic matrix that does not yet reproduce but testifies to itself in a prerequisite to all completed gestures.

The caress seeks out the not yet of the beloved's blossoming. That which cannot be anticipated because it is other. Unforseeability bordering on alterity, beyond one's own limits. Beyond the limits of one's "I can." Irreducible to the other's presence, which is off into an always in the future that indefinitely suspends parousia. Always to come [*à venir*], the other would only maintain the lover in self-love even while making himself loved. Thus resigning from his ethical site, to she who is an opening of, and to, another threshold.

The loving act is neither an explosion nor an implosion but an indwelling. Dwelling with the self, and with the other — while letting him/her/it go. Remembering, while letting be, and with the world. Remembering the act, not as a simple discharge of energy but as a quality of intensity, sensation, color, rhythm. The intensity would be, or would constitute, the dimensions of the dwelling, always in becoming. Never finished. Unfolding itself during and between the terms of encounters.

If the loved one is relegated to infancy and animality, love remains without a dwelling. For the lover as well, who desires the ethical in a return to some transcendent. Building this site in a nostalgia for an inaccessible here and now of love and voluptuousness?

Pleasure is never conceived as an instance of power in act. It expresses itself as an exit, from itself, when tied to the instant, dispersing or rarefying our being — while managing an evasion. It is presented as an amputation of being's ecstasy and not as a fulfillment that surpasses its destiny in the past and in the future. Freeing from being through the affective. Thought as a break, a paroxysm whose promises cannot be kept, a disappointment and a deception in its internal becoming. Doomed to shame through its inability to measure up to the exigencies of need. Never up to what is expected. Never ethical.

In the clamorous display of a presence that foretells nothing, except for its own emptiness, remaining impassive in order to turn to new values, new horizons, without falling into the trap set for a relapse into what has already been seen, known. The impatience of the one who wants something else not being on the same register, musically, with the noise of the one who cries out that he wants me no longer to want. To want what he wants or to nourish myself on his desires, where I can only do so at the price of giving up my incarnation.

An attacking and aggressive appeal from the other, who lets me know that he can no longer tolerate not expressing his will. That he is hungry for my hunger. Is ready to destroy it, in order not to have to hear the place where his hunger might take place — his appeal to the infinite, the unappeasable, the always more. Whose weight he must bear in separation, so that I can take communion with him in a dimension that watches over the mystery of the absolute, without abolishing it. In a demand for regressive nurturing, for example.

The lives of the one and the other are at stake. A future is only possible if this respect for limits is granted, also in the instant. If my hunger is not always turned back in the uncertainty about the other's hunger. If he leaves me to the openness of my quest without absorbing me into his thirst for nothing, or even stifling what I am silently. To exist alone?

One might as well say, to die? To produce, to produce himself instead of me? This impossibility, at once contemptible in its approach and insistent in its manifestations, can cut off my inspiration with its violence. For all that, however, he does not discover its source.

Forgetting that I exist as a desiring subject, the other transforms his need into desire. Desire for nothing — the abolition of the other's willing, which would become a nonwilling. Unless it is for a transcendent — other of the same.

In this way, voluptuousness finds itself set adrift forever. The distraction of transfiguration, transmutation, resurrection. An infinite substitution and spelling out of appearances, the masks falling without parousia? An illumination capable of being buried under showiness, but not signifying a return either to animality or to infancy.

Does the lover not lay upon the loved one what he cannot see in himself? What prevents him from becoming what he is, and from being able to encounter her, herself? Wrapping her up in what he cannot bear of his own identity, he places her, secretly, in the maternal position. A destiny, or maya, hidden in its identifying strata. A net that he cannot pass through and that he lays upon her, in order to rend it — ficitiously. He discovers nothing. And if she surrenders as a child or animal, her finery fallen, God becomes even more transcendent, inaccessible. Out of reach.

Might not the infinitesimal but impassable distance in our relation to death then be that which would take place in the touching of the female sex? Whence the assimilation of the feminine to the other? And the forgetting of a vital threshold — the tactile.

It is the place of my concentration and of his opening out, without vain dispersion, that constitutes a possible habitation. Turning back on itself and protecting me until the next encounter. A sort of house that shelters me without enclosing me, untying and tying me to the other, as to one who helps me to build and inhabit. Discharging me from a deadly fusion and uniting me through an acknowledgement of who is capable of producing this place. My pleasure being, in a way, the material, one of the materials.

Architects are needed. Architects of beauty who fashion enjoyment — a very subtle material. Letting it be and building with it, while respecting the approach, the threshold, the intensity. Inciting it to unfold without a show of force. Only an accompaniment? It only unfolds itself from being unfolded. It is in touch with itself from being touched touching itself. It must be able to persist. To continue to live in itself in order to live with. One must reach the heart of its habitation in order to cohabit. This heart being always in motion and, at the same time, not without a dwelling. A qualitative threshold makes it possible for love to last. For the lovers to be faithful? Not obeying it, the threshold wears out. The house of flesh, which allows them to remember each other, to call to each other — even from a distance — is destroyed.

Letting be and dwelling in the strength of becoming, letting the other go while dwelling contained and persevering, such is the wager that the beloved must make. Not holding back, but dwelling in what wraps itself around a nonforgetfulness. What is reborn, again and again, around a memory of the flesh. Flourishing again around what, in herself, has opened up and dispersed itself in seedlings. Seedlings that are fecund if the one, she who is unique, remembers this impossible memory. Attentive to a time always consecrated to the abyss. Adrift. In an infinite substitution.

There remain only the immemorial interuterine abode and trust in some other. Between blind nostalgia and ethical tension, the lover both loves and despises himself through the loved one (female) — who is the loved one (male). He both allures and rejects himself through this other. Himself assuming neither infancy nor animality.

The memory of touching always covered over by the senses, which forget where they come from? Creating a distance through a mastery that constitutes the object as a monument built instead of the subject's disappearance .

The memory of touching? The most persisting and the most difficult to make comply with memory. The one that brings about returns to an term, whose beginning and end cannot be recovered.

Memory of the flesh, where what has not yet been written is inscribed, laid down? What has no discourse to wrap itself in? What has not yet been born into language? What has a place, has taken place, but has no language. The felt, which expresses itself for the first time. Declares itself to the other in silence.

Remembering and hoping that the other remembers. Lodging it in a memory that serves as its bed and its nest, while waiting for the other to understand. Making a cradle for him inside and out while leaving him free, and keeping oneself in the memory of the strength that revealed itself, that acted.

Leaving free, giving an invitation to freedom, does not mean that the other wants it to be so. And lives in you, with you.

Far away, eventually. Avoiding the encounter, the approach that yields the limits of the flesh. Remaining at a distance, in order to annihilate the possibility of us?

A sort of abolishment of the other, in the loss of the body's borders. A reduction of the other — given up to consuming flesh for the other? Between the memory that preserves in expectation and respects the advent or the eventuality of the other and the memory that dissipates itself in assimilation, the commemoration is lacking upon which the flesh lives — in its mobility, its energy, its place of inscription, its still-virginal power.

Must one have a certain taste? A taste that does not exist or persist in any nourishment. A taste for the affective with, and for, the other. This taste that ought not to remain in an obscure nostalgia, but in an attention to what always forgets itself. As impossible to gratify? What does not exclude the savor of feeling without wanting to absorb or resolve. Between the body and the subtlety of the flesh, a bridge or place of a possible encounter, unusual landscape where union is approached?

It is a question here neither of the preciosity of a fetish nor of the celebratory perfume of some sacrifice. Before any construction of words, any encasement or destruction of idols and even of temples, something — not reducible to what is ineffable in discourse — would keep itself close to the perception of the other in its approach.

The other not transformable into discourse, fantasms, or dreams, the other for whom it is impossible that I substitute any other, any thing, any god, through this touching of and by him, which my body remembers.

To each wound of separation, I would answer by refusing the holocaust, while silently bearing witness, for myself and for the other, that the most intimate perception of the flesh escapes every sacrificial substitution, every resumption in a discourse, every surrender to God. Flair or premonition between my self and the other, this memory of the flesh as the place of approach is ethical fidelity to incarnation. To destroy it risks supressing alterity, both God's and the other's. Thus dissolving all possibility of access to transcendence.

Notes

1. In the original, Irigaray distinguishes between the feminine as passive *aimèe* (here translated as "the loved one") and as active *amante* (here translated as "the beloved"), whose full engagement with the masculine *amant* ("the lover") cannot be rendered grammatically in English due to lack of gender. — Trans.

2. TeI 233/TI 256.

Selected Bibliography

La théorie de l'intuition dans la phénoménologie de Husserl (Paris: Alcan, 1930; Paris: Vrin, 1963, 1970).

> *The Theory of Intuition in Husserl's Phenomenology*, trans. André Orianne (Evanston, Illinois: Northwestern University Press, 1973).

Le temps et l'autre, in J. Wahl, *Le Choix, Le Monde, L'Existence* (Grenoble-Paris: Arthaud, 1947), 125–196.

> *Le temps et l'autre* (Montpellier: Fata Morgana, 1979).

> *Time and the Other*, trans. Richard A. Cohen (Pittsburgh: Duquesne University Press, forthcoming).

De l'existent à l'existence (Paris: Fontaine, 1947; Paris: Vrin, 1973, 1978).

> *Existence and Existents*, trans. Alphonso Lingis (The Hague: Nijhoff, 1978).

En découvrant l'existence avec Husserl et Heidegger (Paris: Vrin, 1949; 2d ed., 1967, 1974).

Totalité et infini (The Hague, Nijhoff, 1961, 1965, 1968, 1971, 1974).

> *Totality and Infinity*, trans. Alphonso Lingis (The Hague: Nijhoff, 1969; Pittsburgh: Duquesne University Press, 1969, 1979).

Difficile liberté (Paris: Albin Michel, 1963; 2d ed., 1976).

Quatre lectures talmudiques (Paris: Minuit, 1968).

Humanisme de l'autre homme (Montpellier: Fata Morgana, 1972).

Autrement qu'être ou au-delà de l'essence (La Haye, Nijhoff, 1974).

> *Otherwise than Being or Beyond Essence*, trans. Alphonso Lingis (The Hague: Nijhoff, 1981).

Sur Maurice Blanchot (Montpellier: Fata Morgana, 1975).

Noms propres (Montpellier: Fata Morgana, 1975).

Du sacré au saint (Paris: Minuit, 1977).

L'au-delà du verset (Paris: Minuit, 1982).

De Dieu qui vient à l'idée (Paris: Vrin, 1982).

De l'évasion (1935) (Montpellier: Fata Morgana, 1982).

Éthique et infini (Paris: Fayard, 1982).

> *Ethics and Infinity*, trans. Richard A. Cohen (Pittsburgh: Duquesne University Press, 1985).

Transcendance et intelligibilité (Geneve: Labor et Fides, 1984).

Contributors

ROBERT BERNASCONI has taught at the University of Essex since 1976. He is the author of *The Question of Language in Heidegger's History of Being* and numerous articles on Hegel, Heidegger, Derrida, and Levinas. He is currently editing a selection of Gadamer's papers on art and aesthetic consciousness.

MAURICE BLANCHOT is one of France's most original and important writers. His work includes essays, literary and philosophical criticism, studies in aesthetics, and several novels. He is perhaps best known for *La part du feu, L'espace litterature, Lautreamont et Sade,* and *L'entretien infini.*

RICHARD A. COHEN teaches philosophy at Loyola College, Baltimore. He has published articles on Heidegger, Merleau-Ponty, Foucault, Derrida, and Levinas and has translated Levinas' *Ethics and Infinity.* His translations of Levinas' *Time and the Other* and a collection, *Discovering Existence with Husserl,* that includes all of Levinas' articles on Husserlian phenomenology, will soon be published.

THEODORE DE BOER is Professor of Philosophy at the University of Amsterdam. His *Tussen filosophie en profetie (Between Philosophy and Prophecy)* is a study of Levinas' thought. He is also author of *The Development of Husserl's Thought* and *Foundations of Critical Psychology.*

JAN DE GREEF is Professor of Philosophy at the Catholic University of Louvain. He has authored more than ten articles on the philosophy of Levinas.

LUCE IRIGARAY is a practicing psychoanalyst in Paris. She has authored numerous articles in contemporary feminism. Her

259

major publications are *Le langage de dements*, *Speculum de l'autre femme*, *Ce sexe qui n'en est pas un*, *Amante marine*, and *Ethique de la difference sexuelle*.

RICHARD KEARNEY teaches at University College, Dublin. He is general editor of *The Crane Bag*, a literary journal. In addition to coediting *Heidegger et la question de Dieu* and *The Black Book*, he is responsible for *Dialogues with Contemporary Continental Thinkers* and has authored *The Irish Mind*, *The Poetic Imagination*, and *Modern Movements in European Philosophy*.

ALPHONSO LINGIS is Professor of Philosophy at Pennsylvania State University. In addition to more than sixty articles on contemporary thought, he has also authored *Excesses: Eros and Culture*, and *Libido: The French Existential Theories*, and has translated Levinas' major works: *Totality and Infinity*, *Otherwise than Being or Beyond Essence*, and *Existence and Existents*, as well as *The Collected Philosophical Papers of Emmanuel Levinas*. He will soon publish two more of his own books: *Phenomenological Explanations* and *Deathbound Subjectivity*.

JEAN-FRANÇOIS LYOTARD is Professor of Philosophy at the University of Paris, Vincennes. He is known for his studies of aesthetics and of psychopolitics. He is the author of, among more than ten books, *Economie libidinal*, *Discours, figure*, *Des dispostif pulsionnels*, and *The Postmodern Condition*.

ADRIAAN PEPERZAK is Professor of Philosophy at the Catholic University of Nijmegan, Netherlands. He has authored many articles on Levinas and has edited, translated, and annotated a Dutch collection of Levinas' articles: *Het Mensilijk Gelaat (The Human Face)*. He is the author of, among more than ten books, *Le jeune Hegel et la vision de morale du monde*, *Verlangen: De huidige mens en de vraag naar heil (Desire: Contemporary Man and the Question of Happiness)* and *System and History in Philosophy*.

CHARLES WILLIAM REED entitled his doctoral dissertation "Method in the Philosophy of Emmanuel Levinas." It was accepted by Yale University in 1983.

STEVEN G. SMITH teaches philosophy and religion at Millsaps College. He is the author of *The Argument to the Other: Reason Beyond Reason in the Thought of Karl Barth and Emmanuel Levinas* as well as articles on Kant, Barth and Levinas.

Index